APPRENTICE TO POWER

A Wiccan Odyssey to Spiritual Awakening

By Timothy Roderick

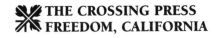

THE CROSSING PRESS
FREEDOM, CALIFORNIA

Copyright ©2000 Timothy Roderick Halphide
Cover art, *Wizard*, by Susan Dorf
Cover design by Courtnay Perry
Printed in the U.S.A.

For information on bulk purchases or group discounts for this and other Crossing Press titles, please contact our Special Sales Manager at 800-777-1048.

Visit our Website on the Internet at: www.crossingpress.com

Library of Congress Cataloging-in-Publication Data

Roderick,Timothy, 1963-
    Apprentice to power : a wiccan odyssey to spiritual awakening / by Timothy Roderick.
        p. cm.
    Includes bibliographical references.
    ISBN 1-58091-077-7 (pbk.)
    1. Witchcraft. 2. Magic. 3. Ritual. I. Title.

BF1566 .R57 2000
133.4'3--dc21   00-030854

ACKNOWLEDGMENTS

It takes many people to write a single book. I would like to thank the following people, who have contributed their wisdom, time, and talents toward the creation of *Apprentice to Power*.

My many thanks to Mead Hunter, my personal editor and good friend. Without his guidance and unfailing insight, this book would never have come to fruition. I am grateful to Caryle Hirshberg of The Crossing Press for believing in this project. Thanks also goes to Lady Varda of Crescent's Shadow for her continued support and magical input. My appreciation also goes to Chani Beeman, who provided inspiration on several occasions, and to Marilyn Odello for her beautiful photographic work. Eduardo Waiskopf provided continued support, long conversations, and listening ears. Without his support, this project would have never been realized.

CONTENTS

INTRODUCTION

A brass bell clattered against the door of the rickety old side street shop as I entered it for the first time. The bell was hung on the inside doorknob from a thin piece of red yarn that had a series of knots, shells, seeds, and tiny brass trinkets tied into it. *This is probably magic,* I thought, as I examined the charm. *Perhaps I'm under a spell right now.* Once I had passed through the doorway I felt that I had entered a world only talked about in fairy tales or in movies. This was the world of enchanters, the realm of witches.

At that point in my life I was like most people in my beliefs about witches. I thought they were heretics, poisoners, spoilers. I thought that they practiced black magic and engaged in unspeakable rites. A chill went up my spine. I was petrified to be standing there in the only shop in town that everyone knew of, yet about which no one would speak. Why was I there? At the time I couldn't really say. I had a vague sense that I was searching and that I was hungry for something unnamable. Perhaps I had the courage to enter the shop that day because, beyond my fear, I felt utterly mesmerized by what I saw.

I looked around the musty old room. Bundled herbs of every sort, which filled the air with a bitter green fragrance, hung from the ceiling. Oversized jars filled with things such as "Dragon's Blood Reed" and "Solomon's Seal" took up every inch of shelf space in the shop.

"Have you seen the back room yet?" a beautiful, dark, elfin woman asked me.

"Yes," I lied. I didn't want to speak to her any further. I was drowning in a mix of emotions that ranged from fascination to dread and the last thing I wanted was to look like a novice. The woman disappeared behind a dark blue beaded curtain that led to the back of the shop. As I stood there watching the hanging strands swing and click together I wondered to myself, *Should I pass through the curtain or not? Where would it lead? What would I find?*

That day I took a breath, braced myself, and passed through that mysterious threshold. To my surprise I didn't stumble into evil, bedevilment, or other dark doings. Instead, I wandered into a world of wisdom, truth, beauty, and above all else, spiritual awakening. When I passed through the curtain that day, I took my first steps on a magical odyssey that continues to this day.

The book you hold in your hands chronicles my apprenticeship along the path of *Wicca*, The Craft of the Wise, which is the name of the spiritual path of contemporary witches. During the years of my training, I learned the ways of a mystic, a healer, a seer, and a magician. Through the guidance of my teachers and by practicing the techniques of this path, I learned how to forge a close relationship with deity and how to align myself with the spiritual power that flows through all things.

This same spiritual journey awaits you as well.

As you read, you may choose to undertake your own spiritual apprenticeship and to awaken the magical power residing within you. For this purpose I have provided the methods that I was taught by my elders and that I still use today.

You may notice, as I did, that at times the practices and techniques feel peculiar and unfamiliar. This is deliberate. The Wiccan path is not intended to soothe or coddle the apprentice. In fact, I found that my training was at times disorienting and even a bit unnerving. I attended mysterious rituals and engaged in unusual customs. However, I discovered that each step of the way was purposeful and designed. Each of the lessons that I encountered pushed the limits of my perceptions, my notions, and my assumptions about life and the world around me. They caused me to become reflective, and consequently, to take note of who and what I was (and continue to be) in the world. Their techniques were aimed at awakening me suddenly to the mystery and power of my being. They worked to ground me in the moment so that I could see for myself that spirit, magic, and power stood before me all the while.

The teachings I encountered compelled me to explore difficult questions like, "What is life?" and "What is death?" It wasn't an easy thing to do. Nevertheless, the practices of Wicca led me to realize the power and magic of living in the present and to recognize the sacredness of each moment. It was a spiritual quest that required hard work, dedication, and a willingness to address the core issues of my life. Through it, I completely reevaluated my understanding of existence.

There were easier options for me. There were spiritual paths available that didn't require the same amount of effort, discipline, or nerve as did Wicca. Why then did I choose to take this path?

In retrospect, I can see now that I chose it because I was yearning for closeness with deity and satisfaction with my life, but everywhere I turned I was unable to attain either of my goals. Mainstream religions failed to bring me into a close relationship with God. No amount of money, good food, sex, fun, or friends seemed to help me feel whole or complete. I chose it because there was nothing left for me to do; I was pressed up against the wall of my own existence and I wanted answers. *What was my life all about anyway?* I wondered. Wicca helped me to locate the gaps in my life and then filled those gaps with spirit and power.

I chose the path of Wicca because its spiritual language and imagery spoke clearly to me. I discovered that its prayers were the wind in the trees, the sunrise, and the stars in the cosmos. I found that its liturgy was none other than the blood that coursed through my veins.

I saw that in the ways of the wise the holy land was everywhere and the spiritual messenger, the prophet, the sage, and the savior was myself.

I chose it because the spiritual practices of Wicca guided me in living my day to day life presently and attentively. They taught me how to live with life as it is — in accord with nature, reality, and spirit. I experienced Wicca as a path that feels as real and alive as this very moment in which you read this page. In fact, it is from this feeling, experiencing and living from moment to moment that practices of Wicca emerge. For the Wiccan, each passing moment holds magic. Each season, each heartbeat, each breath holds power and wonder. All you must do is claim the marvels of your life.

But before you can claim anything, you too must take a breath and pass through the dark blue beaded curtain.

CHAPTER I

HERMES

Magic and power are in your everyday life.

INVOCATION

Ten people stand in a sacred space we've collectively created in one of our homes. One woman brought shells and sea water that sit in a bowl in the west of our sacred space. Another person brought beaded crow feathers that lie in the east. At the northern edge of the space lie gray-blue stones gathered from a nearby hill and in the south is a bundle of dried chili peppers. The flames from the candles that demarcate our sacred space shiver and twist in the faint summer breeze that wafts through a nearby window. We have collected the tools of our magic: the air we breathe, the water that makes up our bodies, the life force within us, and the earth beneath our feet. We are tapping the infinite powers of human life—what it is we think, feel, love, and touch as we dance the sacred round of our existence. We don't need anything more. Magic is here.

A woman rings a bell three times to signal the start of our sacred celebration.

We gather in a circle of community and friendship. Hermes, Hecate, Sin, Muse, Fate, Chaos, Pandora, Saturn, Demeter, and I stand together holding each other's hands. We are a human pantheon standing in a living room. We close our eyes lightly and create a sound made up of woven voices. Then Hermes calls out:

> *O Guide of spirits, messenger of the anointed, bring forth*
> *your wisdom. Enlighten us, winged one of old. Bring forth*
> *knowledge of the divine and ensoul us once more. You who*
> *speak with the voice of ancient magics, teach us that which*
> *is yet unknown. Open for us the path of power.*

THE TALE — *Snow on the Path*

In a time before anyone can remember, there lived the Arch-Druid of Wales. He was renowned for his great magical powers. He could command the heavens and earth. With a simple gesture, he could move the seas and rivers. With his spells, powders, and simples, he could conjure the spirits of the dead and foretell the future. The Arch-Druid was schooled in every glamour and enchantment known in his time.

One day, this sorcerer received word that on the remote Isle of Man there lived a village herbalist who had far greater power than he. Moved by his vanity and indignance, the Arch-Druid took it upon himself to seek out this all-powerful magician. It was the dead of winter; nonetheless, he traveled for twenty days in freezing weather until he finally arrived at the Isle of Man.

When he found the cottage of the herbalist, he found no one but a simple, bent old woman sweeping snow from her front walk. "Are you the village herbalist?" asked the Arch-Druid. "Yes," she replied. With a grand gesture, he flourished his cloak and said, "I am the Arch-Druid of Wales. I am renowned for my great magical powers. I can command the heavens and earth. I can move the seas and rivers. I can conjure the spirits of the dead and foretell the future. I know every glamour and enchantment, yet I am told that you have more power than I."

The woman continued sweeping silently.

The Arch-Druid demanded, "Speak up, woman! I am here to learn from you. What power have you to teach me?"

With that, the woman handed him her broom. "There is snow on the path," she said, "sweep it clean."

MAGICAL LAW — *Magic and power are in your everyday life.*

HERMES' LAW

I wasn't doing anything special when it happened. I was simply standing in line at the grocery store, waiting for my turn at the register. I stood behind a woman who thumbed through a magazine and who occasionally shushed her screaming infant. The man behind me smelled like rotten cigar smoke and he was wheezing on my back. I was waiting for an eternity. It wasn't the most glamorous moment, but it was then that it hit me.

My normal vision changed. It seemed as though I was able to see from every part of my eyes. This gave an odd curved appearance to my environment. It looked as though everything — myself included — was part of a sphere. For that moment I could see the interconnectedness of the people and things around me.

This is it, I realized. *This moment, this screaming and wheezing and waiting and standing — this life — this is it. This is a moment of power.* It was an earth-shattering, jaw-dropping, stomach-sinking insight. But it was the truth.

Standing at the center of that realization, I felt like some lifelong, primal tension had melted away from me. My defenses dropped. Muscles that I never knew existed seemed to loosen. I felt tranquil as though I had never felt real peace before. In that instant, I saw that there was nothing to hope or wish for and nothing to fear. There was nothing that would make this moment more complete or whole or right.

Right here is the sacred place, I thought. It wasn't at my home, at Machu Pichu, at Stonehenge, in a sacred grove, or somewhere else beside the line at the grocery store. It wasn't the parts of my life that I liked or that were pleasurable. I realized that sacredness is everywhere and is everything — whether I liked it or not. *This is where I have power.* It didn't have anything to do with money or career. It wasn't about having authority in the world or gaining control. Power exists independent of these things. *This is where I find deity.* I wasn't going to have a more "sacred" experience during a religious ceremony, or by attending a church, a synagogue, temple, or magic circle. I laughed out loud. *This is it.*

How did this happen? From where did this experience come? My thoughts went back to a conversation I had had some months ago with an elder from my spiritual tradition—a man whom I knew as Hermes. We were in the desert mountains of Anza Borrego some miles outside of the southern California city of San Diego. We were gathering sage for the celebration of the full moon to take place later that night. It was late in the day and we didn't have time to waste, so the two of us busied ourselves, harvesting the best foliage we could find.

At that time of my life, I was heavily involved in my spiritual training. I eagerly poured my energy into participating in the elaborate and mysterious ceremonies conducted by my teachers who were mystics of an ancient Northern European earth-religion. Including Hermes, most of the elders from this circle lived in the city. They held regular jobs, raised ordinary families, and lived modest lives. But these were extraordinary people. They were magical.

In a tribal culture, these folk would have been revered by their peers as conservators of sacred wisdom. They would have been known as honored visionaries, priests, and priestesses. Their people would have consulted them in matters of life and death. They would be asked to ease the pain of childbirth, to heal the sick with herbs, to preside over the tribe's rites of passage, and the seasonal changes. Depending on the culture, their people might have referred to them as *interpreters of the spirits, medicine men and women, or women and men of knowledge.* Anthropologists would call them shamans.

I knew them and their crafts as Wicca, a Middle English word meaning "wise." Wicca also comes from the Anglo-Saxon root word—*wic*—which means "to bend or to shape." Both terms were apropos descriptions of my teachers. Each one was capable of bending and shaping his or her own life to the play of reality. The way that they practiced bending and shaping was through the mystic arts of magic and spiritual power.

When I was first introduced to the terms "magic" and "power" in a spiritual tradition, I thought that these practices would give me influence over other people and the things of the world. I assumed that they were arts that would somehow make life better than it was. However, as I came to learn, neither power nor magic had anything to do with transforming life itself. Instead of changing everything and everyone around me, I learned that power and magic were mystic arts that changed the way I perceived and functioned in life as it already existed.

My teachers were clear with me. There were both ordinary and extraordinary people living in the world, and I learned how to distinguish between the two. "For the most part, people on the ordinary path of life associate the word power with control," I remember being told. In ordinary thinking, power is about "making," "forcing," or "compelling" your personal will on the world. In ordinary life, power means that you have caused something to happen. Ordinary individuals believe it is an extraordinary event when they make things happen according to their personal caprices. They buy something they want. They manipulate people and events until they get their own way. But, as I learned, when your idea of power is linked closely with what you can control, the fall from power is quick and hard.

I discovered on the Wiccan path that *power* is a natural state of being. It is about finding your place within the vastness of nature, uniting with that vastness, and then operating from that experience of accord. The elders taught me that the art of mystic power has nothing to do with maneuvering for personal gain. When you align with power, you act out of each moment, out of whatever life and nature requires. Power is releasing yourself from the shackles of personal expectations and opening to the requirements of your present circumstances.

According to my training, power comes from strength in your actions and in your thoughts. Action is powerful only when it addresses whatever each moment requires. It is natural, sequential action. Power is when one action leads to the next. For example, it is powerless to audition for the Philharmonic before you have taken your first music lesson. It is just as powerless to leave a marriage before ever asking, "Is there anything we can do to make this better?" I remember one spiritual master illustrating the principle of power in natural, sequential order by saying, "If you have finished eating, clean your bowl."[1] Or as the village herbalist stated, "There is snow on the path. Sweep it clean." This kind of power has less to do with taking control of things, and more to do with taking *responsibility* for how you handle each moment of your life.

Magic means trickery in the ways of ordinary living. For most people, the word magic conjures up images of illusionists and slight of hand. I learned that for Wiccans, the term *magic* means powerful thought. Powerful thought is not the usual spinning of ideas, ruminating, and getting caught up in cerebral activity. Powerful thought is about altering, widening, and opening your current mental perspective to include many possibilities. Dion Fortune, a noted twentieth-century mystic, called magic "the ability to change consciousness at will."[2] The elders of my spiritual circle showed me that once I was able to change my consciousness, my mental perspective about what life presented to me, then I would have more options for taking action. I would have more options for living in fulfillment and satisfaction.

For example, I may hang on to a belief that mowing the lawn is a waste of time. As long as I hang on to that consciousness — that mindset — about mowing the lawn, I will feel miserable whenever I have to mow. If I change my thought processes just slightly and remove all of my opinions, beliefs, and running commentary about mowing the lawn, then I have also removed the misery. That is magic. As I came to learn, that is the basis of creating an extraordinary life.

People who act out of ordinary thinking get caught up in personally manufactured limits, rigidity, opinions, and preferences. They lose sight of what is really before them. When the grass needs mowing, they see a miserable, exasperating task that they hate to do. People of magic bypass all of this and live in the moment with a flexible, neutral mind. For these folk, mowing the grass is mowing the grass — nothing more. It is a simple, subtle distinction that indicates whether or not someone lives with magical empowerment.

Of course, up to this point in my training, these were all theories. They were nice ideas and goals toward which I might strive. But that would all change in the desert of Anza Borrego.

As usual, my musings had taken me away from the task at hand. The cry of a coyote awakened me from my internal ramblings. I was absorbed in my thoughts to the point that I hadn't even noticed the change in light. It was already dusk there in the desert mountains. Despite the time of day, it was uncomfortably hot.

Hermes and I continued to work in silence for a long time until he suddenly spoke. "You're ready to learn the laws of power," he said. "What was that?" I asked. I wasn't sure what I was hearing. "Its time to learn the elder lessons," he said, keeping his eyes focused on the sagebrush in front of him.

I had never heard of such a thing. I had been with Hermes and the others of our sacred circle for twelve years. Nobody told me about elder lessons or laws of power. During my extensive apprenticeship I had acquainted myself with all sorts of invocations, rites, and rituals. I knew the principles of astrology, numerology, palmistry, and other divinatory methods. I knew words of power, prayers, and meditations. I learned many mystical secrets over the years. So what was he talking about? I stared at Hermes. "Elder lessons?" I asked.

Without hesitation, he said, "To begin, everyone must answer this question: what is this life?" Like my previous experiences with Hermes, this was all happening a bit too quickly. I didn't have time to think his words through. They caught me off guard. I was even more surprised to discover that after all of my years of study, I could not adequately answer him. If he had asked me about the cycles of the moon and their relation to spellwork, I could quote the key written sources verbatim. If he had asked me about the kinds of herbs one might use to invoke love, prosperity, or good fortune—I could rattle off a whole list of these. But I was stunned by the simplicity and depth of the question he posed. With a few words he had left me in the dust, not knowing what to say or do.

What *is* this life, I wondered. Does anyone know for certain? I tried to justify my ignorance by reassuring myself that religious scholars and teachers from every epoch and every culture of the world had tried to unravel this mystery. How could I ever hope to know?

Without uttering a word, Hermes picked up a stick and drew a large circle in the mud-cracked earth. "Here is where you'll find your answers," he said, and then went back to picking sage. I stood there looking at his circle in the dirt. I couldn't decide if this was a joke.

Hermes was a great prankster, and he often used a cunning and purposeful sense of humor in his teachings. He then startled me out of my thoughts with a stern command, "Sit down!" This was no joke. He pointed to the center of the circle with the stick. After I sat, he instructed me to face the east. "This is only one direction," he said. "One direction teaches one magical lesson. Learn the lesson of the east and the laws of magic will unfold for you."

His statement seemed strange to me. Then he looked at me for a long time as though he was deliberating on what he might say next. He squinted his eyes and locked his gaze on me. "What does the eastern quarter of the world rule?" he finally blurted out.

The question surprised me. It took me a moment to decide what he was asking. Then I remembered something from my magical studies, "It rules thought and ideas."

"That's it," he shouted, "that is where you'll find your answers and the first law of power." "What?" I was completely confused.

"Timothy, sit," he said. "Sit with your thoughts. Look at them. Watch them go by. Once they're all done misleading you, you'll find your power."

That day, for the first time, I sat with the magical question, "What is this life?" What would I find? Where would this lead me? I dared not ask these questions aloud. I had come to this circle of magical elders specifically for training. This is what I got.

For months after that day I diligently sat while facing the east. Each time, I'd ask, "What is this life?" No arcane message came to me. No special secret revealed itself to me. No God or Goddess, no angel or fairy came and explained things to me. I just sat. I sat and watched my thoughts come and go. I watched my opinions and my beliefs march by. Sometimes I would find myself caught up in the drama of my thoughts and feelings. The question and this sitting were maddening.

Over time I got angry; so I sat and fumed. Then I got very sad; so I sat with tears. Day after day I would draw a circle in the earth and sit with this question. Arriving at the answer was a slow and difficult process. But in time I began to notice small changes in my perception.

Some of these changes were disturbing. I would have brief, odd experiences. They were strange sensations and insights that I had never before encountered. For instance, one morning while I was out for my usual jog, I noticed my shadow on the ground. I immediately became light-headed. It felt as though something inside of me woke up suddenly and anxiously. I could feel my face flush. I looked at that jogging shadow of mine and it struck me: *I'm here. I'm really here. This life is really happening. I don't get to do this second over again.*

I had several experiences like this—each one causing me to feel an urgent need to take action. But I would never know quite what to do. Just as quickly as the experiences would come to me, they would fade away. My life would return to normal.

But this time in the checkout line at the grocery store it all became clear. Hermes was right. My thoughts were done misleading me for now. I had a window of clarity and I saw this life. I understood the completeness of this moment which is what makes it powerful. *What is this life?* Just this. Magic is the life you have right now. You gain access to this magic when you embrace this life. There is no other life you can have—live it fully. In that window of clarity I recognized the first of the magical laws. Only those individuals who can recognize the magical experience of their own lives have access to spiritual empowerment.

It can be difficult to believe that what appears to be a problematic, complex, stressful, or humdrum life is actually magical. Most of us are looking for the dramatic and the spectacular when we search for spiritual empowerment. If we pick up a book on magical laws, we want to experience bells and whistles. We want something that will change our lives. Maybe we are like the Arch-Druid of Wales and we want that special something that will set us apart from the rest of the world. Or perhaps we make the mistake of engaging in a spiritual practice, looking for something that will make us feel holy, right, enlightened, or at least different from the way we feel now. We want something to make us or our lives special. We want an escape from the pain that can be part of living. We don't want to be told that power comes from a moment filled with screaming babies, cigar stench, grocery store checkout lines, or anything else that we might consider unpleasant.

Even now, you might expect that the author of a book on "magical awakening" would excite or perhaps even soothe you with talk about angels, fairies, or friendly spirits that are waiting nearby to help you find power in your life and thereby escape your woes. Perhaps you even began reading this book with an expectation of comfort, hoping to learn ways to avoid any of life's unpleasantness. Or maybe you wanted positive affirmations, prayers, or special sentiments that would help you heal emotional wounds or pamper your "inner child." Maybe you wanted to gloss over a life of disempowerment, disappointment, and drudgery with "white light" and nice thoughts.

That is not what you'll find in any of the magical laws.

Instead of an escape from what you have in your life, here you will find a path that leads directly to the heart of it. The first magical law teaches you to come to terms with the reality of your life that is here, before you right now.

Although the reality of your current life may not seem very magical or powerful, it is. You have every magical weapon, every mystic spell and incantation at your disposal in this moment. As I discovered about myself, your own magic may be buried beneath layers of thoughts, beliefs, preferences, and aversions you've built up while living an "ordinary" life. Nonetheless, power and magic are there waiting for you to awaken them. The key to unlock this potential comes when you develop an experiential awareness of the mystery, enchantment, and boundlessness of the life you have in front of you. When you shift your awareness in this magical way, your life transforms. You make the passage from ordinary to extraordinary living.

Living your life in accord with Hermes' magical law may sound inspiring and simple, yet miraculous. Although it is all of these things, it is also not for the faint-hearted. It is a law that requires attention, hard work, and sometimes painful soul searching. It is the life of someone who is willing to challenge ordinary ways of thinking and behaving. Someone who is able to see the magic of the life before him has wandered beyond his personal limits by stepping outside of his known culture, historical context, gender, and family role.

If you choose to live by the ways of Hermes' law, you too will arrive at the boundaries and limitations of whatever you have learned about life to date. It is there that you encounter the truth of your existence and discover who and what you are in reality. In that moment, your old powerless ways and ordinary beliefs that have hindered you will shatter. And once you have opened the floodgates of power and magic there is no turning back. You can never return to your old way of existing in the world. It takes a brave soul to live by this magical law. Consequently, a life of power and magic is, as it always has been, the experience of a select few. But its rewards are immeasurable.

It is important not to fool yourself into believing that by simply reading a book or thinking hard about it you will embrace extraordinary living. The law of finding magic in your day-to-day life comes when you have had firsthand experience with the source behind magical awakening. In other words, you must come face to face with the divine, the universe, "God," deity, or whatever else you would like to name the sacred forces that direct and maintain all of life. Wiccans refer to this source as *nature*.

The first magical law that I encountered implies that power and magic come from linking directly to nature — including human nature. On the magical path, nature is a manifestation of deity. Everything thought of, everything named is a manifestation of deity for beings of power. Magical folk breathe and eat the divine. They walk through it, stand on it, and sleep in it. Power comes from living within this reality. When you arrive at this realization, you can see that every moment that passes is a moment of divinity. Harmony with life as it presents itself is the key to living a magical life.

Fortunately, you don't have to travel very far or go to exceptional lengths in order to connect with nature and deity. Since you are a part of nature, you are also a part of the divine. In its essence, your life right now is a manifestation of deity. This can be a difficult lesson to accept, because our mainstream spiritual traditions tell us that "God" is supposed to be an ideal. It is supposed to be "perfection" that is separate from humanness.[3] It is important for you to circumvent these kinds of ideas in order to claim power. They interfere with the reality that each of us is perfect as we are right now. You are as perfect as any creation.

Look at the trees growing somewhere outside your window and decide which among them is perfect and which is not. Which sunrise is perfect and which is not? Which of the oceans is more perfect than the other? Heraclitus said that for God, all things are right and as they are supposed to be, but for man some things are as they as supposed to be and some things are not.[4] It seems as though living without awareness of divinity in all things is a problem unique to humans living ordinary lives. This is important to know because it means that you do not need to "do" anything special to find perfection.

Perfection just "is." It comes in every shape and size. It looks like things we enjoy and things that bother us. In order to claim the power of your perfection all you need is to accept, to surrender, and to marvel about the mix of life.

This is the power that comes from living in reality. My teachers used the term "reality" often in reference to life as one experiences it in the present moment. If you are living with reality, you are focused on what is happening now. You experience life as an integration of the elements and people that are around you in this instant. The light that illuminates this book, the chair in which you sit, your breath, your thoughts and feelings are integrated, and they inform and empower you within each second. You open to the five senses—vision, hearing, taste, touch, and smell—and take action based on what information comes to you. Living this way is critical to people who abide by the first magical law because they know that reality is a fusion of nature and spirit.[5] In reality, magic and power come from a combination of working and of simply being. They arise from both earthly love and sacred devotion. They manifest when you wash the car, eat your breakfast, have sex, raise your children, and when you realize that each activity of your daily life is an expression of the divine.

The surest way to lose spiritual empowerment and magic is when you see yourself as something outside of nature, outside of life looking in. When we see our lives as something separate from nature and deity, we perceive other people and life itself as objects that we must master. This leads to diminution and fragmentation of the whole of nature, of society, and of our bodies, minds, and spirits.[6] In this frame of mind, we put distance between ourselves, other people, and things. When we live our lives outside of the first magical law, we search for ourselves, our power, and our spirit outside of what we've already got.

Then we start to disrupt the unity of reality and orient the universe around ourselves.[7] We become self-centered, struggling against nature, reality, and deity. In that state, we work to manipulate life so that things always go our way. We think that our needs are more important than everyone else's. Often in that powerless and disconnected state, we adopt a subtle and pervasive attitude of entitlement. We desire, we demand, we insist that life provide whatever it is we personally require.

When we are disconnected from what life is offering to us right now, we use force to get our own way. Or in a more passive mode, we may pray or chant or recite positive affirmations to keep our lives running according to our own personal preferences. In a disconnected state, we all do things that we think will somehow change what life really is. When we act from the disconnected frame of mind we may take the right vitamins, wear the right clothes, or try to say the right things whenever we can. Some people focus on making lots of money, so that they can buy a smooth life. We get caught up in our unique methods of coping with living in a disconnected fashion and believe that these methods are going to save us. It rarely occurs to us that our coping strategies themselves reinforce our disconnection. For example, working to make a lot of money will not change the basics of life. You will still face emotional ups and downs, disappointments, difficulties, pleasure, and tedium. No matter how much money you make, you will still yearn for love, eat, eliminate, breathe, and eventually die. Ultimately, your money, things, hopes, and dreams will not change what is at the bottom of life in this moment. Life itself refuses to change, and when you are disconnected from reality and nature you adopt a powerless stance. Magical folk say that this is the stance of someone who has experienced "soul loss."[8] The only way to recover a lost soul is to relink it steadfastly to nature.

The word "religion" comes from a Latin word, *religare*, which means "to bind" or relink.[9] Religion implies a relinking to deity. Since deity is right here and right now, the word religion also implies that we link to the moment, to nature, and whatever that may bring. The word religion came from the language of the ancient Europeans whose religious work was centered on relinking to deity through nature. Theirs was a pantheon of reality and of human experiences.

Because of their potent imagery, the mythic gods and their teachings continue to serve Wiccans as symbols of the divine working in our everyday lives. They continually beckon anyone seeking magical awakening, calling each of us to join them in the wonders of living presently and powerfully. These are the gods and the ways of the pagan peoples; they are the wisdom of our ancestors, our blood, bone, and flesh. Looking to the old gods for spiritual inspiration is not a return to anything antiquated and lifeless. It is a return to the energies of our present existence. They are waiting deep inside each of us, since they are personifications of our own bodies, sensations, thoughts, feelings, and dreams. They are both symbolic representations and actualities. They are the air we breathe, the water we drink, the warmth of our bodies, and the earth itself. They are not the final word, the Alpha and the Omega, presences for you to bow down to and worship. Instead, they are doorways that open to power; they are presences you can associate with your own life and your own daily experiences.

Psychoanalyst Carl Jung called the ancient gods "archetypes,"[10] symbols of experiences common to all of humanity. They connect us to one another. Each of us experiences laughter, joy, anguish, fear, and sadness. We all have experienced the heat of the sun, the frost of winter, and the mystery of the full moon. As humans, we all have the same bodies and the same structures of mind. Like our ancestors we ultimately face the same baseline life issues such as birth, coming of age, sexuality, and old age. We all laugh, share pain, and are grateful. These experiences are what bind us together in a human community. The ancient gods are presences that personify each of these experiences, and on the path of empowerment and magic you will find a link to each one.

In the magical law of finding power in your daily living, the symbol of the linking force is the mythic god Hermes. The ancient Greeks saw Hermes as a messenger who was a bridge between humanity and the pantheon of divinity. Hermes' secondary role was keeper of magical wisdom. He is a symbolic representation of a linking force that resides within each of us. Hermes represents the possibility of a direct connection between the divine and your daily life. He also symbolizes the opening to magical potential. When you align with Hermes, you establish your own link to the world of wonders and the awakening that is in store for you.

THE ENCHANTMENTS

Learning the Symbols of a Magical Life

If you plan to learn the powerful ways of magic, it is important to learn the picture language of symbols. Symbols are images, words, or actions that have particular meaning and specific, significant connotations.[11] Think of the image of a red circle bisected by a diagonal line. Most of us understand this as a symbol designating something forbidden or not wanted. You might see it in a park to indicate an area where dogs are not allowed. Or you might see it in the streets to warn against littering. This is a symbol that aids you in your ordinary life.

Spiritual symbols aid you in your extraordinary life. A spiritual symbol represents an energy, an idea, or an experience which is beyond the surface image, word, or act. A mandala is not just a pretty, round painting from India. It is an artist's rendering of a spiritual journey through realms of experience. Just as the red, bisected circle conveys a specific message, a spiritual symbol indicates the path toward a powerful and magical life. Every religious system uses spiritual symbols to help its practitioners find their own path toward experiencing reality, nature, and deity.

In primal cultures, a magical, powerful being uses the symbols of the natural world to express spiritual ideas and experiences. Life, the mystery of your own being, is the basis for all symbols of magic and empowerment. Life is sacred, and those things that support life are also sacred: air, fire, water, and earth. These are the basic elements of magic and of life. To the person of power, everything you can see is a symbol of sacredness and you can categorize everything according to the four elements.

Air

Magical people call the power of air the power "To Know." The element of air has to do with any aspect of life related to thought, communication, speech, and knowledge. Writing, self-expression, creativity, ideas, the arts, learning, and all forms of education fall under the symbolic category of the element air. Any time you have a conversation, watch television, read a book, or have a brilliant idea, you experience life through one aspect of deity, embodied by the element of air.

Fire

The power "To Will" is what magical people call the power of fire. Fire and will power have to do with physical energy, spontaneity, force, drive, ambition, and passion. Action, movement, work, sexuality, and physical strength are all tied into the power of fire. Any time you physically move—whether drumming your fingers or working out at the gym—you ignite the element of fire. When you go to your job, engage in sexual activity, or play, you experience deity through the magical ring and power of fire.

Water

The element of water is the element that connects with your emotions, feelings, cycles, memories, compassion, and understanding. It also links with the movement of your unconscious mind. It governs areas such as dreams, intuition, hunches, and premonitions. Magical folk call the power of water, the power "To Dare." When you recall an event from the past, or when you find compassion for another person, you have connected to deity through the element of water. Likewise, when you have a premonition that something will occur, or when you feel love for someone, you have entered the magical pool of water.

Earth

The power "To Be Silent" is what magical people call the power of earth. Earth symbolizes the material world: goods, property, money, and gain. But it also represents qualities like solidity, unity, and stability. Whenever you work with money, whether you are paying off your credit cards, learning how to invest, or making a purchase, you align with deity as it expresses itself through the element of earth.

Each of the elements also symbolize aspects of deity within human beings. For example, people who are reliable, stable, and dependable are earthy people. Individuals who are emotional or compassionate carry the energy of water. Passionate, active, and intense people align with the energies of fire, while talkative, social, and imaginative people align with air.

The four elements correspond with many other aspects of life: the four compass directions, the seasons, colors, senses, and stages of human life. Knowing each symbolic aspect of the elements helps you to understand how deity manifests through them. For your convenience, I have provided a brief list of several correspondences with each element in the chart on the following page.

Making Sacred Space

In order to find the sacred in everyday experience, you can create sacred space. You do this by aligning with all four of the elements the aspects of deity. All space is sacred space to people of power. The earth, the town where you live, the room in which you sit are all sacred when you open yourself to magical consciousness. The act of creating sacred space is a process that helps you to open up to seeing the wonder and magic of the life you have before you right now.

The Elements and Their Correspondences

ELEMENT	AIR	FIRE	WATER	EARTH
DIRECTION	East	South	West	North
SEASON	Spring	Summer	Fall	Winter
COLOR	Yellow	Red	Blue	Black
LIFE CYCLE	Birth	Youth	Maturity	Old Age
TIME	Dawn	Midday	Dusk	Midnight
SENSE	Hearing	Seeing	Taste, Smell	Touch
EXPRESSION OF	Breath, directed thought	Physical energy, physical force	Feelings, directed compassion	The body, silence

Most of us live in denial about what is really happening in our lives. We do this because the actuality of our lives may be painful, boring, or unpleasant. The practice of creating sacred space will make you come out of your hiding place and expose you to the moment and whatever it may bring. It will center you in the reality of what is happening right now. It does this by helping you ask the questions raised by each of the elements and their corresponding compass directions.

The east asks you, "What are your thoughts right now? Are they real? Are they necessary?" The south asks you, "Who are you? and

What are you?" The west asks the question, "What do you feel? What do you sense?" The north asks the question, "What is your place in the world?" When you ask these questions and keep them in your heart—not only when you cast the circle but when you mow the lawn, wash the dishes, eat, play, and work—eventually the mysteries of these questions and of your life begin to unfold.

Many magical people call creating sacred space "casting the circle." A circle is an important symbol shared by most cultures to represent the infinite, spirit, and deity. The circle is a geometric shape representing perfection and simplicity. With the practice of casting the circle, you will begin to see the truth of your own existence, which is also a manifestation of perfection and simplicity. Casting the circle brings you in touch with the simplicity of being, of existing from one magical moment to the next. It helps you see the perfection of your own life. Through this practice, you will discover that your life is the circle. You are made up of the circle, and your existence is a powerful continuum of all that exists internally and externally.

Casting the Circle

To begin, close your eyes and take several deep, slow, relaxing breaths. Imagine that you face the east of your sacred space. As you imagine this, take a moment to monitor your thoughts. Do not follow them along their path. Just see what is going on inside of your head and take note of it.

Now imagine that you face the south of your circle. Take time to feel the beating of your heart and the inhalation/exhalation of your breathing. To align with the south, ask yourself the question, "Who am I?" Shorten the question to "Who?" which you ask as you exhale on three consecutive breaths. Do not attempt to answer the question consciously. Simply ask it without any expectation.

Imagine that you turn to face the west. As you do this, monitor your feelings. What are you feeling and sensing right now? What emotions lie just below the surface of the current moment? Allow them to bubble up, whatever they may be: sadness, anger, happiness—whatever comes up. Do not edit them. Instead, take the time to feel them without adding any thought to them. Do not cling to any of the things you perceive or feel, but simply allow them to be whatever they are as they transform from moment to moment.

When you have done this for a few minutes, imagine that you turn to face the north of your sacred space. Take a moment to feel the seat, floor, or bed beneath you. Feel the weight and balance points of your body. Where does your body bend as its sits? Where does it make contact with the surface beneath it? Listen to the sounds around you. As you breathe through your nose, take note of the sounds you make (if any). Feel your abdomen expand and contract as you inhale and exhale. Take this time to become truly present to your environment and your place within it. Is there any difference between "you" and your "environment"?

When you have centered yourself in all four directions, open your eyes and stretch your arms and legs to be certain that you are fully alert. Try this practice twice daily—once when you awaken in the morning and once before you retire in the evening. However, keep the question of each direction in mind as you go about your daily routine. Wherever you are, take note of the direction you face in each moment and raise the question of that direction to yourself.

1. David Scott and Tony Doubleday, *The Elements of Zen* (New York: Barnes & Noble Books, 1992).
2. Quoted by Starhawk in *The Spiral Dance* (San Francisco: HarperCollins, 1989), p. 32.
3. Arnold Joseph Toynbee, *Choose Life* (New York: Oxford University Press, 1989), p. 321.
4. This is a paraphrase from Joseph Campbell, Betty Sue Flowers, ed., *The Power of Myth* (New York: Doubleday, 198), p. 66.
5. Toynbee, *Choose Life* (New York: Oxford University Press, 1989), p. 25.
6. Erwin Chargaff, *Serious Questions* (Boston: Birkhäuser, 1986), p. 154.
7. Toynbee, *Choose Life* (New York: Oxford University Press, 1989), p. 23.
8. Mircea Eliade, *Shamanism: Archaic Techniques in Ecstasy*, (New Jersey: Princeton University Press, 1974), p. 310.
9. Noah Webster, Jean L. McKechnie, ed., *Webster's New Universal Unabridged Dictionary* (Cleveland: Dorset & Baber, 1979), p. 1527.
10. Jung calls archetypes "instinctual trends," which are turned into symbols, such as gods. See, e.g., Carl G. Jung, *Man and His Symbols* (New York: Dell Publishing, 1964), p. 58.
11. Carl G. Jung, *Man and His Symbols* (New York: Dell Publishing, 1964), p. 3.

CHAPTER II

HECATE

When faced, fear becomes a power.

INVOCATION
▼ ▲ ▼

Hermes moves through clouds of smoke that rise from smoldering, dried, white sage. From where I sit in the circle, it is difficult for me to distinguish the white of his long, loose hair from the smoke that surrounds him. Ceremonially he carries a large, brass bowl around the circle three times. Hermes speaks not a word but presents the bowl to each of the four compass directions. Someone else shakes a rattle and whispers a chant to the goddess Hecate. I am there in the circle with two other postulants who are about to be initiated into the mysteries of our own darkness. The air is cold and I feel a tingling sensation move across my arms and down the back of my neck.

Then Hermes stops in front of me. He lowers the bowl to the level of my eyes so that I can peer inside of it. "Look and learn"; he breathes the words into my ear so softly that it tickles. The smoke from the sage makes my eyes water a bit, but I look into the bowl and see an odd reflection. It appears to be a face other than my own staring back at me. The vision is startling and I can feel my heart race.

Although the sight makes me want to run from the circle, I am riveted and cannot look away. The longer I stare, the more I can see that this is the face of an elderly person. The eyes look familiar to me. Then it dawns on me — this is my own face. This is the face of my old age, of my death. I am shocked.

Hermes chuckles, and pulls the bowl away. He holds it up high and calls out to the night sky:

> *Dark Mother, we stand at your crossroads of magic. We open ourselves to the transformation of our fears. Be our guide, O Lady of Night, as we search for your cosmic mirror. Be with us and teach us to see through the shadows. Help us know what is not yet known. Whisper to us the words of strength that open wide the gates of your power.*

THE TALE — *The Potion*

Long ago there lived a wise man in a village. In the course of his lifetime he had taken on two apprentices, one clever and the other foolish. Over the years of his training, he taught them the healing arts and the ways of magic, but neither apprentice had demonstrated true power.

One day he brought the apprentices into his private chambers. He closed the door behind him and placed a green corked bottle on the center of a table. "I have taught you the healing arts and the ways of magic," he said to them, "yet neither of you shows your power." The two apprentices were speechless. The old man continued, "I have decided to give each of you the gift of power. I have here a potion that, if drunk, will unleash the wisdom of the ages. It will give whoever drinks it power far beyond ordinary human beings. He who drinks of this potion shall have the ability to do whatever he pleases."

The foolish apprentice said, "That's for me. I wish to have that power." But the clever apprentice remained silent.

"And you may have that power," said the wise old man. "However, if you drink the potion with the slightest shade of fear in your heart, the potion will act as a poison and you will die a slow, agonizing death. This is my final lesson to you both." And with that, the wise old man left the two apprentices alone in the room with the green corked bottle.

The foolish apprentice said, "I cannot drink this for surely I will die. The old man himself causes me to be afraid — let alone his noxious elixirs. What foul sorcery is this that one must face his own death?" The clever apprentice remained silent. "I cannot bear the disgrace that this teacher has brought upon us," said the foolish apprentice. "I must leave this place," he shouted as he stormed out the door without even taking his belongings.

Without a word, the clever apprentice uncorked the green bottle and drank the potion. Within moments, he was filled with the wisdom of the ages. He gained power far beyond ordinary human beings, and he saw that he had the ability to do whatever he pleased.

The old wise man entered the room. "Ah, I see one of you still stands." "Yes master," said the clever apprentice. "But tell me why you drank the potion," inquired the old man.

The apprentice said, "In one life there is but one death. I saw that I could no longer fear what is assured." The old man burst out laughing, "Then did you enjoy the tea?"

MAGICAL LAW — *When faced, fear becomes a power.*

Hecate's Law

Hecate always caused me anxiety. She certainly lived up to her goddess' namesake. The ancient deity known as Hecate, the mother of darkness and fear, was a symbol for the Greeks and Romans of the power that resides beneath that which has not yet been faced. Making you confront your fears was this goddess' specialty.

It was sometimes hard to believe that this petite, bony woman from our circle could cause me so much worry. She was charming and humorous most of the time. Still, she had a way of teaching that always cut to the heart of any matter. She had the ability to tell the truth ruthlessly, no matter what the outcome.

It was especially difficult to keep all of this in mind as the two of us sat atop her favorite grassy hill in the foothills of the San Fernando Valley. It was a warm, breezy day and as we settled into the grass I noticed two hawks making slow, patient circles in the air above us. Hecate called this hill a "teacher" of hers, a statement which never really made logical sense to me. "Everything here keeps you alert," she said to me as we looked around at the view below us. "It keeps action in your mind. Life stands still for no one." That was Hecate's approach to the world. She was always on the move. She was quick-witted and sharp-tongued.

The other students from our circle usually did their best to avoid Hecate. "She's trouble," I remembered one younger man telling me. "She's always testing the limits."

"That is true, Timothy," said another student, a plump woman in her late thirties. "If I were you, I'd be careful." They knew that I had been summoned by our High Priestess. "But why does she want to see you—and in private?" asked the young man. I just shrugged. "She didn't say." Hecate had simply said that there was something that she wanted to show me on that hilltop.

"Trouble!" he replied and jabbed his elbow into the plump woman's side.

She pushed him away. "Knock it off," she snapped at him. "He needs us to help him now." Then they burst out laughing together.

As we sat on the grass, I couldn't help but notice that Hecate's hair had the look of coarsely loomed fabric. It was wavy and blue-black with thick strands of white running through it. The sun made the full length of her braided, salt-and-pepper hair shimmer. She was a vibrant, beautiful, earthy outdoors woman in her late forties. Her olive complexion and angled features reflected her Mexican-American ancestry.

I must have been staring at her because she turned her head and met my eyes. She took a deep breath as though she had something to say, but then exhaled slowly and deliberately. She looked down toward the bottom of the hill. "Look there," she said in a hushed tone.

Two rabbits had stuck their heads out of their underground dwellings. Both of them seemed to sniff at the air a bit and then they dashed out on to the prairie. Hecate stared at the scene and said, "The hawks are about to have their meal."

"That's terrible," I managed to say.

"It is only terrible when you have not confronted fear," Hecate commented without missing a beat. "It is only terrible if you are in hiding."

How was she able to do that, I wondered. It always felt like she was able to see through me to my secrets and my vulnerabilities. But I had to admit that she was right. The natural flow of life can seem terrible when one has not confronted fear. I also had to admit that it was difficult for me to acknowledge my own fears, let alone confront them. I began to tune out Hecate, the grassy hill, and the circling hawks, and I started to spiral into my own thoughts. I wanted to sort through my feelings. I knew that, like most people, I had my own catalog of fears. I was afraid of loss. I was afraid of my own anger. I was afraid of never having enough — and I was even afraid of getting what I really wanted. Hecate touched my arm gently and I awakened from my ruminating.

"Don't worry Timothy, you wouldn't be the first to hide," she spoke. "But hiding will keep you from ever knowing true power," she said, as she picked a blade of grass and placed it between her teeth.

"But how does somebody confront fear?" I asked her. She looked up to the sky and watched the hawks for a while before speaking. Finally she said, "The trick to working with fear is that you must first learn to see it for what it is. Do you know what I mean?"

"No," I quickly admitted. "Not really." Was she saying that fear was something more than fear? This seemed like nonsense to me. Maybe I didn't want to know what she meant. I started feeling annoyed. I found Hecate's words confusing and anxiety-provoking. My palms started to sweat and I wiped them on my pants. I wasn't sure I was going to ask her anything more. I didn't like where this conversation was going.

But I knew Hecate would tell me what she thought anyway. She relished telling people exactly what she saw in them. She smiled with one side of her mouth and she looked at me out of the corners of her eyes. "To put it bluntly, fear is a reflection of your own self. Life is just what it is: hawks, rabbits, eating, breathing, dying. It is all the same energy. When humans enter the picture, they filter life through their thinking and suddenly it has terrible and not terrible parts, good and bad, desirable and undesirable elements."

I stammered. "I think death is a terrible part. To say the least, it is undesirable."

"So death is at the bottom of your fears. I should have known." Hecate laughed. "I've noticed death hovering near you many times, but instead of learning from it, you run. You cannot be initiated unless you stand still for the initiator."

I knew that she was mocking me now. The elders of my training often seemed to teach in a way that aroused my anger. I was never very skilled at expressing anger, but now I felt my face getting warm and I could hear my voice raise as I spoke. "Come on, Hecate. What is death going to teach anyone? I know I am not alone when I say that I find death frightening. Most people fear death."

"And that is why most people will never find their power," she said, sounding a bit saddened. "Death awaits you every day," she said. "You are on the road to it even now. This very moment is what the throes of death feel like. It is nothing more than what you have in your life right now. So what is there to be afraid of?"

She was right. Her words jarred me into a profound realization. The end of physical life was not necessarily the thing to fear. It was existing in my life without really living that was the most dreadful. I had a sinking feeling in my stomach. The truth was that my fear of death had stopped me from living fully. It was difficult for me to accept this. The fear had intimidated me into living a false life. It was false because I believed that all of my precautions, my worrying, and my safe choices would protect me from death. I couldn't speak, so we both sat in silence.

After a while, Hecate said, "No matter your wealth, age, status in life, or accomplishments, the physical body must wear out eventually. Why let that time of wearing out, that one brief moment in the entire history of your life control you? The dog is taking the master for a walk!"

"I know, I know," I said shaking my head. I was embarrassed by the way that she was able to strip me of my defenses so cleanly and quickly. "I need to resolve my fear of death," I said. "But how should I do it?"

Then she said something that I will never forget. "Resolution is not what you should really seek since another problem, another fear, another topic will come into your life. And then what? No, resolution sounds permanent, but nothing about the life we live is permanent. You may cut the grass today, but tomorrow it will have grown again. That is the way of nature. The problem comes when you try to find permanent answers to impermanent questions."

"But isn't it human to want to have permanent solutions, Hecate?" I asked her. "Now that you've pointed out my fear, I'd really like to fix it, or I'll just feel uncomfortable."

Hecate looked hard at me and took a moment before she spoke. "It doesn't matter how you want to feel or wish you could feel. There is nothing to fix. Living in harmony with your death or with anything else you fear is living with reality. There is no other way to be. Either you face your life and move through it freely with full knowledge, or you live in fantasy and ultimately become inflexible when you feel burdened with a moment of truth. I suggest you embrace truth, which begins with facing what you fear. It ends with facing your fears too. That's just how life is. It's only a problem if you see it that way."

I couldn't help but feel a bit sad. Her words carried a stinging truth: fears are nothing but what we make of them. I realized that I had piled my fears into a towering monument, and that monument ran the whole show. Then I started to recall the major events of my life and took notice of how fear had controlled my decisions at each turn.

"Here come the hawks," Hecate said pointing to the ground.

Without my noticing, the hawks had circled around the hill and were sweeping low to the ground. Before long, the two rabbits that had left their hole caught sight of the hawks closing in on them, but it was too late.

They came plunging for the rabbits. One of the rabbits was quick to take action. It darted around until it found another hole in the earth where it swiftly took cover. It was safe for now. The other rabbit became immobile, frozen, staring at its fate.

I couldn't watch anymore. I turned away from the scene. Hecate stood up and began walking down the slope, shaking her head. As she walked, I could hear her say, "Which way will you live your life? You need to choose."

Hecate's lesson was clear: fear creates a major stumbling block to the person of power. Fear is a natural feeling, because there are many aspects to living a human life that can cause anxiety and fear. The threat of "hawks," of death, destruction, danger, uncertainty, calamity, misfortune is always present in everyone's life, no matter how he or she chooses to act in the world.[1] That is simply how life is. In the course of one life, you can certainly count on one death. You can also count on facing a number of situations that will evoke a response of fear. It is only natural. Everyone feels fearful at one point or another. Even without some particular event to prompt people's overt fearfulness, beneath the surface of most people's lives they hold a low-level, basic fear that manifests as tension. It is not the natural feeling of fear itself that creates the stumbling block, but rather the actions they choose based on this feeling. Like the rabbits, you can either freeze in your tracks or move into nimble and appropriate action.

That day I learned the second of the magical laws, which points out that people who avoid their fears also avoid their power. Avoidance is the manifestation of the consciousness of the immobile rabbit. Immobile rabbits work to camouflage themselves. They don't make sudden moves. They don't take any risks. Consequently they keep themselves from ever living fully, extraordinarily, or powerfully. Out of avoiding fear, ordinary people act in ways they believe will protect and shelter them from the difficulties of living. Immobile rabbits think that hiding will keep them from harm. They live in their own "underground dwellings" hiding from reality, from themselves, and from life. Just as I did, they make "safe choices" in their lives. For example, they go to work each morning so that they can avoid poverty. They eat the right foods so that they can avoid illness.

Going to work and eating the right foods are not the problem. It is the perspective, the motive behind these actions that transforms the simple events of everyday living into desperate requisites, demands, and protective devices.

The problem is that danger never goes away. Life itself is dangerous.[2] There is no place where humans can hide from the ultimate danger of living. Ordinary people use denial as a means of coping, staving off this reality and quelling their fears. But the person who chooses to live by the second magical law knows that staving off fear is not only a waste of time but also a restriction of power. The person of magical ability actively drops the buffer between the self and real life. When the buffer between yourself and your experience of life drops, you too become a person of power.

The second magical law teaches that every fear holds a secret power. Power resides underneath layers of fear that accumulate over the years. Fear is a signal that there is untapped and unexplored potential residing somewhere within the being of magic.[3] For example, hiding within a fear of death you may find an unrealized ability to live fully. Under a fear of being different and thereby ostracized, you may find untapped originality and uniqueness. Under a fear of loneliness, you may find a hidden yearning for independence. Moving toward one's fears is a manifestation of the consciousness of the active rabbit.

The ancient cultures of our ancestors understood the link between moving toward fear and coming into power. The wise ones and myth-makers of ancient Greece and Rome symbolized this principle with a goddess—Hecate. Both the Greeks and Romans used the symbols of night and crossroads to imply the heart of her power.[4] These symbols and the goddess herself all point in the same direction. They point toward things that make you fearful.

Both night and crossroads are symbols of things that raise your anxiety. Night puts you on edge because physical darkness won't allow you to see where you are going. It can be dangerous too because you might stumble, hurt yourself, or run into something unforeseen and unpleasant. Night is a primal symbol in mythology that relates to fear and the unknown.

Similarly, crossroads are places that can raise anxiety. When you come to a crossroads you always have to face the question, which way do I go now—here or there? It is the process of making a decision about unknown factors that prompts fearfulness at crossroads. No one wants to make the wrong choice. The road you take now might set you back from the journey you intended to take, or it might lead into some unforeseen difficulty.

In primal cultures, a being of magic—a shaman—spends a lifetime facing and exploring his or her fears and the unknown. The shaman does this not because he or she likes feeling the discomfort of fear and anxiety, but because there is nothing else to do, there is no other way to live. Mystery, fear, and the unknown are simple facts of being alive, and avoidance of these facts is an act of disempowerment. The shaman knows that each moment is mysterious and unknown, and that there is no other way around reality.

Ordinary people believe that there are ways around reality. They think that if they brace themselves, resist, or plan for the uncertainties of life, they will somehow remain untouched. People of ordinary lives don't want to face the mystery of each moment because they might have to face moments of pain or anxiety. In a misguided attempt at power, ordinary people take action toward controlling the unpredictability of life. They spend time speculating about what may hurt them if they face the unknown unready and unprotected. They stay poised, ready to strategize and manipulate life instead of confronting their fears and discomforts. Another way they try to control the uncontrollable is when they externalize their fears and blame them on other people or events outside of themselves. For example, someone may identify homosexuals as the cause of AIDS and therefore the cause of trouble in the community. Or they may blame minority groups for violence and therefore oppose those people.

As this commotion goes on inside the minds of powerless people, beneath their feet is the road that can lead to empowerment. They don't look down at the road because they are focused on the things that they believe are the cause of their fears. As a result, they avoid power when it presents itself. They shield themselves from the very thing that will make them whole.

The second magical law teaches us that we claim power through the very mystery of life. If you seek the wisdom of magic it is important to realize that right now you are at the threshold of the unknown. Whether you are standing in familiar surroundings or somewhere unexplored, each moment holds something new. This newness can be either an opportunity or a curse. The newness and unpredictability of each second is a dreaded experience by ordinary people. From Hecate's perspective, the newness of each moment is an opportunity for change in any direction. People who seek spiritual empowerment find limitlessness where ordinary people find struggles.

The fact that you are reading this book means that you have come to the edge of your power, enticed by Hecate and spurred by some discomfort you may be experiencing in your own life. Perhaps you have had difficulty in your relationships or maybe you are facing illness, loss, or uncomfortable emotions. Perhaps your life didn't turn out as you hoped it would. Whatever manifestation of Hecate's power you face, when you confront the "unconfrontable," you face an initiation into your full human potential.

The word initiation means "to begin something." On the magical path, initiation means both a beginning and an awakening to something. What are we supposed to awaken to? The unpredictable mix of life. It is an initiation into the consciousness that moves you into action whenever fear comes along. This is the consciousness that understands that each moment, no matter what it brings, is full of magical potential.

Getting into this agile frame of mind by confronting your fears can be hard magical work to do. No one likes facing the things that make him or her fearful. However, it is of some comfort to know that the initiation into power is the same across the globe. No one can claim power and experience true life change without going through the jarring effects of an initiation. Part of the initiation ceremonies in primal cultures is usually psychological shock and fear. Some of these initiation rituals include such practices as scarification of the body, circumcision, subincision, burning of the skin, cutting with knives, or even knocking out the initiate's teeth.[5] Such stress can engage an initiate's fear and can cause him or her to open up to the realities of living with power. Sometimes it takes extreme discomfort, a brush with danger or death, in order to shake someone up and cause him or her to live outside of the controlling grip of fear. It is not unusual for people who have experienced a life-threatening situation to become fully engaged with life later. Once fear is out of the way, they often take chances, make the most of each moment, and start living more fully. When you open to Hecate, she strips away the illusion that life will continue as you expect. When this happens it becomes easier to set aside the ordinary, defensive, strategic, or fearful ways of existing.

When I was initiated by my teachers onto the magical path, I was first blindfolded and then led to the edge of a sacred space. Then I felt the point of a sword at the base of my throat. I heard a stern voice warning me that in order to move into the realm of power, I had to journey past the barrier of my own fears. "It is better that you thrust yourself upon this sword then to enter the realm of spirit with fear in your heart," the initiator concluded.

The message of these symbolic actions is clear. A life lived under the dominant force of fear is not worth living. If you cannot penetrate the barrier of fear, then you are as good as dead. Worse, you are alive but powerless. If you remain like an immobile rabbit, you will live your days as a slave to the gatekeeper of power, your fear.

Once you descend into the realm of Hecate, the mythical "underworld," you undergo a form of initiation. Through that experience, you come to realize that the realm of spirit is not some special place. It is not the edited version of your life that you fill with people and things that you like, or that make you feel secure, special, or holy. The realm of spirit is within each gritty second, whatever that second brings. Things that are joyful and things that are painful are both aspects of spirit. You know that you have slipped back into ordinary consciousness when you freeze in your tracks as Hecate raises her intimidating, initiatory sword. When fears arise, remember that you cannot be initiated unless you stand still for the initiator.

THE ENCHANTMENTS

Hecate's Mirror

This exercise is part a meditation with guided imagery and part written. Before you begin, either select someone to assist you as a reader of the meditation, or prepare your own audiotape. Also, it is important that you have on hand paper and a pen or pencil. I have found that it is best to begin writing immediately after you complete the meditation portion of the exercise.

Find a place in your home or in an outdoor, natural setting where you will be undisturbed. Sit in an upright position that you can maintain for the duration of the guided imagery meditation.[6] When you find a position that you can sustain for 15–20 minutes, close your eyes and turn on the tape or have your partner begin reading.

Take several slow, deep breaths that feel as though they begin just below your belly. Inhale slowly and exhale just as slowly. As you do this, imagine that mist begins to swirl around you, lifting your body, taking it to a far off place. [Pause]

Eventually the mist will clear and when it does you will see that it is night. You stand at a crossroads of three paths that converge on a grassy moor.

There is no moon in the sky and the crossroads are quite dark. Nevertheless you can still note the features of the surrounding landscape. You can see three giant stones standing next to each of these roads at the place where they all converge. You stand just outside of this mysterious place. Walk until you stand at the center of all three stones. Once you are there, an old woman dressed in black emerges from behind one of the stones and approaches you. She is silent. This is Hecate.

Ask her to show you something from your life that makes you uncomfortable, yet which is the thing that you must face at this time. She reaches into her cowled sleeve and draws out a silver hand mirror. She holds it up to your eyes and instantly you see a person, event, or scene from your life that represents your discomfort. If you see nothing, Hecate will speak a single word in your ear. This word represents what it is you fear.

When you hear the word, mist will cover your body again and rapidly transport you back to the place where you began this meditation. When you are ready, open your eyes.

Take a few moments to ponder the scene and/or the word Hecate revealed to you. Take time now to write about what it is you saw. Here are some questions to help you with your writing.

- What was the scene that appeared? Or, what was the word Hecate spoke to you?
- How did you get to the point in your life that this fear became a powerful influence on you?
- What effects does this force have on your life?
- What can you do you minimize the effects of this fear?

Initiation Celebration

This is a celebratory rite that you can use to initiate yourself into the mysteries of spirit, which manifest as your own life. Through symbol and action, this celebration announces to your deepest self and to the spirit realm that you are ready to take on the responsibilities of a spiritual life. It is the beginning point on a journey toward a life more fully lived.

Initiations into spiritual traditions or magical paths generally focus on the theme of death and rebirth. When you participate in an initiation, you follow a pathway of symbols that help you to disengage psychologically from your old, dysfunctional ways of living in the world. The result of initiation is that you no longer become numb to the parts of your life that you don't like or that you cannot bear. An initiation celebration announces to all levels of your being—spiritual, physical, emotional, and psychological—that you vow to live your life in its entirety. Since a genuine life is where you will find spirit, you are subsequently reborn to that realm.

In this ritual I included a temporary sacred marking or tattoo on your body using henna. In Morocco, the art of henna painting on the feet, hands, and shoulders is called *mehndi*, and is primarily used for ceremonies and spiritual practices.

Sacred body marking is not only fashionable in the Middle East, but throughout the globe. Joseph Campbell compares the markings on the body of a mystic with the stained glass windows of a Catholic cathedral. Symbolically speaking, the mystic's own body is comparable to a church. It is within the body that the mystic experiences deity. Campbell says that sacred body markings allow a mystic's "church" or sacred place to be mobile. When the body is the sacred temple, then every experience with which it comes in contact becomes a rite of passage. Daily life transforms into something sacred when a mystic understands that his or her own body is the temple of deity. When you mark yourself with spiritual symbols, you place yourself in the center of spiritual life. You become the center of the sacred experience, not only for yourself, but for those whose paths you cross.

Prior to the ritual, try going to the library to research various sacred designs. There are many symbols from around the world that would be appropriate. Try to do this research with mindfulness. Eventually a sacred symbol will emerge and appear to you. You can either copy an existing symbol or create your own.

One practical point to keep in mind about this ritual is that henna will stain your skin (and everything else) for at least a week. If you choose to do this part of the ritual, you will live with your mehndi for that time. Keep that in mind and do only what feels comfortable for you.

What you'll need:

- Four pieces of white or "natural" color parchment paper
- A pen or felt-tip marker
- A fireplace, large ashtray, or some other burning vessel, such as a deep metal bowl, a pot, a stone bowl, or something that can withstand heat
- Matches
- A small bottle of henna
- A fine-point artist's brush or fine makeup brush

Three weeks before you do this ritual, there is a task to complete. On an ongoing basis throughout the three weeks preceding the initiation, create a journal for yourself. You can use a blank book for journaling or a notepad. The purpose of the journal is to pay attention to those parts of your life that you find difficult to embrace.

Each day for three weeks, pay very close attention to your thoughts and your actions. Ask yourself these four questions as you go along throughout the day:

- What is it that I am avoiding?
- What is it that I am trying to gain?
- What emotions am I holding back?
- What are the thoughts to which I cling?

Keep these four questions in mind as you pay attention to the usual proceedings of your life—as you watch television, argue with a friend, drive to work, go to the grocery store. At the end of each day make an entry into the journal regarding your findings. Attempt to answer each question. If you do this well enough, by the end of three weeks, you will begin to see a pattern in the four questions. In other words, themes will emerge.

On the day prior to the ritual, read over the journal and see if you can answer the four questions succinctly. Try to give definite answers to the best of your ability. If you are unable to answer these questions, it is best to continue with the journaling process until the answers become clear and honest.

Once you have the answers to each of the four questions, see if you can compress these four themes down into single words. For example, if I were to answer the question "What am I trying to avoid?" I might compress my three weeks of findings down to the single word, "death." The word might be anything for you, poverty, rage, sadness, loneliness, etc. When you are finished, you will have four single words that answer each of the questions.

The night of the ritual, make sure that you are completely alone and have continued privacy. Create sacred space by using the method you learned in the previous chapter. Some people like to create a more dramatic effect by lighting four candles and placing them on the floor at each compass direction.

Write down the four answers to your questions, one answer for each piece of parchment paper. Place all four parchment squares aside.

Stand facing the eastern edge of your space and say aloud:

I stand before the powers of the east,
The powers of my own mind.

Next, walk to the edge of the southern part of your sacred space. Say aloud:

I stand before the powers of the south,
The powers of my own energy and passion.

Walk to the western edge of the sacred space and say aloud:

I stand before the powers of the west,
The power of my emotions and feelings.

Finally, go to the north of your space and say aloud:

I stand before the powers of the north,
The powers of my own existence.

Next, take out the parchment paper squares on which you have written the answers to the four questions. Place the one with answer to the question "What am I trying to avoid?" on the floor at the north point of your sacred space. Place the answer to the question "What am I trying to gain?" on the floor at the south point of your sacred space. Lay the answer to the question "What are the thoughts to which I cling?" in the eastern point of your sacred space. Finally set the answer to the question "What emotion am I holding back?" in the western quarter of your sacred space.

Before you set each parchment square down, say aloud:

"I cling to _____. (Use the word for each specific direction/question.)

"And I seek to release it."

Sit in the center of your sacred space, surrounded by all four parchment squares and close your eyes. Imagine that you face the east of your sacred space. Take deep breaths and imagine that a great wind carries a symbol toward you. Do not force the image. Simply sit until an image or symbol emerges. When one comes, know that it is the symbol of how you can release that to which you cling in the east. When you see the symbol, open your eyes, take out the pen, and draw it on the reverse side of the parchment with the word lying in the east.

When you are done, sit again at the center of the space and imagine that you are facing south. There, in that quarter of your sacred space, a great fire burns before you. Again, simply breathe deeply, and eventually a symbol will emerge from the center of that fire. It is the symbol of how to release that to which you cling in the south. Open your eyes and draw the symbol on the back of the parchment paper lying in the south.

Sit at the center once again, close your eyes, and imagine that you sit at the edge of a great sea that flows at the western edge of your sacred space. A symbol will soon emerge from the sea that will represent the way to release what you cling to in the west. Open your eyes and draw this on the parchment paper that lies in the west.

At this point, take out the bottle of henna and your fine-point paintbrush. You should now choose one or more positions on the body to paint the sacred symbols of release you saw in your visions. Choose body points that have special symbolic meaning to you. Below I have listed some body parts and their traditional symbolic values.

Heart: Place the sacred symbol here to symbolize empathy and openness to each moment as it comes along. If you place the symbol here, you awaken feelings of love toward others.

Throat: Place the symbol here if you want to open, give "voice," or expression to your sacred feelings. This placement symbolizes the ability to realize your inspiration.

Third Eye: The spot at the center of your brow, sometimes called the "third eye," opens you up to a sacred vision of your life. It symbolizes clear insight into the truth of your life at all times.

Top of head: You would need to be either bald or have a shaved head to place your design here. This placement symbolizes an opening to genuine understanding and enlightenment.

Hands: Your hands can symbolize your daily work. Place the symbol here to realize the power of spirit in your daily routine.

Feet:	Feet often represent "grounding" or the ability to remain level-headed in life.
Arms:	Arms can represent your strength. Place the design on your arm if you want to develop spiritual strength.
Legs:	Your legs represent motion and the ability to get from one place to another. Place the symbol here to represent movement in your spirit life.

Be creative in discovering a symbolic spot to draw your mendhi. Remember that once you paint your mendhi you will have this symbol with you for at least a week—maybe even a bit longer—so position it wherever it will be powerful and allow you to function as you usually do.

When you are finished with painting your mendhi, gather together your four pieces of parchment paper. Set them into the fireplace (or some other safe burning vessel) and light them on fire with a match or lighter. The rite is finished.

Magic to Neutralize Fear

It is important to have weapons to help you cut through fear so that you do not become immobile. This is a technique that helps cut through anxiety and fear for the purpose of moving into action. This technique can be done at any time. The only magical trigger for this charm is ordinary rock salt.

What you'll need:

- Rock salt
- A small leather or cloth bag

If you have ongoing anxiety that you wish to neutralize, try the following technique.

Begin by filling a small cloth or leather bag (even a plastic baggie will do in a pinch) with rock salt and carry it around with you. Whenever you feel overt fear or anxiety, pour a small portion of rock salt into the palm of each of your hands. Sit down with your back erect. Hold your hands, palms up in your lap. Close your eyes and begin to feel the full force of your anxiety without editing from the critical mind. During this, be sure to breathe deeply and naturally. Start to become curious about the feeling of anxiety. Follow it to its source in the body. Find out where the feeling originates. Each time you feel anxiety, it feels different in the body. Try to name the sensation exactly. Perhaps it feels like a buzz in your stomach, or maybe it feels like a throb in your head.

Many people's anxiety dissipates after noting its place of origin and the exact feeling of the anxiety. If it has not dissipated, your next step is to imagine that you are able to move the feeling of anxiety from one place in your body to another. Wherever you hold the anxiety, roll it toward your arms and down to your hands. Squeeze the anxiety into two small balls, one inside the palm of each hand. Now, imagine that you push the anxiety out from your palms into the salt, where it is captured. Make sure that all of the anxiety is balled up and pushed out into the salt.

Open your eyes and brush the salt away into a sink or toilet and flush the salt with water, so that it carries your anxiety far from you, never to return.

1. Joseph Campbell, Betty Sue Flowers, ed., *The Power of Myth* (New York: Doubleday, 1988), p. 66.
2. Carlos Castañeda, *A Separate Reality* (New York: Simon & Schuster, 1971), p. 113.
3. See, e.g., Verena Kast, "How Fairy Tales Deal with Evil" in Mario Jacoby, Verena Kast, and Ingrid Riedel, *Witches, Ogres and the Devil's Daughter* (Boston: Shambala, 1992).
4. Janet and Stewart Farrar, *The Witches' Goddess* (Custer: Phoenix Publishing, 1987), p. 125.
5. Campbell, Betty Sue Flowers, ed., *The Power of Myth* (New York: Doubleday, 1988), p. 81.
6. Although lying down is a valid and useful meditative body position, unless you have sufficient practice with it, most likely you will fall asleep.

CHAPTER III

SIN

Acceptance holds great magic.

INVOCATION

It is time for the fall equinox. This time is an important spoke in the great Wheel of the Year. It is the time of transition from growth to harvesting. Our sacred circle is decorated with many colored leaves and acorns at the four directions. Squash, melon, and all forms of gourds lay on the altar that the whole spiritual community has created. We all know what we are here to do—to reap, to go within ourselves, and harvest the truth of our lives. We must come to terms with our lives as they are now, as opposed to what we might want them to be or what they once were.

Hermes stands in the west, raises his arms to the spirit world, and calls out to the Goddess:

> Come to us, O Goddess. We are in need of truth. Be here with us and wash self-deception away in order to reveal the truth of our lives. Your power is the stone upon which all magic must rise. Without your presence, there is no change, there is no movement. Be with us now!

THE TALE—*The Secret*

Once there was a man living an ordinary life until one day he had a vision. The man stood dumbfounded, looking at this vision. "Who are you?" the man asked. The vision spoke, "I am God. I have come to give you the secret of living." The man couldn't believe what he was seeing or hearing, but became quite excited. He rushed to the nearby home of his sensible sister. He explained all that he had seen and then asked her, "Should I believe it?" She laughed. "You know you've always been overly imaginative. That was just a figment of your overworked imagination," she said. Then she continued, "If I were you, I'd go see a psychologist."

Heeding her advice, the man made a few quick phone calls and immediately set up an appointment with a psychologist. The psychologist looked worried after the man told him what he had seen. "Should I believe it?" asked the man.

"This is a manifestation of repressed fantasies and urges and is well beyond what I can treat," the psychologist announced. "Let me refer you to a medical doctor." Within an hour, the man found himself in a doctor's office explaining what he had seen. "Should I believe it?" asked the man. Without uttering a word, the doctor wrote prescriptions for antipsychotic and anti-depressive medications.

The man left the doctor's office with prescriptions in hand and felt more lost than before. Just then he noticed a church across the street. Before he knew it, he was inside the church speaking to a priest. He told the priest what he had seen and then asked, "Should I believe it?" The priest was indignant. "I have sought God all of my life! What you are saying makes a complete mockery of who I am. That was not God, sir. The days of visions and miracles are over. What you saw was a demon."

With that, the man left in tears, filled with doubts and fears. He stumbled along the city streets until he found himself sitting on a park bench next to a little girl. Suddenly, the vision appeared again and said, "I am God. I have come to give you the secret of living." The man became hysterical and broke down sobbing. The little girl turned to the man and asked, "What's the matter?" The man replied, "I am overly imaginative. I am full of repressed fantasies and urges. I am depressed. I am psychotic. I am seeing demons!" Then the man shouted at the vision, "I shall not believe in you! Go away and never come back to me again!"

The little girl sat on the bench and watched the man race away from the scene. Then she turned to vision and said, "So what is the secret?"

MAGICAL LAW — *Acceptance holds great magic.*

SIN'S LAW

*God offers to every mind its choice between truth and re-
pose. Take which you please; you can never have both.*
                                        —Ralph Waldo Emerson[1]

I couldn't believe it was happening to me. The angel of death existed
and he was standing inches away. "Keep cool or I'll blow your fucking
head off," this man with dead eyes said to me. The long barrel of his
gun was pointed at my temple. My heart stopped. This was the end of
my life—I was sure of it. "What do you want?" I asked. "I need a
ride," he said, "and you're coming with me." I could feel the blood
drain from my face. I looked wildly for a witness in the dark parking
lot. *Somebody, please see me; please help me.* But no one saw what was
happening. The angel of death had come for me and the world continued on as it always did. There would be no mercy for me.

   Then another voice spoke. It was Sin. "Breathe deeply. Stay with
this, Timothy." I felt a tear roll down the side of my face. I was in the
center of Sin's magic circle. I was lying on my back on the cold earth
and I could smell wisteria all around me. Sin was guiding me though
a hypnotic vision.

   "Open the fucking door, or I'll kill you now," the angel of death
snapped at me. He jammed the barrel of the gun into my cheek. I fum-
bled with the keys. *Somebody please see me; please help me.* I felt cold
and nauseated, my hands and legs felt numb. My emotions were raw.
This is the pain I did not want to bear. But it was real. It was the truth.

   My brush with death happened a year ago, but I decided not to
talk about it since that day. I wanted to move on with my life. I
thought that it was important to bury that memory as soon as

possible. There was no point in dwelling on painful events. Life was too short and I wanted to be positive. I wanted to lose the truth of that awful night.

But it wouldn't stay hidden, buried, or lost. Nine months after the event and my attempts at denial, I began to have terrifying dreams. Soon I couldn't sleep or eat at all. I would weep suddenly and inexplicably. All I wanted was for this experience to go away, but it had grown inside of me during the last nine months. I was pregnant with emotional distress.

The elders knew what was happening. They saw the danger of my state of mind and emotions. They convened in secret on the full moon and assigned a woman named Sin the task of healing me. Sin was a beautiful, blond woman in her early thirties. She had a strong jaw line and well-defined, rather masculine shoulders and arms. I always thought of her as both the physical and emotional strength of the group of elders. Sin descended from a family of healers and wise women in northern Italy. Her grandmother taught her the magical uses of herbs, and she often helped the members of our group with her herbal wisdom.

A month passed after the elders had met before Sin approached me and announced that she had an old recipe for an elixir that would banish my anxiety. I was so desperate to get some sleep that the prospect of some painless, instant cure thrilled me. Sin said that the main ingredient was a substance that her grandmother called Verita. "What is it called in English?" I asked her. "The power of Verita is in her name," Sin replied. "I cannot speak her innermost name. It is for you to discover. She will reveal herself to you when you are ready."

"Where do we go to find Verita?" I asked Sin.

"It is something that you can find everywhere. Right now, she is strongest in Topanga," Sin replied. Topanga Canyon was well-known with local magical folk as a place to find wild herbs of every kind. "Only you can handle Verita," Sin said to me. "It might be bitter but it is the way to power. You must take it all—roots and everything—at midnight." I knew that I needed to do something, so I agreed to her plan and that night we drove to Topanga Canyon.

"Here," Sin said, "Pull over." I drove the car onto the dirt shoulder of the winding canyon road. We had driven for forty minutes or so before we found the right place. It was a moonless night and we needed flashlights to find a pathway through the scented thicket of reeds and wild anise. "Verita is never far away. It pervades everything," Sin said as we started to walk carefully along the narrow path. She turned around and said in a hushed tone, "Keep your hands free now. You cannot take hold of Verita if you grip onto other things."

"Yes, Sin. But what does it look like? Help me out a little." I asked feeling a bit confused.

"It's hard to describe. It doesn't look like anything special. In fact it looks like a lot of things. I've seen people walk right through it and never acknowledge its presence. But it is there nonetheless. Keep your eyes peeled. It is easy to see only what we want to see. That's when we miss the thing we need."

"Are we talking about a plant or something else, Sin?" I asked.

Sin did not reply and kept on hiking through the dark. I started to look around for something that looked like a common variety of plant. But after fifteen minutes of squinting at plants in the darkness, I felt foolish. It was then that I noticed that Sin was far ahead of me on the trail. I could barely see the glow of her flashlight through the brush about one hundred yards ahead of me. "Over here!" Sin shouted. "Here is a spot of Verita."

I pushed excitedly through the winding path heavy with overgrowth until I found Sin standing in a clearing. There was a heady, sweet aroma that filled the air in the clearing, but I couldn't see from where it originated. It seemed to come from all around me. Sin pointed her flashlight at a blob of dried cement on the ground at one end of the clearing.

"This was once an ancient wisteria," Sin said. I recognized the scent now. Sin continued to speak. "It grew tall. It was Verita." "So wisteria is Verita, Sin?" I asked.

Sin ignored my comment and continued with her story. "One day, someone didn't want the wisteria. They wanted to develop this land—to change it from what it was. But Verita would not let them. This place is what it is. No one can change what is. They chopped the wisteria to the ground and poured cement over it to seal its fate. But you cannot keep the power of Verita away. Look!"

She pointed the beam of the flashlight all around us to reveal wisteria growing in all directions in a perfect circle that formed the edges of the clearing. It had traveled by its roots and popped up to climb across every tree and shrub in the vicinity. Purple cone clusters hung over our heads like heavy bunches of grapes that were ready for harvest.

"Verita never dies," Sin said looking into my eyes now. "She never goes away. She lives and each must learn to live with her. Verita can become a destroyer when she is not allowed to be. Now she will climb the other plants and she will choke and kill everything in her path. But you know this already. Verita has taken this path with you."

"What do you mean?" I asked.

But I knew what she meant. Verita was not a plant. It was not something that I needed to find in Topanga Canyon. Verita was truth. I looked down at the ground. Without saying another word, Sin gently placed her hand on my heart. I could feel a swelling of emotion; it was a mixture of pain, rage, sadness, and relief. "Here is Verita," Sin whispered in my ear.

My stomach wrenched and I could hear someone sobbing uncontrollably. They were deep, ancient, profound sobs. I realized it was my own weeping and I wept with every muscle of my body. "I...almost...died," I choked on the words. Sin silently held my hand and looked intently into my eyes.

I was changed forever and we both knew it.

On that moonless night I encountered the third magical law: the necessity of facing the unedited truth of your life as it happens in each moment. This is the power of the goddess Sin,[2] who is the Teutonic goddess of "truth." In ordinary, mainstream religions, sin means transgression. It is the breaking of some spiritual law. For people of power and magic, the goddess Sin is the *keeper* of a particular spiritual law. Her law is called acceptance and the effect of her law is "presence," or grounding.

Acceptance means to know who you are in your entirety, with all of your strengths and weaknesses. It means seeing what you have in your life in its entirety, with its advantages and drawbacks. It is knowing that every part of your life is complete just as it is. Knowing, in the magical tradition, is an experience rather than an intellectual exercise. You keep the law of presence by seeing, tasting, touching, smelling, and hearing your life in each second.[3] When you break the law of presence, you step outside of experiencing.

Experiencing is key to unlocking the secrets of Sin. In a stance of power we come to our senses and focus on our experiences in the present moment. When you break the law of presence and move away from experiencing your life, you create a vacuum. What fills the void of experience are your concepts and imaginings about your life. Once you fill your head with concepts, theories, and ideas, you start to think your way through life. The action that you take based on your concepts is often inappropriate because it does not match reality or the experience of the moment. Experience might be telling you to act in one way, but because you operate from your concepts and imaginings, you act in another way and start creating problems. In truth, for the goddess Sin, life is more than whatever it is you think or mentally conceive.

Thoughts and concepts are limited and they tend to freeze fluid experience. Thinking is a valuable tool when you employ it wisely, but the ideologies and running opinions of the critical mind obscure experience.[4] When you limit experience in this way you create unrealistic postulations about your life like: "My marriage is sound," when it may not be. Or you rigidly operate from the premise of "we are a happy family," when reality is something other than that. Or you may think "my life is difficult," or "I am unlovable," when the facts do not support your theories. Perhaps any of these were truth somewhere at one time or another in your life. In contrast, reality in each moment is much more fluid and diffuse than the narrow labels that you might try to create for it. This means that none of your ideas are truth, experientially speaking. In experience, life is beyond frozen tidbits of ideas and descriptions like "sound," "happy," or "difficult." Experience reveals a life that is a mix of these things. Outside of experience, we often force the round peg of our experiences into a square hole of our concepts.

Acceptance is a law of power that moves us into something we fear. Most of us fear facing our lives in their entirety. If we do so, then we have to own up to our behaviors and decisions. It can mean the shattering of unrealistic hopes and dreams. It might mean acknowledging that you have no power except over your own life. It might mean seeing that the difficulties you face each day are not always the result of external events, but of your own inner turmoil. There is power in knowing these things.

If you invite the magic of acceptance into your life, you've opened the door to action. Powerful action begins when you accurately assess the facts of your life through careful observation and through heightening your senses. The power of acceptance is allowing the directness of the moment to come in contact with you. When you make contact with the power of Sin, you make contact with reality. Through that contact you can detach from the usual judgments of the critical mind and honestly assess both your strengths and your limitations. Facing reality gives you the power to make realistic choices. Real, substantive change cannot happen unless you know what needs to be changed. You need some sort of map to know how to get from here to there. Acceptance is that map.

There are two kinds of spiritual practice that result in a greater and a lesser form of magic. The greater magics are those of the extraordinary people who are shamans, healers, and wise ones. Acceptance and living in accord with the law of truth are two of the shamanic, greater magics. The magic of the shaman comes from a change in consciousness. Something shifts inside the shaman, not the outside world.

The lesser magics are those of sorcerers who focus primarily on the creation of illusion, the concealing of truth, and living outside of the third magical law. The path of the sorcerer is the path of misguided souls and the ordinary minded. Sorcery and illusion result in manipulation of the outside world. In this craft, nothing changes internally for the sorcerer.

The first and the most common sorcery is the foggy haze of denial. It gives someone who chooses to live outside of truth the ability to hobble along in his or her life. Denial is a sorcery of desperation, covering up truth through mental avoidance or minimization. It is the refusal to come to terms with reality.[5] Mental avoidance means distracting yourself so that you don't have to face anything. Minimization is diminishing the truth so that it cannot hurt you.

Disempowered and fearful people work the sorceries of denial whenever something difficult, hurtful, or displeasing comes along. Instead of facing it, knowing it, experiencing it, sorcerers desperately try to banish it.[6] If the problem itself won't go away, they take steps to avoid the problem. When denial is in place, sorcerers can pretend that their lives are what they want. They can edit out the parts of themselves that are troublesome or less than honorable. They can edit out the difficult behavior of their children. They can make believe their marriage is good all the time.

Sorcery has some effect, but it also exacts a price. When you split your life into fragments of wanted and unwanted pieces, it is only a temporary solution. Reality demands wholeness, and eventually the truth of our lives shines through the foggy haze of denial. That is when you face great disappointments. That is when you have horrifying insights that your life is not what you pretended it was. The price of denial comes when the sickening moment of truth eventually emerges and causes anxiety and depression.

Many people on the path to acceptance stop short once they lower the barrier of fear and begin to come to terms with who they are and what they have in their lives. If you hesitate on the path toward acceptance, you will most likely encounter two other illusory, lesser magics. The first one is called anger. The sorcery of anger allows you to justify yourself. It allows you to express your disappointment that life isn't everything you hoped and dreamed. Blaming others is the greatest weapon of anger. Through it you can shift the focus of disappointment and frustration on to someone or something else. "He is to blame for my life." "If that had never happened, I would be so much happier." This is how to use blame. Just like denial, the sorcery of anger also exacts a price. Its price is rancor and isolation.

The second and more poisonous sorcery is called resignation, and it comes when the initiate faces the second gateway of acceptance. The first gateway of acceptance is when you take responsibility for the consequences of your actions. The next gateway is when you know that often you are the cause of your own pain or suffering. This can be unbearable to face, so often people work to defend themselves by giving up. They allow inertia to take over, and they allow any circumstance to take hold of their lives. It is a form of masochistic self-punishment that comes from the shattering of unrealistic fantasies we may have about our lives. People who are resigned angrily pretend that acceptance means tolerating abuse or harm. The sorcery of resignation is a refusal to take appropriate action. The price of resignation is a life of victimization.

The lesser magics are those of illusion. You can fool other people with them occasionally. For example, you can make people believe that you are a nice person, or a polite one, or that you are tough as nails. You can even weave the illusion that you have control over the circumstances of your life and over other people. Illusions are fine, but they are not real and mostly they fool no one but yourself.

The first step to the power of the third magical law is observing—becoming curious—about what your life is all about. It means being meticulous about watching every detail, hearing every word other people say to you, feeling every emotion as it arises. It means mindfulness in each and every moment of your daily activities.[7] As you go to the grocery store, clean the bathroom, walk the dog, or talk to your partner, pay close attention. Let every second penetrate you without slipping into the commentary of the critical mind. As you observe, keep that extra commentary out. The trick to accepting lies is opening fully to your life. In order to do this, it is wise to ground your-self in time and space.

Time, Space, and Power

Awareness of time and space are both central to the third magical law. Present time and space are of particular importance. Time for the shaman is right now. There is no past and there is no future of any consequence for the shaman. On the other hand, sorcerers live at either end of the time continuum, past or future. They rarely settle on what is happening right now.

Space refers to the physical body and where you are in this moment. Shamans pay close attention to their bodies in each moment. They watch for whatever they sense and feel, like emotions and bodily tensions, which are expressions that can lead them to their power.[8] On the other hand, sorcerers ignore or repress their body signals and their emotions. They cut them off for fear of shattering one of their illusory magics. In examining each of these aspects of acceptance, you can come to a clearer understanding of how you might best arrive at this power.

The matter of time for a person of power is almost irrelevant. This is because in reality, in the ways of magic, there is no time. Clocks and calendars are devices that have meaning only in the ordinary realm. Of course, it is important to know what time to begin your meeting or when to pick up the kids from school. Without knowing the days of the week you could create a chaotic mess of your life. Everyone needs to function in harmony with his or her society, and clocks and calendars are ways in which communities agree on the terms of everyday, functional harmony. However, in the realm of magic and power, wise ones know that past and future are only conventions.[9] Clocks and calendars are only concepts. They are ideas in our minds. That is not to say that progress or causality does not happen. But both of these are matters for the ordinary, critical mind, which tries to order things and attempts to make sense of life using logic. There is nothing we can do about the events that have happened in the past; likewise we have no power over the future. Ultimately, neither the past nor the future is real or even useful for the person of magic. Only the moment at hand and the circumstances of what is happening right now qualify as reality and a time of empowerment for the shaman.

What happens when you mentally stray in the direction of past or future? When you venture down the path of the past, you weave another sorcerer's illusion. As always, the illusion of sorcery comes with some minimal benefit combined with a heavy price. The primary benefit of living in the illusion of the past is that it helps you to justify the life you have now. It soothes you with excuses about your mistakes and behaviors. It absolves you of responsibility so you don't have to worry about why your children are screwed up, why your marriage is screwed up, or why you are screwed up.

Another way the past may weave its spell is to keep you ruminating on an event. It may play a scene over and over out of nostalgia or regret. As always with sorcery, both of these feelings are illusion because they do not correspond to what is happening in your life currently. They are based on ideas, not actualities. What happened ten minutes or ten years ago is not what is happening now.

Illusions of the future also keep you from power. They fool you into believing that they are guiding you or keeping you from harm. Sorcery that keeps you in the future ends in anxiety and hypervigilance. There is tension when you strain to predict what may happen next. That tension blocks any realistic decision making. What will happen ten minutes from now is not what is happening right now. You might be worried about a test that is coming up or a date you are supposed to have tomorrow night. Or you may be dreaming about what you are going to do with the rest of your life. You might even be thinking about where you would rather be right now. None of these are real. They are distractions from the main event.

I remember a tale that the Priestess Sin told me so that I would remember the importance of grounding myself in present time and space.

Once there were two Druid priests who were on a pilgrimage to a faraway sacred grove. As part of their strict regimen of vows, they kept silent throughout the journey. Halfway to their destination they happened upon a young woman kneeling beside a swiftly running stream. She was weeping into her hands. The older of the two priests broke his silence and asked, "What is the matter?" "My mother lies sick on the other side of this stream, but the current is so swift that I cannot cross," replied the woman. "Oh please, if you can help me, I would be grateful."

The younger priest stepped forward. "Woman, we cannot touch you, we have made vows of chastity. We cannot speak to you, for we have made vows of silence. We cannot be bothered by your problem."

The older priest, without saying a word, picked up the woman, put her on his shoulders and crossed the stream, setting her down on the other side. "Oh thank you, great one," cried the woman. "No matter," said the older priest. "Just go about your business now." He left the woman and headed back to the younger Druid who stood on the opposite bank, mouth open and completely astonished. When the older priest reached the bank, he continued walking in the direction of the sacred grove. The younger Druid caught up with him and they walked silently for twenty more miles. Finally, the younger one burst out, "How could you have done that? We have made vows!" The older one said, "She was on my shoulders for twenty seconds and she has been on yours for twenty miles. Which of us has broken vows?"

The message of the story is clear. Neither past nor future holds any power. Staying in either place is a form of denial. Acceptance allows you to act with purpose and reason because it grounds you in the moment. Each moment tells you what is required. If it is time to eat, then eat. If it is time to sleep, then sleep. If it is time to pay the bills or sweep the floor or take a bath, then do so.

When you evoke the power of acceptance, another consideration is your space. People of power define space as the place where your body manifests in the field of time. No other space except where you are right now counts if you want to empower your life. Of course, all space is sacred and, like deity, power is everywhere. However, the shaman's prime connection to the power of acceptance is through his or her body. It is in the space of the body that you actualize your power. In other words, your body is the "space" that takes action in the world. Powerful action, of course, comes from aligning with nature, with life as it is.

When you are in kinship with nature, you sense and feel the moment. Breathing, tasting, touching, smelling, hearing are all vehicles to power. The magical being works to heighten his or her senses and bring them into alignment with present space.

Another bodily sensation is emotion. Emotions also have a strong link with the critical mind. Whenever the mind wanders into either the past or the future, your emotions can easily fluctuate and you lose any power in the moment. When you feel your emotions as an event happens, you take a stance of power. When an image is not in your field of vision, you don't see it. When a sound is beyond your range of hearing, it is inaudible. Likewise, when a stimulus for your emotions is not present, those too should subside. These are the ways of acceptance.

The Enchantments

In order to bring acceptance into your life it is necessary to come to your senses—literally. The following enchantments awaken you to each of your senses. Initially you may feel as though these exercises are too simple for you, but try them for a while and see if you notice the results.

Seeing Sin

Begin by creating sacred space as outlined in the first chapter, or create your own way of designating a sacred time and place for this work. When you are finished, place a single lit candle at the center of your sacred space. Sit in front of the candle and observe it. Try to focus only on seeing. If you notice sounds or smells or other sensations, allow them too, but maintain your focus only on seeing. If thoughts or judgments come up, try not to get caught up in them. For example, if the thought, "I have to do the laundry next" comes up, just allow it. Try not to follow the thought or get caught up in critical thinking such as "I hate to do the laundry. Why do I always have to do it..." and on and on. Observe the thought as it emerges. Be present for it, but concentrate only on seeing the lit candle. Do this exercise for ten to fifteen minutes each day for five days and then move on to the next sense exercise.

Hearing Sin

Once again, begin this exercise by creating sacred space. When you have finished, turn on an audiotape or a CD of some kind of sacred music. All music and all sound is sacred, but for the purpose of this exercise, choose music that feels soothing and sacred to you. It can be choral, instrumental, classical, new age, whatever appeals to you.

When I practice Hearing Sin, I choose percussive music such as that of Gabrielle Roth or Jim McGrath.[10] In doing any of the sense exercises, it is easy to drift off into my imagination and I find that the percussive, rhythmic, tribal sound of these drumming artists helps me to stay focused as I listen.

As in the seeing exercise, focus solely on hearing. Sometimes it is helpful to close your eyes, since visual input can distract you from being completely absorbed in hearing. Again, allow your thoughts to come up as they normally would, but try not to follow them. If you catch yourself thinking or following thoughts instead of hearing, just return to the sensations of the sound. Do this exercise for ten to fifteen minutes a day for five days and then move on to the next sense exercise.

Smelling Sin

Begin this exercise by creating your sacred space. Before you begin, place a single essential oil or an incense within easy reach. For this exercise, I like to use a floral essential oil like jasmine or gardenia.

The chemicals of the essential oil may change your own body chemistry. It is best to research the essence you choose in order to know what effects it may have on your body. Some oils create healing states, while others can alter your moods. Choose with care. If you don't like oils or incense, select a particularly fragrant flower or herb. One person I know likes to use orange peels for this exercise. It is fine to be creative in choosing a scent upon which you can focus for this exercise.

Sit in your sacred space and again close your eyes. Bring the fragrance to your nose and focus on the sensation of the aroma. Try not to inhale in any special way. Instead, breathe normally. Thoughts may come up during this exercise. If they do, allow them to surface.

Observe them and return to your sense exercise. Do this for ten to fifteen minutes for the next five days before moving on to the next sense exercise.

Tasting Sin

Before you begin, select a piece of fruit or a vegetable that is particularly flavorful for you. Divide the fruit or vegetable into small pieces and set them within reach. Create sacred space as outlined in the first chapter. Close your eyes and place one of the small vegetable or fruit pieces into your mouth. As in the other exercises, try to focus solely on tasting what is in your mouth to the exclusion of other senses. Where do the flavors go in your mouth and across your tongue? After a minute or so of pure tasting, begin to chew. Swallow the fruit or vegetable and begin again. If thoughts come up, then try not to follow them. Continue with this exercise for fifteen minutes for the next five days before conducting the last of the five sense exercises.

Feeling Sin

For this exercise, select a piece of cloth or something that has an interesting texture. Velvet is one of my favorites for this exercise. Something coarse like sandpaper would work just as well. You may select any item that appeals to your sense of touch.

After you create sacred space, close your eyes. Next, touch the textured material and focus only on your sensation. Once again, do not follow thoughts that invade your sacred touch exercise. If you follow a thought, simply correct yourself and refocus on what you are touching. Do this exercise for fifteen minutes for the next five days.

Integrating the Senses of Sin

Once you have completed the twenty-five days of sense training, it is important to know how to apply the exercises to your daily life. Seeing, tasting, touching, hearing, smelling are fine to do in a sacred space as practice, but what does it mean in the real world? As you go through your usual day, open yourself to what is happening right now by allowing the senses to emerge. For example, during your lunch hour try to focus solely on the flavors and aromas of the food. Or if you are grooming your dog or cat, use that time to really feel the texture of the animal's fur. Or if a co-worker comes to you with a problem, really see and hear him or her. Not only will you improve your relationship, but you will continue to hone your skills of remaining present and responding to the moment.

The Sachet of Truth

This is a magical technique to help you keep focused on the truth of your life in each moment. You can use this in combination with the exercises above or use it in your daily life. The key component is cinnamon bark. According to Scott Cunningham in his book *Magical Aromatherapy*, cinnamon has the ability to increase one's physical sensory focus.

What you'll need:

- A 3" x 3" square of cloth (or felt)
- A 5" piece of ribbon or string
- One cinnamon stick (or ground cinnamon bark)
- A 3" x 3" square of blank parchment paper
- A pen

Begin by creating your sacred space. Take out the parchment paper and pen. Write down a time during which you commit yourself to stay focused on the truth of each moment. Keep the commitment short because it is difficult to stay focused for long periods of time. For example, you may commit to stay focused for eight hours, or for an entire day or more. If you completed the Initiation Celebration of Chapter One, you can also inscribe the parchment paper with your sacred symbols of the four compass directions. Fold the parchment paper into a tiny wad.

Crush the cinnamon stick and place it in the center of the cloth square. Place the wadded-up parchment paper in the center of the cloth also. Gather together the four corners of the cloth until you form a small bundle. Tie the bundle shut with your piece of ribbon or string. Some people like to make the bundle into a neck pouch. Whatever you do, keep the bundle with you during the duration of your focus-work. Whenever you find yourself drifting from the moment, squeeze the little bundle and breathe in the aroma. That should be enough to get you back on track. In some instances, this may not be enough to help you refocus. What I do in these cases is to vocalize a small rhyming chant:

> *Truth be known; truth be shown,*
> *Awaken me in flesh and bone.*

Rites of Passage

Every culture assists its members as they make transitions from one phase of life to another. Some do this in an informal way. For example, in mainstream American culture when a teenager drives a car for the first time, it marks an important transition to a more independent and adult life. Other cultures address the transitions from one stage of life to another with rituals and celebrations.

A rite of passage is a ceremony that marks your personal passage through time and denotes your current reality. A rite of passage provides you with a "time map," pointing out where you are now. Each phase of your life evokes certain behaviors and attitudes. For instance, you act and think differently when you are forty-two from when you are twenty-two. A rite of passage helps you to acknowledge this difference and to stay focused on each moment of your new life phase. It also reminds those who conduct the rite of where they are in their own lives. One of the benefits of such rites is that they ground participants in the moment. They help everyone recognize the sacredness of what is happening right now.

Most rites of passage center around important occasions: birth, adolescence, adulthood, marriage, old age, and death. It is important to recognize your own transitions from one life stage to another whether you mark these with the ceremonies provided below or with your own special celebrations.

Birth

Power comes from celebrating life. A birth is therefore cause for ceremony and festivities. It is a reminder to all who are present that life is a "round." Birth leads to death. Without death, there cannot be new life. There is no end to this holy round of existence.

Across the globe and throughout time, birth has been surrounded with superstition and custom. For example, in Old Europe, many mothers believed that the placenta of the baby held magical power, so they kept it after birth. One odd custom was to hang the placenta on a young tree to assure the growth of the baby. Another custom was to save the placenta in a secret, safe place to assure protection for the baby.

Below is a birth ceremony to bless a child with the four elements and their symbolic qualities. It is an adaptation of these older customs from ancient Europe.

What you'll need:

- Rose petals
- A length of white cord
- A special box large enough to contain the cord
- A small dish of salt
- A small bowl of warmed water
- A candle
- A baby blanket

Place the baby blanket on the ground. For safety and health reasons, it is best to do this rite indoors with a newborn. Place the baby on his or her back on the blanket with the head at the north and feet pointing south. Make a circle with the rose petals around the baby's body.

Stand on the east or the baby's left side. Inhale deeply once and blow across the baby from head to toe. When you finish say:

May you always act with knowledge.

Light the candle and set it at the baby's feet. (Be careful!) After you set the candle there say:

May you live your life with passion.

Next take the warmed water and sprinkle it clockwise around the perimeter of the baby's body. Dab a bit on the child's forehead and feet saying:

May you always touch others with your understanding.

When you finish, place the bowl of water near the baby's right hand. Next take the dish of salt and sprinkle it around the baby's body. Touch the child's forehead and feet with a dab of salt, and say:

May you open to your wisdom.

Place the dish near the top of the baby's head. Lastly, take the white cord and measure the circumference of the baby's head. Tie a knot in the cord at the circumference point. From that knot, measure the circumference of the baby's chest and tie a knot at this next circumference point. Finally, from this knot in the cord, measure the entire length of the baby's body from head to toe and cut the cord so that it reflects this measurement. Have each person blow on the cord to bring forth the powers of air. Then, each member takes a turn holding the cord over the flame of the candle to bless it with the element of fire and then dabs a bit of water on the cord and touches the cord to the dish of salt. Place the cord in the special box and then say:

Blessed be this place and this time,
And this newborn child!

Put the box with the cord in some secret place to keep the child safe.

Coming of Age

What does it mean to come of age? For boys and girls it means something very different. For girls, the time comes with their first menstrual cycle. At the moment of menstruation, the role of a young woman in a tribal culture becomes clear. She is now the vehicle of life. Nature has taken over her body. The initiation into the mysteries of regeneration happens naturally for women.

Boys have a more complicated transition. Instead of becoming the vehicles of life, boys are inducted into society. They become vehicles of their society. Their bodies do not offer blood as women's bodies do. Because they do not offer the blood that transforms them from youth to adulthood, in tribal cultures the society exacts a blood offering. Young men are symbolically and physically "cut away" from childhood, and so young men throughout time have experienced rites of scarification and circumcision. Part of the initiation rites of young men in tribal cultures includes cutting and battering by the elder men's group, which is comprised of the tribe's social leaders. They are also separated from women, especially their mothers, to demonstrate to the young men that they are no longer a part of the women's world as they once were in boyhood.[11]

In some tribal settings, when a young woman comes of age she might be separated from the others in the tribe and placed where she can reflect on what she has become. Alternatively, young women can be taught the secrets, mysteries, and crafts of womanhood. Many times young men are taken on a hunt for a particularly wild game animal. Or they can be left in the wilderness to fend for themselves for a period of days. In either case, a transformation of body, mind, and spirit is the common theme in the rites of passage from youth to adulthood.

Young Woman's Rite

I recently interviewed an initiate of the Moontydes women's spirituality circle in Riverside, California. A priestess, who goes by the magical name of Varda, taught me the purpose and meaning of the rites of menarche, a young woman's onset of menstrual cycles. At this auspicious time, the young woman becomes identical with the energies of life. She is analogous with the mythical earth goddess and her powers, which include fertility, bringing forth new life, and nurturing that life. The rites around this passage are meant to awaken the young woman to the fact that she has been overtaken by this power. They are meant to open a young woman to the knowledge of her own power.

Among some of the lost California tribes of Native Americans, this special rite was administered by the young woman's mother or another significant elder female among the tribe's people. The elder woman would praise the girl and pamper her. Then the girl might have fresh flowers woven into her hair and might be given a warm bath to ease cramping. Gifts and laughter were essential to this rite of passage.

The light-hearted, airy feelings presented by the rites of menarche are similar to those that represent the archetypal, symbolic quality of woman in her aspect of maiden. The maiden is the symbol of youth. In this symbolic aspect, the young woman represents innocence, purity, and virtue. She is full of potential, and the young woman's archetypal power is that of inspiration and renewal. The onset of the menstrual cycle begins the period of timekeeping for the young girl, and if she were a member of a tribal folk, she would learn about the cycles of the moon as they might correspond to her monthly physical cycling. This practice of timekeeping for women is as ancient as mythological thinking itself, which by the most recent academic consensus might have begun some 60,000 years ago. In one archeological dig in Europe, there were found a series of staves with notches in them. Careful study of these notches under a microscope revealed that the notches were made with different instruments. This variation in notching suggests that they were time-factored counts, made at different points within a year's cycle. The number of counts on the staves also seemed to correspond with the count of lunar cycles. The moon, menstrual cycles, and women are all mythically and spiritually linked.

The moon, the earth, fertility, nature, and the mythic goddess are all tied into this passage for a young woman, and each of these many aspects can be incorporated into your own celebration. Varda of Moontydes suggests that red is a powerful color for this time in a young woman's life. Give a gift of a special red necklace, perhaps one made of garnets for her "moontime." Another appropriate gift might be a beautiful article of clothing in soft cloth—perhaps a red sweater or sweatshirt—something lovely and comforting for her moontimes. Another appropriate gift can be a new purse or book bag to carry her new necessities.

The most important part of the rite is to tell stories of places where this rite of passage is a celebration, because many cultures (particularly in the West) brand it as a nuisance at the very least. Regularly a woman's cycle time is thought of as ugly, dirty, and shameful. The truth of this cycling is that it is a central and honored part of womanhood. It is important to do this rite when the girl first notices the appearance of her menstrual blood. Even if you never had this kind of honoring of your own when you came of age, you can still commemorate this cycle of your life and this phase of your power at any time.

The rite I have provided below makes use of Celtic names for the lunar cycles. You might read a bit before the ritual to research alternative moon names that might best suit your needs or current experience.

What you'll need:

- Thirteen cowrie shells (or other shells with holes or crevices)
- Four candles (optional)
- A large, flat rock (try to find slate if you can; it is very useful for this ritual) or a rock that has a large, smooth surface
- Red paint (try poster or acrylic paints; Varda suggests a blood-red color)

To begin, the elder woman should create her own sacred space. When she has finished, she can light four candles and place them at the four directions, thus designating the sacred space for the ritual. The elder woman then brings the young woman into the center of the circle, sits her down so that she faces north, and then says:

> You have entered the circle of the thirteen moons.
> You are one with nature.
> Power runs deep within you now and
> It flows out upon the land making it whole and sacred.
> I will teach you the powers of your circle of thirteen moons.

The elder woman then places the thirteen shells in a circle around the young woman. To begin, she sets one shell on the east or right side of the young woman. The elder woman continues:

> The first moon is called Fearn.
> Her time brings to you strength, courage, and passion.

The elder places the next shell (and each of the others after this) in a clockwise pattern around the young woman. When she sets the next shell down she says:

The second moon is called Saille.
Her time brings to you sensuality and sexuality.

The third shell is placed, continuing clockwise around the youth.

The third moon is called Uath.
Her time brings to you innovation and new ideas.

Place the fourth shell.

The fourth moon is called Duir.
Her time brings to you expansion, humor, and vision.

Place the fifth shell.

The fifth moon is called Tinne.
Her time brings to you virtue and integrity.

Place the sixth shell.

The sixth moon is called Coll.
Her time brings to you truth and knowledge of all things.

Place the seventh shell.

The seventh moon is called Muin.
Her time brings to you love, kindness, and social artistry.

Place the eighth shell.

The eighth moon is called Gort.

Her time brings to you loyalty and the bond of friendship.

Place the ninth shell.

The ninth moon is called Ngetal.
Her time brings to you visions of things to come and
The power to penetrate the depths of all mysteries.

Place the tenth shell.

The tenth moon is called Ruis.
Her time brings to you self-discipline and patience.

Place the eleventh shell.

The eleventh moon is called Beth.
Her time brings to you trust and humor.

Place the twelfth shell.

The twelfth moon is called Luis.
Her time brings to you compassion and selflessness.

Place the last shell.

The thirteenth moon is called Nion.
Her time brings to you healing and deep faith.
Know these times and their powers,
For there is great magic within you!

To finish the rite, both the elder woman and the one coming of age will create a petroglyph, a painting on the rock that symbolizes the significance of this day. The symbol can be of anything, but it should spring from the young woman's sense of vision. Perhaps she might try closing her eyes and evoking an image that can represent her passage into the power of the thirteen moons.

Young Man's Rite

The appropriate time for a young man to make his transition from boyhood to adulthood varies from person to person. In tribal cultures, the shaman or the head of the men's hunting group decides what will happen based on the young man's behavior. This is important to ascertain because the transition does not happen with the onset of a young man's first ejaculation, in correspondence to a young woman's first menses.

When a young man becomes ungovernable, then the elder men's group—sometimes dressed in nothing but their own blood—will come to claim him. How a young man becomes ungovernable or acts out his assertion of manhood is different for every young man. It also varies from culture to culture, and if you are a parent, you will have to use your spiritual judgment on this. In the United States, I have found that "ungovernable" behavior can take several forms. Between the ages of thirteen and seventeen, a young man may attempt his first sexual encounter, or he may experiment with substances like alcohol or drugs. He may want to take on his first job, drive a car, or move away from home. Whatever behavior he acts out with consistency, be sure to consider it well.

This rite is to help the young man face the responsibilities and challenges of adulthood. This is a difficult psychological transition for everyone involved because the youth is making a transition from being protected by his parents to taking his place beside them. In Western cultures, I find that parents have difficulty facing this transition themselves. This may be based on their own experiences in their mid-teens. Nevertheless, it is critical for a young man to face responsibility and begin detaching from the protective parental hold. It is important to remember that this passage should not only be a ceremony, but an actuality for the youth. Try to let the other adults in the young man's life know that he will be making this passage and that everyone is to treat him accordingly afterward.

Traditionally, this rite is performed by an elder man or a group of elder men.[12] Optimally, the young man's father and other male relatives including older brothers are present for the rite. In the event that there are no blood-related males, find other elders to whom the young man has some attachment.

What you'll need:

- Three essential oils blended in equal parts: patchouli, musk, and myrrh[13]
- Tea lights or small votive candles, one for each man present
- Optional: drums

You might consider performing this ritual by candlelight or by the light of a fire either in a fireplace or outdoors. The symbolic quality of fire is important to this rite.

To begin, the men present should sit in a circle with the youth seated in the center. If anyone has a drum, he can begin to drum softly at this time. Allow the young man to sit for several minutes facing each of the elder men. The young man looks into the eyes of an elder for several minutes until each sees in the other's eyes what it is that makes him laugh and what makes him cry. Each of the men in the outside circle tells the youth what he "saw" in his eyes. Then the youth reciprocates and tells each elder what he saw in his eyes.

Then the youth's father or a chosen elder speaks:

The time has come that we must claim you for our tribe.
Gone are your boyhood days and ways.

Then the elder leads the youth to the east of the circle and says:

Learn as a man.

Then they proceed to the south and the elder says:

Work as a man.

Then they proceed to the west and the elder says:

Love as a man.

Then they proceed to the north and the elder says:

Grow as a man.

Then the two move to the center of the circle. The youth should remove his shirt, shoes, and socks, so that his upper body and bare feet are exposed. The elder takes out the anointing oil, puts a droplet on his finger, and then presses it onto the top of the youth's head. The youth then says:

I open to the wisdom of manhood.

The other men repeat this phrase.

Then with another drop, the elder makes a mark at the center of the youth's brow. The youth says:

I open to the vision of manhood.

The other men repeat this.

The elder anoints the hollow of the youth's throat. The youth says:

I open to the voice of manhood.

The other men repeat this phrase.

The elder anoints the center of the youth's chest. The youth says:

I open to the compassion of manhood.

The other men present then repeat this.

Next, the elder marks the youth's two forearms with the oil. The youth then says:

I open to the strength of manhood.

The other men repeat this.

The elder anoints the young man approximately two inches below the naval. The youth says:

I open to the potency of manhood.

The other men chant this phrase.

Finally, the elder marks the soles of the youth's feet. The youth says:

From this day forth,
I walk the path of my manhood.

The other men chant this phrase.

The youth may then replace his clothing, if he chooses. He sits in the center and, one by one, each male lights his tea light (candle) and tells the youth an aspect of becoming a man in which he vows guidance over the coming years. The men might vow such things as, "I bring knowledge to you," or "I bring honesty to you," or "I bring empathy to you." As they say this, they place their candles around the youth to make a circle of light.

The ritual can conclude with the men taking turns relating stories from the time they first realized they had become men.

Love Union

When you begin to share your life with a partner, you have arrived at another important time-marker in your life. It shows that you are ready to commit to a relationship with another human being. It shows that you are able to care for another fully and release a good portion of self-centeredness. The "other" becomes the focus in your life beyond this celebration of union. An alliance such as this is an initiation into love.

My own teachers called a coupling ceremony a "handfasting." The focus of this ritual is that of the sacredness of joining two lives. A handfasting can be between any two individuals, male or female: two men or two women can be handfasted as easily as a man and a woman because the central theme of the rite is commitment and caring—two aspects of humanness that have no specific gender or sexual orientation. Also, because this ritual is meant to generate awareness for the participants, there is no officiator presiding over the rite. It is self-administered.

What you'll need:

- Two long-stem wine glasses (or, my preference, two chalices)
- Red wine (or red grape juice for a non-alcoholic alternative)
- A large bowl
- Four feet of red or white ribbon or cord

- An essential oil that represents love, such as rose or jasmine
- Two long-stem, red roses

To begin the ritual, both participants should face the east. It is important to have two small tables or floor mats, one on your right and one on your partner's left. On these tables, place chalices filled with red wine and a corn dollie that will represent each of you. On the ground in front of you place the large bowl. Stand shoulder to shoulder, so that you will both have a "free" hand, which is on the outside, and a "bound" hand which is on the inside. Pick up the ribbon and jointly hold it in your free, outside hands. Pull the ribbon so there is some tension. Raise your inside "bound" hands and place one on top of the other, palms down. Pull up the ribbon so that it touches the wrist of the bottom, bound hand.

When both hands are together, one on top of the other, one of you should have a right hand free and the other should have a left hand free. Assuming that you are standing on the right, begin by loosely folding your end of the ribbon over the tops of your joined hands. It is important that each fold is done loosely, because these folds will need to slide off your hands later. After you make the first fold, you say:

With trust, I commit.

Then your partner takes a turn folding the ribbon over your joined hands, crossing the ribbon end over the other. Then your partner says:

With passion, I commit.

Grab your ribbon end, bring it underneath the hands, and continue the wrapping, saying:

With respect, I commit.

Then your partner grabs the other ribbon end and continues this wrapping, saying:

With love, I commit.

You make the next wrap and say:

With tenderness, I commit.

Your partner makes the next wrap and says:

With spirit, I commit.

Then you make the seventh and final wrap. Say together:

With all these things we commit for as long as love shall last
Which in the eyes of the Mighty Ones is
The wholeness of time.
Hands, neither bound nor free.

Next, take your individual wine goblets with your free hands and simultaneously take a short sip. Then take turns vowing what you promise to bring into the union. You might say such things as, "I vow beauty," or "I vow to provide," or "I vow to listen." When you have said your vows, you both pour the contents of your goblets into the large bowl on the ground in front of you.

Then say:

Can you take the wine that was once yours?

Your partner responds:

No. Can you take the wine that was once yours?

Then you reply:

No.

Then you both say:

Then they shall mingle and become one!

Lift the large bowl with your free hands and assist each other in drinking from it. Slide the ribbon off your bound hands, but be careful to maintain the loops. Set this on one of the side tables. Then tie the two long-stem roses together with the ribbon. While you both hold the tied roses, you kiss. Then anoint your partner with the essential oil on his or her heart and say:

I bless our union with perfect love.

Your partner responds by anointing you and saying:

I bless our union with perfect trust.

Old Age

The rite of passage from adulthood into senescence is called a "croning" for women and a "saging" for men. This can be a difficult passage for both men and women because of its many implications. Old age means that the initiate is closer to death. It may also mean a decline in health and status. The initiate also faces life without the beauty or the vitality of his or her youth. Each of these can mean feelings of loss for the elder. Before you begin any ritual, be certain that your feelings associated with old age are neutral.

At this transition, women become the archetype of the crone. The crone represents the woman past childbearing and mothering years. The time of the crone begins for most women at the same time as menopause. Men transitioning from adulthood to elderhood become the archetype of the sage. This is the symbol of man no longer pursuing his role of provider and protector for others. He is no longer preoccupied with his sexual pursuits. He has released his push toward personal conquest. Both the crone and sage are archetypes of human beings turned inward.

In tribal cultures both the crone and the sage are elders who join the inner circle of initiates. They are the wise ones and law givers. They are the ones who bring justice, balance, and insight to others. No matter what the culture of origin is, those who make the passage to elderhood face the challenge of adapting these traditional roles into their own lives.

The following ritual format is, once again, a template for you to expand upon. Find what is meaningful and significant to you and add or subtract according to your personal taste. After all, you should know what is best — you are becoming the crone or sage.

For this rite, you'll be giving two "gifts" to people present in the circle. One "gift" will be something from your youth and the other will be something from your adult years. In Native American cultures, these are called "giveaways." Select some simple item — a photograph, a baby blanket, a piece of artwork or jewelry — that has some particular significance, or that seems to represent a past period of your life. If you have no memorabilia, try an antique store or an arts and crafts store to make something that represents these various times of your life.

What you'll need:

- Your two "giveaways"
- A length of silver cord long enough to tie around your waist
- A spool of string
- A purple candle
- Optional: drums

To begin the ritual, you will make a sacred "maze" with the spool of string. The maze you create is not meant to be sophisticated or elaborate. It isn't meant to be a puzzle. Sacred mazes are walkways that one can use ritually to denote a sacred journey from one state of consciousness to another. You will create a spiral with the string that is a symbol of the double spiral. You will need a large enough space to create the maze, so you might choose an open field or a beach setting. The appropriate, symbolic time of day to create and walk the maze is dusk.

In order to create the maze, begin by laying the end of the string at what will be the center of one spiral. Then create larger consecutive rings that encircle each other. Make no more than three rings. Each ring represents an archetype of the gods. The innermost ring represents the symbolic life phase of the maiden for women. For men the symbolic phase is that of the inseminator. The second ring represents the symbolic aspect of the mother for women and the symbolic aspect of the provider for men. The last ring represents the crone and the sage.

When you have made the three rings, then pull the string across the ground to begin your second spiral. This second spiral begins with the outside, larger rings and spirals inward to the center point. Your double spiral should look like this when you are finished.

Next, lay down on your back across the string that connects the two spirals. Close your eyes and take several deep breaths. Release any stored tension that you may sense. Next an officiator (preferably someone who is already an elder) will lead you through a guided meditation. (*Note to the officiator:* Throughout the meditation and this rite in general, choose the word "crone" or "sage" as is appropriate for the initiate.)

Officiator: *You are awakening to your age of wisdom. It is time to meet the (crone/sage). A purple mist begins to form around your body. You can feel its warmth surround you. It begins to make your body feel light, weightless. It begins to carry you to a place that is beyond time and space, but all you are aware of is movement. [Pause]*

The mist now sets you down and dissipates to reveal the moonless nighttime sky. You are at the foot of a steep, rocky mountain. From above on the rocky peak, you can see the light of a fire. You begin to search for a pathway that might lead to the fire. From behind a large boulder, a cloaked figure approaches you. (Her/His) face is obscured by the hood, but you can see that (her/his) hands are old, thin, frail as (she/he) reaches out toward you. You are not afraid and you take the hand offered to you.

The cloaked figure does not utter a word. (She/He) takes you to a hidden path behind one of the rocks and begins to lead you upward. You follow wherever the cloaked figure leads as the path zigzags back and forth along the rocky cliffs. [Pause]

You now approach the top of the mountain. You know this because you can see the bonfire at the mountain top. The hooded figure, still holding your hand, leads you to the fire. Within the fire's light, you can see that you too are wearing a long, dark robe, just like that of the hooded figure before you. Finally this figure removes (her/his) hood to reveal the face of an old (woman/man). This is the presence of the wisdom deep within you. The old (woman/man) speaks a single word to you. This word represents a power of yours that will come to fruition as you pass into your own (croning/saging) time. After the elder speaks to you (she/he) backs into the fire. (She/He) beckons for you to follow. As you approach the fire, you once again take the hand of the (crone/sage) and you are pulled into the flames. At that moment, you are quickly transported back to the place where you began the journey. You arrive back to your body on the ground, laying between the spirals.

You may open your eyes now. When you return from the journey, those who are present can begin a pulsating drumbeat that sounds once every four seconds, to create a slow "march" rhythm. While the others drum, you now use a pin or a sharp knife to inscribe a symbol or a word on the purple candle that represents what the crone or sage will bring to you in your elderhood. For example, you might write the word "balance" or "peace" or "silence." When you are finished, place the purple candle unlit in an appropriate holder at the center of one of the spirals.

Then, stand at the center of the other spiral and begin walking the line of the string, taking one step for each drumbeat. If there is no one to drum for you, take one step for every exhalation. The most mindful, meditative walk is usually quite slow and each step is deliberate. Feel the weight of your body press down as you transfer from foot to foot. You might even take very small steps that are half the length of your foot. As you do this be mindful of your passage from the years of your adulthood to the wisdom of older age. With each step, embrace the power of your wisdom.

When you reach the center of the second spiral, where your candle lies, pick up the candle and light it. Hold it with both hands over your head and say:

I embrace the time of the (crone/sage)!
I have come into my elderhood.
I walk the path of the waning moon.
I offer the power of (word revealed in vision)
To the people around me.

Finally, give away the item from your youth to the youngest member present. As you give the item, say:

I release my youth so that I may ripen to elderhood.

To another elder, give the item from your adult years and say:

I release my adulthood so that I may ripen to elderhood.

If you complete this rite of passage alone, give the two gifts away after the ceremony and remember why you give them.

Death

The passage from physical life into the mysteries beyond is assured to each of us at the moment of our first breath. Passing from one state to the next is as natural as breathing. Metaphorically speaking, physical life is as simple as your inhalation, and death as simple and easy as an exhalation. The spirit knows what to do when the body can no longer house it, it does not need instruction. Neither did it need instruction on how to inhabit the body at birth. Consequently, the main focus in a "rite of passage" for one's death is an initiation into the reality of death for those who continue to live—as opposed to some sort of ritual of spiritual release for the departed.

Many times death brings up long repressed feelings in us, such as anger or sadness. A death of a loved one makes us feel as though it has cheated us and taken away those whom we love. The following rite of passage helps to remind us that death does not cheat us out of life any more than life cheats us out of death. Both are threads woven into the same infinite tapestry.

Imagine for a moment a wooden sailing vessel on a journey around the world. If along the way a plank begins to rot, it must be replaced. Does the captain despair at the loss of that particular old plank? No, he orders the carpenters to take out the old wood and replace it. If you equate yourself, your existence, with the rotted old plank of wood, then death becomes unbearable. But when you equate yourself with the whole ship or the voyage (which is life itself), then you have identified yourself with the part that is truly everlasting.

What you'll need:

- Butcher-block brown paper or other art paper at least 3' x 3'
- A black felt-tip marker
- A candle in a holder

It is best to gather together at least five people for the rite. Ideally, the facilitator is someone who was closest to the deceased. The facilitator draws a large five-pointed star on the 3' x 3' piece of paper, big enough to touch all four edges of the paper, and places the unlit candle at the center of the star.

The five attendees sit at each of the five points of the star on the floor. The facilitator gives each of the five people a pencil or pen, lights the candle, and says:

_____ *(Name of deceased) has passed from the world*
Of the seen to the world of the unseen but lives on.

The facilitator instructs each person to think of words that describe the deceased's best traits. For example, "joyfulness," "humor," "courage," or "artistry," and each person reads the traits.

The facilitator then instructs the members to select a trait that they themselves wish to attain. Each member takes a turn and says:

_____ *(Name of deceased) has passed from the world*
Of the seen to the world of the unseen but lives on.
In the days to follow, I vow to bring forth in myself
And in others his/her (name the trait here) _____.

When all have finished expressing the traits, the facilitator instructs them to write down the less-than-honorable traits about the deceased, for example, "fearfulness," "possessiveness," or "hostility," and each person takes turns reading the traits.

Then the facilitator instructs the members to select a trait that they wish to decrease in themselves and in others. Each member says in turn:

_____ (Name of deceased) has passed from the world
Of the seen to the world of the unseen but lives on.
In the days to follow, I vow to bring an end to
(name the trait here) _____
In myself and in others.

The five attendees then inhale together and collectively blow out the central candle. The facilitator then says:

The round of life continues.
That which was lit is now unlit.
And it stands to be lit again!

The candle and the star can either be buried or cremated with the deceased.

1. Ralph Waldo Emerson, *Essays,* "Intellect" (first series, 1841).
2. Janet and Stewart Farrar, *The Witches' Goddess* (Washington: Phoenix Publishing, 1987), p. 273.
3. Shunryu Suzuki, *Zen Mind, Beginner's Mind* (New York: Weatherhill, Inc., 1996), p. 41.
4. Roshi Philip Kapleau, *The Three Pillars of Zen* (New York: Anchor Books, 1989), pp. 32–33.
5. Melody Beatie, *Codependent No More* (New York: HarperCollins, 1987), p. 122.
6. Jacqueline Small, *Awakening in Time* (New York: Bantam Books, 1991), p. 41.
7. Barbara Ardinger, *A Woman's Book of Rituals and Celebrations* (San Rafael: New World Library, 1992), p. 31.
8. Jamake Highwater, *The Primal Mind* (New York: Meridian, 1981), p. 133.
9. Highwater, *The Primal Mind* (New York: Meridian, 1981), p. 91.
10. See the listing of sacred music in the back of the book for more details.
11. Joseph Campbell, *The Hero with a Thousand Faces* (New Jersey: Princeton University Press, 1973), pp. 8–11.
12. Jerome S. Bernstein, "The Decline of Masculine Rites of Passage in Our Culture: The Impact on Masculine Individuation" in Louise Carus Mahdi, Steven Foster, and Meredith Little, *Betwixt and Between* (La Salle: Open Court, 1987), pp. 138–144.
13. I have substituted essential oil for the youth's own blood. Typically, the young man's finger will be pricked with a sterilized blade or pin. The facilitator (usually the boy's father) uses his son's blood as the anointing oil. This is the method we use in the EarthDance Collective.

CHAPTER IV

MUSE

Actions done on behalf of the self hold no power.

INVOCATION

It was wintertime and several of us continued our training even though we had been initiated. "There's too much to learn in one lifetime," said Hermes. The three students and I piled into the back seat of Hermes' beat-up, rusted-out car, but we had already gotten soaked from a downpour of rain that had started just before we could take shelter. Hermes was the driver. He looked too old to drive us anywhere. "Where are we going?" I asked politely. I couldn't feel it, but I could tell by the sound of my voice that I was nervous about Hermes driving us. He laughed until he almost choked. He kept his face turned from us. "What's the matter? You afraid of a little old man driving?"

I laughed out of nervousness with the rest of the apprentices in the back seat. "Maybe if I were a bit younger?" he asked. Then he turned around to face us and I couldn't believe my eyes. His face looked different — younger. His features didn't look like the old man whom I had known from training. It looked firm and full of life. He turned his face away from us again, "There is more to life than youth," he said with a small laugh. We had been silent for an hour of the trip, when Hermes spoke abruptly. "There are many faces that each of us has. Some are young, some are old. Some of our faces are sad and some are content. You can choose any face you like by the story you tell." The four of us in the back seat were dumbfounded and we all remained silent while Hermes drove us to the home of another elder.

Later on, during the training circle, Hermes moved to the center of the circle and invoked the spirits:

> Hear me, ancient ones, women of the art! Be with us to teach of your skills. Show us the magic of the stories and tales of our own weaving. Reveal to us that which lies beyond our tales and open us to your power!

THE TALE—A Father's Treasure

Once there was a great sheik who had two sons. The eldest was particularly stupid and greedy and the youngest was particularly clever. One day the sheik asked his two sons to go to a faraway kingdom that had fine markets. "Go there and return with whatever you find of value. The son who returns with the finest treasure will be richly rewarded." This, of course, excited the eldest, who could not sleep many nights afterward as he spent his time dreaming about his life of independent wealth. The youngest said not a word, but agreed to his father's wish.

Since the kingdom was a long way off across a vast desert, the sheik equipped each boy with a camel, flasks of water, food, and large purses of gold coins. So the boys set off to the faraway kingdom. It took them three days of travel across sand and searing sun, but finally they arrived at the markets. The eldest bought many silk rugs, jewelry, golden urns, robes of spun cloth, herbs, spices, and every other treasure he could find. The youngest bought nothing except three flasks of water. This only made the older son laugh. "You will see how our father will reward me for all of my finery," said the eldest boy. Once they had finished at the markets, the oldest son had to hire four men to carry the goods back to the waiting camels.

"What shall I do to bring these goods back?" said the eldest son, "I cannot carry these riches back to father." The youngest said, "Load them on to the camels and we shall walk alongside them." The eldest was angered at this, for he did not want to walk back across the searing desert sands for three days. Since he had no other choice, he agreed. They loaded both camels and the youngest tied the three flasks of water to his belt. The eldest was so loaded down with goods that he did not have room for more than one flask of water. This did not bother him, though. He was certain that his father's reward would more than compensate him for his trouble.

On the first day across the sand, one of the camels died under the weight of the rugs, golden urns, and other goods. The eldest son said, "I cannot leave these things behind. I will need them for my reward." The youngest said nothing, but opened one of his flasks and swallowed its contents. The older son said, "You have wasted one of your pitiful gifts for father. He will disown you when you return."

The second day across the sand, the eldest bundled the goods from the dead camel and began dragging them behind him. He grew very weary and begged his brother to help him carry the load, but the youngest refused. Finally, the second camel gave out under the heat and weight of the goods. The oldest said, "I cannot leave these things behind. I will need them for my reward." The youngest said nothing, but opened the second of his flasks and swallowed its contents. The older son said, "You have wasted the second of your pitiful gifts for father. He will disown you when you return." The eldest then opened his only flask of water and poured it down the camel's throat hoping it would revive the beast. However, it did not, and the camel could not budge from the ground.

On the third day, the eldest son was weary from the heat and parched from drinking no water. But he bundled up the goods from the two camels and dragged them behind him as best he could. "I will need these for my reward," he said to himself as he shuffled through the burning sand. Not long after that, the eldest son collapsed and died from exhaustion and lack of water. The youngest son, who was far ahead, was unaware that his brother had collapsed. Focused on his task of returning home, the youngest opened the third flask, drank its contents and continued on.

When he returned home, he was met by his father, who said: "Where is your older brother?" "I do not know," said the son. "What of value have you brought back to me?" asked the sheik. The youngest son handed him the three empty water flasks. The king then began to weep. "Why is it that you weep father? Have I disappointed you? Shall you disown me?" The sheik said, "I weep because only one of my sons knew what was most valuable to me."

MAGICAL LAW — *Actions done on behalf of the self hold no power.*

The Wisdom

"There is no such thing as a self." I was a bit shocked at Muse's bold words. Muse and I had struck up a great friendship from the moment I became part of the magical group. After so many years of knowing her, I was used to her wit, but this statement didn't seem to come from her sense of humor. As she spoke, she had a pensive look on her pale, fragile face.

Muse and I were wandering through the Arroyo Seco Canyon, which was usually dry and a bit dusty, but now after a long rainy winter the creek bed was swollen and fast-moving. As we journeyed, we listened to the water and watched for mockingbirds. In her mid-seventies, Muse walked with a cane, but she was able to hike with ease along the dirt path that ambled next to the creek bed. This was her favorite place in the early spring. "This is when the stream starts to teach," she said to me.

"What does the stream teach, Muse?" I asked while looking at a round river stone move along beneath the swift current.

"It knows how to teach about the no-self," she said.

I wasn't sure what she meant and my mind began swirling with questions. "Why would we ever attempt to improve the self, if it were not there?" I asked. Sometimes I wondered about the effects of age on Muse's mind. She had retired as the active High Priestess of our circle, but to me she still wielded great power and influence. Out of respect, I gave her the benefit of the doubt and I asked what I would have asked any other teacher who would have uttered such statements. "I mean, I am here; aren't I a self?" I asked.

"I don't know, Timothy. Are you a self?" she asked and then giggled a bit.

"Muse, are you speaking to me from a magical perspective or a psychological one?" In her earlier years, Muse had worked as a psycho-analyst, and because of my own training in clinical psychology, we often discussed theory. But this conversation was starting to sound odd.

"Both," she said in a serious tone. "Even Freud said that ultimately, there is no such thing as a 'self' — at least not as you would ordinarily think." I had to admit I was intrigued by her unusual statement. I had done my share of self-exploration, self-growth, and work toward expanding the consciousness of this "self." I wondered for whom I had done the work, if not for myself.

I protested, hoping to hear more. "Nevertheless," Muse continued, "you are not who you think you are." She eased herself down to sit on an unusually square boulder along the side of the creek. "Look here," she said grabbing my arm and pointing to a spot where rocks and moss had gathered in the stream to form a two-foot cascade. "What would you say that is?" She asked this in a tone that demanded an answer.

"It's a small waterfall," I said flatly. I couldn't see where she was going with this question.

"Well, I say it is the creek. Waterfalls come and go with circumstance. The creek is constant."

Her words rang with truth. Then a small breeze picked up some stray leaves and it sent them spinning by us. "And what was that?" Muse asked again.

"It was a breeze, Muse."

"I say it is the air. Your problem is that you look for fragments, events, things to hold on to: a breeze, a waterfall, a self. But you lose what these things are in reality. You say you are a self; I say that you are something more — something beyond a self."

Muse made logical sense. But I could not understand what could be beyond the self.

Then she spoke again, "Each of us has a self which is nothing but our own creation. It is made up of whatever we assimilate from birth. I guess you could say we collect stories about who and what we are based on our experiences with family, friends, home environment, history, community, and culture. Once we have our collection of stories, we weave them together and assume they are the solid entity we label self."[1] Her words carried power for me and I began to question some of what I assumed to be reality. Who was listening to the gurgle of the creek water if it was not myself? Wasn't it myself that felt the chill of the early spring air as we sat?

I began to recall pieces of information from my graduate studies. It was true that raw experiences form the basis of our stories. Experiences are multidirectional and multifaceted. Simultaneous stimuli are difficult for the limited, ordinary mind to apprehend. The ordinary mind strives to make logical, sequential, two-dimensional sense out of three-dimensional experiences. Something gets lost in the translation when the ordinary mind works to find order and coherence in order to define what it is experiencing. When a raw experience gets trapped within the confines of the ordinary mind, it is what we call a story.[2]

Muse cupped her hands and took a handful of the cold creek water. She told me to hold out my hands and then she poured the water into my palms saying, "The stories you tell yourself about your life begin to define who or what you are in the world. They begin to define a self. It is like an optical illusion." I regretted ever doubting her now. Muse was penetrating in her insights.

"But Muse, if it is only an illusion, why can't people see through it?" I asked her.

"Tell me what you think could be beyond the illusion," she said.

I thought for a while before speaking. "I don't know."

Muse laughed a little and rubbed my back with her small hand.

"That's right, you don't know. I don't know either. And it is hard to face what we don't know. Ordinary people have difficulty seeing through the illusion of the self because outside of that illusion is the unknown. It is frightening for ordinary folk to imagine what they might be beyond what they call the self. So, like most of us, they cling to the stories we all tell about ourselves."

"So what are we beyond the self, Muse?" I asked.

"Knowing what we are in that state does not help us. It is simply a matter of returning to the experience of that state of 'I don't know.' There is great magic there in that unknown place."

"But what makes it such a magical place?" I wanted to know.

"When you find yourself existing beyond your own stories, you have found out how to live limitlessly. Magic is change and in that limitless state, you can move with life's ever-flowing changes."

After that, she sat silently watching the creek and poking at the water every now and then with her cane.

As we sat, I began to formulate my own understanding of her teaching. Her words made sense. In an effort to sustain our own illusions, we often look for (or even manufacture) evidence that supports our storytelling. We give our "selves" definition, dimension, character, personality.

Say, for example, that you have had experiences that your ordinary mind has placed into a sequence or a story that describes your "self" as a "loner." Maybe you were left out of some group games in childhood. Perhaps you had friends who moved away and left you feeling lonely or perhaps there were other events that could give the loner story logical credence. Reality and experience may have included many other possibilities, but because you relied on the narrowly focused conscious mind to define your life, you were stuck with a sequence that created a self called loner.

Despite this, life is never one-sided. A loner story (or any other story for that matter) is always accompanied by a range of diverse life experiences that potentially could also go into defining a self. You may have had countless other experiences that suggest a different narrative altogether. Perhaps the reality was that you were surrounded by other people who wanted to be your friend. You may have functioned well in groups all of your life. But often, unconsciously, we choose our stories and edit out what does not fit the narrative story-line. Once a story is selected, the limited critical mind does not allow for flexibility. It demands a certain order and a certain structure. If it says you are a loner, and it works to keep you there, it ignores or edits out the experiences that fall outside of its totalizing story.[3] The treachery in this is the subtlety and control that this belief has over your life. The critical mind keeps each of us locked into patterns and stories, even though there are new stories waiting for us in each moment.

This realization gave me an unearthly feeling, like I was standing on sand that was slipping away beneath my feet. At the same time, I knew that Muse's teachings were all true. In the course of my own spiritual practices, I had had brief, sudden realizations that nothing about my "self" was really all that solid. I had vague sensations that my personality was nothing more than a shadow of what I had seen, heard, felt, tasted, touched, and learned from the past. It was difficult and a bit intimidating for me to follow this thread of consciousness. After all, it would lead to the ultimate question: "Who am I, if not myself?"

I started to feel self-conscious and I squirmed. Muse observed my obvious discomfort, but instead of sitting in silence, she pinned me down once again. "Do you remember the story of the wild boy of Aveyron?" she asked me. From my graduate work in psychology I was well aware of a late eighteenth-century study which focused on a feral boy who was found living in the French wilderness.[4] Evidently, specialists had found this boy after his formative years, when his learning was already woven together into stories that defined him outside of the confines of human culture and language.

"He did not have a self as you might define it," Muse said. I had never thought of the study from this perspective. "The self is not real," she said, "and that is why it can be anything and everything—including an animal self. That is because it is mostly a reflection of the past caught by memory."

I could no longer follow her words or their weighty implications. I had to excuse myself from the conversation and take her back to her home. For days afterward, I had lingering thoughts.

It was time for me to face the truth. I had encountered the fourth magical law which reveals that the self is not solid at all, despite whatever it is we might think. Mystics of all ages have arrived at the same conclusion. This self that you and I constantly refer to is nothing but a group of thoughts, ideas, and stories. It is, at best, a reflected self, a collection of impressions that have been ordered, categorized, and processed through the critical mind.

Because of this, the fourth magical law also hints at the importance of storytelling. To people of power, a story can be a tool. It is through storytelling that shamans and people of power learn to alter their reflected selves. Through this power, they learn to weave any story of their choosing. Storytelling shatters the mirror that reflects a "self" and helps the shaman gain access to the creative forces beyond the mirror and behind their stories.

The ancient Greeks referred to the powers of creativity as the Muses. The nine goddesses of creativity governed a diverse range of disciplines including history, music, comedy, tragedy, poetry, writing, dance, art, and eloquence.[5] The Muses were the daughters of

Mnemosyne, the goddess of memory,[6] and Zeus, the supreme god, who was master of every other god and goddess.[7] The two generative forces behind the Muses symbolize two potential power paths.

The first path of the Muses involves creativity with Mnemosyne, your memory. The power of the Muses here lies in their ability to teach you that you can weave any story from your memory. People of power know that stories and memories are not fixed constructs that have definitive powers. In reality, they are fluid descriptions that can change with a turn of the head or the glance of an eye. Wherever you stand, there is a new story ready to arise. The person of power learns never to fixate on one particular story because it is only one of an infinite number of possible stories within each moment.[8] To the person of power, a story of tragedy can just as well be one of comedy, strength, or wisdom. Power comes with the telling of the tale. Because people of power live by the rules of creativity, spontaneity, and art, they tap into the powers of the Muses. Through the Muses, magical people learn how to tell and retell the stories of their experiences in creative ways.

For example, an individual who carries a cancer diagnosis can easily create variations of his or her experience. On the one hand, the diagnosis can begin a story of victimization and defeat. In the grip of this story, the cancer patient can dredge up memories and experiences that can verify his or her past experiences with victimization. The diagnosis of cancer is the final chapter in a long history of difficulties and struggle. The title of this story could be called, "Dying with Cancer."

On the other hand, the cancer diagnosis can confirm a story of survival and courage. The cancer patient can begin to look for memories, stories, and evidence from the past that verify the skills of a survivor. The patient might remember times from his or her own history that demonstrated strength, nerve, and the fortitude to carry on in the face of adversity. The title of this preferred story could be called, "Living with Cancer."

Storytelling is the creative power path of the Muses. Zeus is the other influential power behind the Muses. If you follow the path of Zeus, you learn how to move beyond the realm of your stories altogether. Zeus is the supreme god—he is beyond the limited forms of the other gods and goddesses. Zeus represents limitlessness, which is the point at which stories and skills with storytelling are no longer necessary.

Through the path of Zeus, the Muses teach us that life is not the personal, individual story that our ordinary critical minds might lead us to believe. It is simply the intertwining of stories. It is a shared story. Through the Zeus path, the Muses reveal that there is no "person" to take things personally. Our bodies, animals, plants, the sun, and moon all appear to be separate entities, but they are all part of the same flow of energy. They are all manifestations of the same force, which is deity. The force that guides and shapes these forms is also the force that binds everything together in unity.

When you live your life believing in the substance of an individual self, which is separate from other selves, then you act accordingly.[9] In this disempowered state, you act to preserve the self. You close yourself off from other people and the events of the world. You notice differences in people and things. You believe that your self-focused desires are important to fulfill and you open the door to selfishness. In that state, all magical power is lost. The current of life is gone; you see yourself as a waterfall and not as part of the flowing creek.

The Muses in their Zeus aspect help you to take a step back and detach from your ongoing story line. Without them, it is easy to get caught up in a single story line, follow it too closely, and then believe that it is "real" or important. "I am a failure," "I am a success," "I am special," are all examples of story lines in which you can become entrapped when you leave your stance of power. Once you become lost in a story line and then start acting on behalf of the self, you obstruct your ability to experience the flow and magic of each moment.

The self is as solid as a cloud. With just the right amount of wind and sun, the cloud disappears. When the sun and wind, the limitless moment of Zeus, strip us of all of our stories, the clouds—the self—blow away and reveal the same shining power that moves the stars and gives life to the universe. When you realize that the self is not real, then you realize that focusing on yourself is a foolish and disempowering enterprise.[10]

The Enchantments

Letting Our Stories Go

The stories we all collect from our personal history affect each of us on all levels of our being. This spell helps to release your history on the thinking, feeling, action, and practical levels of our lives. You will evoke the elements of the sacred wheel along with each of the corresponding powers. This ritual is one that takes several nights to perform. Dedicate each night to releasing your personal history in each direction with the aid of each magical element.

What you'll need:

- A balloon
- A felt-tip pen
- A cup or chalice filled with spring water
- A bonfire, fireplace, or barbecue (some place to burn something)
- Colored sand[11] or dried, ground flower petals and herbs
- 1 sheet of 8 1/2" by 11" white paper

Choose four nights that are within the waning phase of the moon. This is a good time to remove and release old patterns in your life that no longer work for you. It is a good time because the moon sheds its shadow as you magically shed your history. Begin with the element of air.

Night One

Create sacred space. When you are done, choose a balloon color that represents the thought processes from your history. For example, blue might represent sad thoughts. Red might represent angry or even disjointed thoughts. Be creative and choose a color that best suits your usual thought patterns. Begin to inflate the balloon using your breath. As you do this, close your eyes and imagine that your old thought patterns fill the balloon with each exhalation. Continue until the balloon is filled. Tie off the balloon with a knot.

With a felt-tipped pen, write the following couplet on the balloon.

> *Creature of air, bring me peace*
> *My history I now release!*

On the opposite side of the balloon, draw the symbol for air:

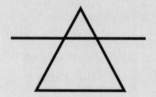

The Symbol for Air

Take your balloon to a spot in nature that feels airy and open to you. It could be a cliff or a meadow—any place that feels like it resonates with the element of air. Bring a pin with you. Hold the balloon over your head, face the east, and recite the words on the balloon three times:

Creature of air, bring me peace
My history I now release!

Finally, pop the balloon, allowing your old thought patterns to dissipate and merge with the air around you.

Night Two
Create sacred space. Then face the south in a seated position. On a clean sheet of 8 1/2" x 11" white paper, draw the alchemical symbol for fire. The symbol for fire is a triangle with one point upright:

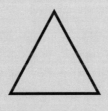

The Symbol for Fire

Beneath the fire symbol write the following words of power:

Creature of fire, bring me peace,
My history I now release!

Turn over the paper and draw a line that divides the paper in half. On one half list actions that you have taken in your life about which you are particularly proud. On the other half, list your actions that have been less than honorable. Try not to judge the length of the list.

Take the sheet of paper to an open space for the next part of the exercise. You will also need a vessel that can safely contain a fire. Be certain that you use a fire-safe space such as a fire pit, or fireplace—even a barbecue will do. For my own magical workings, I use a large, cast-iron cauldron. Begin by facing the south and holding the sheet of paper over your head. Recite the words of power written beneath the fire symbol three times:

Creature of fire, bring me peace
My history I now release!

Light a match and set the parchment on fire, allowing your history of actions to bring light and warmth to the open space around you. Know that the power of fire has dissipated your past actions. Know now that action from your past has no meaning. It dissolves into the night sky.

Night Three
On the third night, gather together your sacred cup or chalice and plenty of spring water. You may also need a bucket. Create sacred space. When you are ready, fill the chalice with clear, spring water. The use of spring water is purely symbolic. It is a form of moving water, as opposed to lake or pond water, which is more stagnant and unmoving. In this part of the spell, you are striving to move beyond your emotional history. Once the

cup is filled with water, begin by stirring your deepest emotions. This may take some time. Reach into your past history and recall strong emotional states. As you dredge up your old emotions—anger, sadness, happiness, fear, etc.—hold your hands over the water in the chalice. Imagine that you fill the water with your emotional state by passing it through your hands and into the cup.

When you sense that the cup is filled, empty it into the larger bucket (or cauldron) beside you. As you do this recite the words of power:

Creature of water, bring me peace
My history I now release!

As you speak, trace the alchemical symbol for water on the cup using your right index finger.

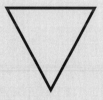

The Symbol for Water

Fill the chalice again and repeat the procedure of filling the cup with old emotional states and emptying them into the bucket until you feel drained of your emotional past. This may take some time, so be patient with yourself. Once you feel completely drained of past emotion, find a body of running water, such as an ocean, river, or stream. Cast the contents of the bucket into the larger moving waters and say:

Creature of water, bring me peace
My history I now release!

Watch as your emotional history merges with something larger than itself until it is no longer something solid or real for you.

Night Four

On the last night of the spell, you will need to have colored sand with you. Create sacred space. Seat yourself facing the north. Using the various colors of sand, create a "painting" that represents your past existence in the world. Be as creative as you like. You do not have to be an artist to do this in a powerful way. In fact, artistic prowess might hamper uninhibited expression. Instead of concerning yourself with how detailed or accurate the picture can be, focus on simply expressing yourself and representing the feeling of your past existence. Many people create sand paintings that are abstract, full of sweeps of color. Others are detailed and representational. Always keep in mind that the point of this exercise is to generate power and release, not to develop great artistic skill. As you develop the sand painting, imagine that each grain of sand represents part of your personal history. As you sprinkle the sands, you also release your history.

Once you have completed the sand painting, use some of the leftover sand to draw the symbol of earth either above or below the sand painting:

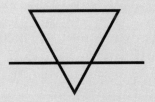

The Symbol for Earth

As you draw the symbol recite the words of power:

Creature of earth, bring me peace
My history I now release!

With one sweeping gesture of your left hand, destroy the sand painting. Sweep together the sands so that all of the colors mix. Place the sands in a jar and close it tightly.

Finally, go to a natural setting and bury the jar that contains your personal history. When you complete the burial, hold your hands over the spot in the earth and repeat the words of power:

Creature of earth, bring me peace
My history I now release!

Dissolving the Self

The self is the key barrier that keeps each of us from experiencing beyond the boundaries of our personal history. In this spell, you symbolically and magically remove the barrier. To do this you will first
create a doll—which is a magical representation of a human being.
In this case, it will represent you.

What you'll need:

- A handful of beeswax or softened paraffin wax
- A cooking pot

Create sacred space, then soften the wax between the palms of
your hands. Work with the wax, alternating between using
your palms and your fingers until it is malleable. Next, mold it
into the basic form of a human being. Take your time to sculpt
the wax as best you can into your own image. This magical
working is not about artistic prowess. If proportions are wrong
or out of alignment, this is fine and expected. What matters
most is that you feel that you have created a good link—a
good representation of your self.

When you are done, hold the image in both hands and
show it in turn to the east, south, west, and north, saying at
each quarter of the circle:

Sacredness of the (east, south, west, north),
In my hands, I hold the self I have created.

Next, place the image into the cooking pot, put it on the
stove, and set the burner on low. (This is important, because a
high setting can cause the wax to catch fire!) Watch as the wax
begins to melt. As it does, recite the following words of power:

> *The separate one must be undone,*
> *I open the cocoon.*
> *The path is open to the mystic one*
> *By way of the waning moon.*

When the wax is melted completely, turn off the heat and pour the wax into a jar or a mold to make a candle. In the days that follow, light the candle whenever you recognize that you are acting solely on behalf of the self.

1. Henri F. Ellenberger, *The Discovery of the Unconscious* (New York: BasicBooks, 1970), p. 404.

2. Michael White, David Epston, *Narrative Means to Therapeutic Ends* (New York: W.W. Norton & Company, 1990), p. 10.

3. Mary Sykes Wyle, "Panning for Gold," *Family Therapy Networker* (Nov./Dec., Vol. 18, no. 6, 1994), pp. 40–48.

4. See, e.g., Jean-Marc Gaspard Itard (translated from the original 1799 study by George Humphrey and Muriel Humphrey), *The Wild Boy of Aveyron* (New York: Prentice Hall, 1966).

5. Janet and Stewart Farrar, *The Witches' Goddess* (Custer: Phoenix Publishing, 1987), p. 250.

6. Thomas Bulfinch, *Bulfinch's Mythology*, (New York: Avenel Books, 1989), p. 928.

7. Farrar, *The Witches' God* (Custer: Phoenix Publishing), p.121.

8. Shunryu Suzuki, *Zen Mind, Beginner's Mind*, (New York: Weatherhill, 1996), p. 117.

9. Starhawk, *Truth or Dare* (San Francisco: Harper & Row, 1987), p. 164.

10. Jamake Highwater, *The Primal Mind* (New York: Meridian 1981), pp. 169–170.

11. You can purchase colored sand at any well-stocked craft store. Children use this sand to create "jar landscapes." If colored sand is not to your liking, try the traditional method of grinding up herbs and flower petals of various shades.

CHAPTER V

FATE

Life has its own needs; follow them closely.

INVOCATION

Hermes stands in the south, within our magic circle. Two other group members create a smaller circle around him made of votive candles while a woman ties glossy black feathers into his hair. Hermes places a beaked mask over his face and then grasps more of the feathers in each of his hands. He shall become the power of the Raven, a familiar, the spirit-animal of the trickster.[1] He shall abandon himself to the powers of life. Silence fills the room. A priestess calls out,

> *O sisters three! You, daughters of Zeus, triple goddess Fates,*
> *be with us. We call upon you, O powers of surrender.*

Drums begin to pound out a deep, rhythmic pulse and Hermes dances with his eyes closed. The priestess continues,

> *Teach us of what lies at the end time of our desires. Teach*
> *us to be one with the will of the universe!*

Hermes caws as the Raven does, ruffles his feathers, and the transformation is complete.

THE TALE—*The Date Palm*

Once there was a rich traveler who was journeying by camel across the desert. He came upon an oasis in the middle of the desert and there in the oasis he found a little old man who was kneeling in the sand digging a hole. The old man did not pay much attention to the traveler, who got busy pitching his tent.

"What are you doing with such keen interest?" asked the traveler. "I am planting date seeds to grow date palms," replied the old man, who continued at his task. "Why would you bother with such a foolish task?" said the traveler. "If you plant a date palm you will never gain any benefit. You will not see its fruit, nor will you get coins for selling the dates. You are an old man and a date palm takes thirty years to come to maturity to give its fruit. Do not continue with this waste of time. Come to my tent and I will give you plenty of wine to drink."

The old man stopped his task only long enough to say to the traveler, "When I arrived here, there were date palms old enough to give me food to eat. Someone planted this tree without thought of himself. I too must plant a tree for someone else who may come to stay in this oasis. It is what is needed, so I must do it."

The traveler was so moved by the old man's words that he filled a bag with gold coins and presented them to the old man. "You are wise," said the traveler, "you have taught me well. Here. Take these coins as your pay for this teaching." The old man held up the coins to the traveler saying, "See here, traveler, sometimes when you do only what needs to be done there is a reward."[2]

MAGICAL LAW — *Life has its own needs; follow them closely.*

FATE'S LAW

There was nothing to be done about it. I had no control. There must have been an accident somewhere along the Santa Monica freeway because there wasn't a single car moving for miles. The midday July sun was scorching the car and I was trapped inside without an air conditioner. The man in the vehicle to my right had his turn signal blinking for at least twenty minutes. He wanted to change lanes and get ahead of me. But there was nowhere to go and nothing to do.

"I have lost my faith," I had told Fate earlier over afternoon tea and tarot cards. "I have made the decision to give up my spiritual practices. I no longer feel as though I am walking the path of magic. I think I need to end my apprenticeship." The memory of my words made me feel a bit sad and lost.

I caught myself daydreaming. The car in front of me had inched up a couple of feet and the man to my right aggressively dove in ahead of me. I felt a surge of anger, but then I remembered Fate's words. "Nothing ever gets anywhere," she had said to me. "Where are you going to go? What are you going to demand that will change life?"

Fate was a tarot master and I always enjoyed her card reading lessons. But now that I had announced my intention to leave the group, I felt uncomfortable as she casually spread her deck of tarot cards across the width of her kitchen table. I wasn't sure that she had heard what I said. She closed her eyes and began randomly flipping over cards one at a time. "Putting your faith away is a powerful action," she said. She turned over one card that had "The Fool" printed in bold across the bottom. "The path of magic has no place for faithfull people. How can you learn if your mind is jammed up with faith?" She traced the figure on the card with her fingertip and then took a loud sip of sage tea.

Her words were like a sudden, awakening flood of light in a dense fog bank. But I wasn't certain whether she was trying to lead me toward safety or planning to dash me against the rocks of my own emotional discord. I was anguished over my decision to leave the magical path, yet I sensed that from the intense fire of my emotional turmoil could come transformation, just as sand could become beautiful glass under heat. I kept quiet and listened.

Fate flipped over another card with the words "The Devil" printed on it. "Hmm," she said, and her eyes bugged like a witch doctor who had just discovered the cause of her patient's illness. She propped up her head between her thin, pale hands and tightened her lips. Her curly, unkempt, red hair covered her face. Her demeanor was typically as easy and comfortable as her worn, brown Birkenstocks. She was a wholly natural woman. But now, her usually casual demeanor stiffened a bit and she assumed a more serious tone. "The Devil means illusion," she said, "and illusion only comes to those who conjure it."

I explained to Fate that the only thing I had conjured was a spell to achieve a personal goal some months ago. I had carefully followed the methods outlined in the magical texts passed down to me by the elders of our group. "I did everything that I was supposed to do according to our Book of Shadows," I complained, "but nothing ever happened." I told her that I had felt cheated by my spiritual path, so I had stopped my magical practices and carried resentment around for some time.

Without even looking at the deck spread out on the table, Fate almost accidentally turned over another card. It had no name on it, but it depicted a man looking at the contents of several goblets that had spilled onto the earth. The man hung his head as though he was in despair. "Vain regrets," she said, and she seemed to mock me with an exaggerated pout. Then she laughed. "You demanded something from the powers of life. In the end, deity, nature, life never responded. And why should it?" she asked and then poured herself some more tea.

I didn't understand what she meant. Up until now I had the impression that one purpose of magical practice and the cultivation of power was to help people attain their dreams and goals.

I decided to speak up in my defense. "What good is the path of power if you can't manifest the things you want?" I asked, but then I swallowed hard. I didn't like how my own words sounded.

Fate grabbed another card and flipped it over. The card depicted a king who had a large gold coin propped up atop his crown. He appeared to be clutching another gold coin with his two hands, and he pinned down two other gold pieces beneath his feet. The card had no name, but from our previous lessons I remembered what it meant. I was clinging to something.

"Shall we ask the sun to stop rising because that is what you want?" she asked in all seriousness. "Shall we ask a river to change direction? Or have the stars disappear from the sky—because you have a goal?" Her statements stirred me from my self-centered oblivion. I instantly became very alert to my surroundings. I wanted to speak, but I knew it was better for me to remain silent. "This is the dangerous path of the sorcerer, Timothy," she said with a tone of warning.

"I followed the procedure that was in our own book," I said in my defense.

"Then you have read some words, but do not understand their meaning," she said and tossed another card at me. I turned it over and saw the image of a lightning-struck tower that was engulfed in flames. "You need to destroy fruitless notions," Fate stated bluntly. "Powerful magic only comes to those who align with life itself. Life has no planned ambition. It has no personal motives. A follower of the magical laws learns to live just like this."

Her words sounded nice, but they didn't seem realistic. "Fate, people who would live in that way would never be able to get anywhere in their lives," I said emphatically.

She put down the cards and laid her hands flat on the table. "Nothing ever gets anywhere. Where are you going to go?" Fate asked as if she really didn't understand something. "What are you going to demand that will change life?"

Then Fate looked down at the table. She stood up, gathered her cards together, and wrapped them in silk. She said, "A tree does not have a demand. It doesn't get ahead in the world, yet it still stands." Then she looked me over and said, "The others were right. They told me that you couldn't see reality. I didn't believe them. But now I see that it is wise for you to give up." She left me sitting alone at the kitchen table.

The car behind me honked, bringing me back to the present, but there wasn't anywhere for me to move. My tee shirt was stuck to my back and chest with perspiration; I was confined to my own private sauna. The man in front of me got out of his car and stood up to get a better look at what was causing the road block up ahead. "Shit! God damn it," he yelled and slammed his hand down on the top of his car.

I was frustrated too by the way Fate had dismissed me. My mind dropped back to thoughts of our interaction.

After a few minutes by myself, I realized that she was not coming back to talk to me. I got up and roamed around her house until I found her in a back room spinning fine yarn on an antique spinning wheel. At her feet was a fluffy pile of loose, white wool. She seemed to be in a trance as she twisted the yarn with her fingers. She held the spun wool with some tension as it passed through the wheel. It was an unusual hobby, but it seemed to suit Fate.

"I didn't mean to upset you, Fate," I said while standing in the doorway. My words seemed to have broken some sort of spell. Fate looked up at me with owl eyes. "I don't want to give up," I said, "but I'm feeling as though I've become lost along this spiritual path."

She tilted her head and curiously smiled at me. "But you *should* give up," Fate said. Then she snipped the length of yarn she held between her fingers with a large pair of scissors. "Don't you see that your only chance at winning over magic is by giving up?" she asked me. For a moment I couldn't believe what I was hearing. Then she went on to explain, "You need to agree to life on its own terms. Otherwise you are caught in a trap of your own making. When you insist that life turns out how you demand, you force, twist, and distort it. Give up on spells that compel life. Magic is meant to attune you to the world and nature, not the other way around. An amulet for love? Give up— you must attune to the love in this moment. A charm for abundance? Give up—what about the abundance you have before you right now? If you want to live a magical life—a life lived in unity and harmony—it is necessary for you to participate with a willingness and an understanding that not everything will go your way. Should we teach a child not to participate in a game unless he wins? Of course not. Playing the game is fun, interesting, and exciting in and of itself. Ultimately you will lose in the end of this life-game. That's how it ends—in case you didn't know. If you are going to lose anyway, you might as well play the best that you can with as much enthusiasm and joy for the game as you can muster."

Neither of us spoke for a while. I watched Fate nimbly thread the spinning wheel again. Her words made some sense to me, but I still had strong doubts.

"Isn't there some way to have what I want and still be in union with life?" I asked.

"Yes, there is a way," said Fate. "When you learn to want what life itself wants, then you have achieved your mission." She pulled the wool tight in between her fingers and began to spin more yarn. "It would be a mistake for you to leave the magical path just as it was a mistake to work magic for self-centered gain. Instead, you need to find a magical ally to show you the way to true power. Wise ones should have strong allies and spirit helpers."

This was news to me. "Fate, what is an ally, and how do I find one?" I asked.

Fate was quick to respond, "An ally is a power-teacher. Sometimes an ally takes the form of a spirit, a rock, a tree, or an animal. An ally can even appear as an experience or an idea that can guide and inspire you to achieve the true magical way. You have allies around you right now. Look! Look!" She pointed into the air. I didn't see anything.

The fumes of the other vehicles around me made it difficult to breathe and that brought me back to a conscious focus on the heat of my car. I realized that I felt tense and a bit nauseous. "Nothing ever gets anywhere." I remembered Fate's words as I looked out at the sea of traffic. A gray cloud of diesel fumes cleared from around me and in a sudden rush of insight and emotion, I realized that I had already met my spiritual ally. It was there in front of me all along. My own disappointment and frustrations were pointing the way.

My eyes began to well up with tears. The anger and resentment I had bottled up during the last several months drained away from me. The noise, the fumes, the confusion around me became a single point of wisdom and enlightenment. I could not escape the realities of life any more than I could escape the traffic. In that moment I understood that life continues on as it is despite my efforts to achieve my personal wishes. I saw that it was powerless to strain in order to realize some individual gain; nothing was ever separate from me in the first place. My inability to compel the world around me with magic was not a sign that I had lost power and spirit. It meant that I was much closer to it than ever. Instead of walking away from the path of magic that day, I had stumbled upon my ally: the power of the fifth magical law. This was the law of Fate.

From the ordinary perspective the word "fate" does not have powerful associations. It does not seem a likely ally. Most of us think of it as an unavoidable event. An accident is the result of fate; an untimely death is caused by fate. It implies a loss of control of the external world of people and things, which is a state that ordinary people fear. Within the confines of the customary definition, fate is no power at all. If anything, it is an enemy from which we should protect ourselves.

When you approach an extraordinary practice, such as magic, from an ordinary perspective, there is bound to be confusion. From that ordinary mindset of non-power, people can make all kinds of mistakes in their magical practices. For example, I thought the point of a spiritual discipline like magic was about conforming the external world to my personal wishes. From that perspective one would naturally try to make everything and everyone compatible with one's own needs and desires. People who do not follow the fifth magical law often begin their spiritual observances with the words "I want." "I want love." "I want money." "I want serenity, or a happy home, or a spiritual experience." The list is endless. Underneath the words "I want" are often the sentiments of "I deserve," "I expect," and "I am entitled." When you begin magic from an ordinary standpoint, you always arrive at the forceful and self-centered ways of the sorcerer.

Sorcery has no real power, but it can help ordinary people feel as though they have some semblance of control over the world. Meanwhile, reality teaches us again and again that the forces of life are in control of us, not the other way around. Life, nature, and reality have their own force and gravity. Life has its own timetables and concerns. The immense, impersonal flow of life rarely addresses human desires that are self-serving. When the sorcerer occasionally manages to manifest some personal whim, it usually comes at great expense to the resources, people, and things of the world. Likewise, when a society works to manifest its own desires, the expense is one that all must pay—for example, war, global warming, depletion of natural resources, air or water pollution.

We can never have any lasting or meaningful control over external events or people. The person of power learns this lesson quickly and chooses to act in the world accordingly. People of power therefore find an ally in fate, which is the power inherent in relinquishing your grip on the external world. In order to fully understand this power, it is important to understand the three goddesses who are vivid symbols for its workings.

The modern word "fate" comes from the Fates of Greek mythology. The three goddesses who govern human destiny are also called "the *Moerae*." The first of the three goddesses is named Clotho. She is the one who spins the thread of life. From the start of our lives, Clotho teaches us to release the fantasy that we "own" anything about ourselves. Human beings participate in the process of creation and of life itself, but they do not own it. Clotho reminds you that your body, your life, and the people you know are all lent to you. When you act from this knowledge, you achieve the first of this ally's magical powers, which is called gratitude.

The second Fate is Lachesis, who measures the thread of your life with her rod. She represents the element of chance. Lachesis' power of chance causes ordinary people to feel vulnerable to the effects of life. In reality, life is chancy. Pain, pleasure, joy, and terror are all part of the mix from which no one is immune. It is sheer fantasy to think that you might be able to abstain from the effects of life and reality. She teaches you that it is an impossibility to control the world, life, and therefore deity. The person of power cuts through the fantasies inherent in manipulating the external world and aligns with reality. Running from reality is a debilitating and fruitless exercise. When you surrender yourself to the mix of life, you achieve the second of this ally's magical powers, which is effortlessness.

The third Fate is Atropos, who snips the thread of your life with her shears when it is completed.[3] She shows us that the final reality of living, death, is also something out of our control. She reminds us that in the end as in the beginning the processes of living have their own ways that operate outside of human interests, resistance, or desires. Death takes no account of human concerns. Death is part of nature and comes as a matter of course, like a sunrise or a sunset. A person who does not understand the power inherent in nature will resist the uncomfortable inevitabilities that come with life, such as death, pain, or sorrow. Someone who observes that fifth magical law knows that resistance to reality simply makes for frustration. When you act in alignment with Atropos, you achieve the third of this ally's magical powers, which is tranquility.

When you choose to acknowledge fate as an ally, you acknowledge the power inherent in releasing yourself to life's processes. Your actions are transformed when you know that you are only in life for the ride. The ride can be exciting, wild, and turbulent, but it is only a ride. With this in mind, you no longer struggle to be effective. Instead, your actions are driven by the requirements of life within each moment. This action comes from knowing that birth, growth, cessation, decay, and death are a cycle in which we participate, but do not control. As Chief Seattle said, "Man did not weave the web of life, he is merely a strand in it."[4] People who practice the fifth magical law see that they are made up of the energy of this cycle and understand that working to manipulate these energies would be useless. When you take action to manipulate life, you take action against the source of your own being. When you release your grip on manipulating life, you assume the combined powers of the Fates called freedom.

The underlying magic of the fifth magical law is change. This is not external change. Even when you have powerful allies, the traffic lights don't all turn green for you. The weather outside does not become perfect. A pile of lead does not turn into gold for you. The underlying power of the allies prompts a change from within the magician. From the ordinary perspective, this makes the powers that come with the allies something unexpected. At the core of the allies' magic is a shift from ordinary to magical consciousness. It is a shift from living your life led by personal desire to surrendering to something larger than yourself. The allies teach you to align your personal will with the will of deity, which reflect the demands and necessities of life itself.

Each of us has the ability to guide our magic in either of two directions. You can guide magic by your wishes and your personal will. This is called the left-hand path. It is the path that has no allies, since it is focused on the self. You can also guide magic by releasing your will and following the "will" or direction of life itself. This is the power of the allies, and it is called the right-hand path.

The left-hand path of magic means sustaining and insisting on the fulfillment of personal fantasies. Its practices consist of weaving a web of mirages for yourself that help keep you feeling safe from reality (or at least numb). You can pretend that you have the financial resources to take an exotic trip around the world, but the reality of your bank account may prove otherwise. Despite the temporarily pacifying mirages of the left-hand path, reality continues to exist.

If you choose to allow your personal whims to lead you, you must necessarily take action against reality. For example, you might take that exotic trip despite the fact that you cannot afford it, resulting in the acquisition of more difficulties. You might choose the left-hand path because you fear that living in each moment might also mean living through unpleasant experiences or disappointments. The left-hand path usually begins with a belief that if you change life as it is, you will be safe, or happy, or content. Instead of working to have power with life in all of its reality, pleasant or not, you aim for power over life in one tiny aspect. You want life to look and feel how you like it. So you focus and work toward forcing life into your little corner.

Consequently, you force a gap between yourself, life, and deity. You strain against the flow of life, and in the process you lose power. In the end, you set yourself up for disappointment because reality moves independently of your momentary wishes.

The left-hand path is seductive, but ultimately it does not deliver. It is like drinking sea water when you are thirsty. The water may fool you for a while into believing that you have quenched your thirst, but meanwhile your body dehydrates. It needs something else. On the left-hand path there is no end to the thirst of wishing and wanting. Acquisitions and immediate gratification can temporarily quench your thirst, but soon you'll need more. The left-hand path is a cruel master, teaching you to follow behind your desires blindly. You are powerless in their grip. Any satisfaction you obtain occurs coincidentally, as the random effect of personal caprice and shifting life circumstances.

True power and magic are not about filling your life up with everything you've ever wanted. They have nothing to do with *having* something. They are about *losing* something—namely the demand that your will be done. The power of the fifth magical law implies that you are not in charge of the universe.

A seed is not in charge of the universe. It has no other choice but to be true to its nature. A seed needs to yield to nature in order to claim its power—to become a plant. When it surrenders itself to life, it becomes a sprout, a tiny leaf, and eventually a full-grown plant.

The seed doesn't worry that it may grow to be a weed. It doesn't worry that it may get crushed beneath someone's foot. It doesn't try to become a dog, a person, or an ocean. There is a simple, basic wisdom inherent in nature that the seed taps into and then follows. If the seed tries to do anything beyond its nature, it will never grow into its full power. The same applies to each of us as we look for our own power. The first step of the right-hand path is yielding to nature.

The right-hand path is about *releasing* personal desires. This is the path of one who does not make demands of life, but appropriately interacts with it moment by moment. The right-hand path means coming into accord with reality and nature. When you follow this path, you become open to the intuitive experience that you and what you desire are the same thing. In this consciousness, you are at one with life around you; you have no need to possess anything or anyone. If you travel the right-hand path, you know that the wishing well of the left-hand path exists, but you do not drink from it.

A contemporary magical poem called *The Charge of the Goddess* reveals the secrets of the fifth magical law. In it deity speaks, "Know now the mystery: that if what you seek, you do not find within yourself, you will not find it outside of yourself either. For behold, I have been with you from the beginning and I am that which is attained at the end of your desire."[5] On the right-hand path, you no longer seek fulfillment externally. You realize that what you seek is waiting within you. Along the right-hand path the individual will and the will of deity merge. In that merger, you establish a center point of power. To want something for your individual fulfillment does not make sense to someone who experiences deity in everything. Deity is waiting for you there at the "end of your desire." When you release desire, you find an ally in deity. Releasing your will, your insistence, your wishes, fantasies, and "faith" can be a heartbreaking and disappointing moment. Paradoxically, it is in that cutting moment you restore freedom and empowerment to your life.[6]

THE ENCHANTMENTS

The Circle of Release

Keep in mind that the point of learning the lessons of the Fates is to learn how to surrender to the necessities of life around you. It is important to contribute to the stream of life that flows impersonally through all things. Either you can be a rock that impedes the flow of life or you can contribute and become an active part of the stream. The following exercise will help you clarify what aspects of your life keep you from surrendering to the stream.

What you'll need:

- Five blank pieces of paper
- Five taper candles (6" to 12" in length)
- A pen
- A sharp knife

Create your sacred space. Light the five candles and place the first four at the compass directions, creating a sacred circle. Place the last candle at the center of the circle. Put one piece of paper next to each candle and the fifth piece of paper in the center of the circle. Sit in the center of the circle and think about one situation in your life that is currently important to you emotionally, intellectually, physically, or spiritually. Once you have a situation in mind, turn to the paper in the east and write down all of your thoughts about the situation. For example, you might say, "I think a lot about paying my bills. I think about various ways that I might be able to pay them." Continue writing until you complete an exhaustive description of the thoughts you have regarding your situation.

Next, turn to the south and list all of the actions you are taking regarding this situation. For example, you can say, "I am working eight hours every day. I am taking a loan at the bank." Continue with this until you list each action you have taken in this situation.

Turn to the west, and on that piece of paper, write your feelings and emotions about the situation. You can say, for example, "I am feeling worried and anxious. I am feeling overwhelmed." Continue with this list until you have explored each emotion that arises from this situation. Be as honest as possible, so that you obtain emotional clarity.

In the north, write down the physical manifestation, the thing or situation you want to obtain. For example, you might say, "I want to be debt free." Finally, on the last piece of paper in the center of the circle, write down the state of being you want to achieve by obtaining your goal. In our example, I might say, "I am trying to gain peace of mind."

Begin to identify which aspects—thoughts, actions, feelings, or manifestations—do or do not contribute to the stream of movement toward the state of being you listed. In my example, I don't recognize any aspect of thought, action, feeling, or manifestation that would move me toward gaining peace of mind. Peace of mind seems to be something that I should have regardless of my finances.

Next you will release each aspect that you have identified as an impediment toward movement to your desired state. If you find your thoughts are impeding your movement, stand facing the east. Hold the eastern candle in your hands and say:

I release my hold on thought.

Blow out the candle and set it down.

If you have discovered that your actions obstruct the flow toward your desired state, stand facing the south. Hold the southern candle and say:

I release my hold on action.

Blow out the candle and set it down.

If you have found that your emotions hold you back from attaining your preferred state of being, stand facing the west. Hold up the candle and say:

I release my hold on emotions.

Blow out the candle and set it down.

If the thing you want to manifest does not help you move toward your desired state of being, stand facing the north. Hold the candle in front of you and say:

I release my hold on the physical world.

Blow out the candle and set it down.

Turn over the sheets of paper that correspond to those aspects that appear to impede the flow toward your preferred state of being. The writing on each page you turn over should now be facing the ground. In my example, I would turn over all four pieces of paper.

Take out your pen. If you have flipped over the paper in the east, write down a new set of thoughts and concepts (if any) that you believe would best contribute to your preferred state of being. If you have flipped over the paper in the south of your circle, write down a new set of actions that you believe would move you toward your preferred state of being. In the west, write any new feelings that would best contribute to the preferred state of being. In the north, write any situation, person, or thing that you think would result in your preferred state of being.

Create a symbol to represent each revised aspect and carve that symbol into each corresponding candle. For a revised set of thoughts carve a symbol into the eastern candle. For revised actions carve a symbol on the southern candle. Carve a symbol in the west candle for any revision in your emotions and feelings. Carve a symbol in the northern candle, if you have made revisions to the aspect of manifestation. In my example, I would carve a symbol on all four directional candles. When you are finished, relight the candles.

Face the east and call out:

> Powers of air, O you who inspire,
> There is no thought that I require.

Then turn to the south and call out:

> Powers of fire, of strength and drive,
> I release my action, I do not strive.

Then turn to the west and call out:

> Powers of water, of ice and mist,
> There is no emotion on which I insist.

Turn to the north and call out:

> Powers of earth, from where I stand,
> There is no thing that I demand.

Allow the candles to burn down completely as you ponder your renewed approach to life.

Stream of Consciousness

Whenever you sense that you are struggling with the circumstances of your life, take time to try this guided imagery meditation. Either have a friend read it to you or record it.

Close your eyes and take several deep, slow breaths. Relax all parts of your body—from your head to your toes. When you are relaxed, imagine that you stand in a warm, slow-moving stream. You are in the water up to your knees. Feel the warm current as it swirls around your legs and flows past you.

Face the water as it moves downstream and imagine that you lie down in the stream bed on your back. Feel your body as it lies across the soft, silt bed below. You are able to lie comfortably so that the stream passes around your body. As the stream flows around you, your body gradually becomes transparent. Continue to breathe deeply and slowly.

Now, imagine that your toes have become so transparent that they painlessly dissolve and join with the stream. Slowly, with each breath, parts of your body effortlessly join the stream. Your feet join the stream first, followed by your calves, knees, thighs, hips, stomach, chest, arms, shoulders, neck, and finally your head. Become the stream.

When you have successfully surrendered to the stream open your eyes. For the rest of the day, move and think, feel, and act as the stream.

1. Timothy Roderick, *The Once Unknown Familiar* (St. Paul: Llewellyn Publications, 1994), p. 176.
2. Adaptation of "The Date Sewer" in Leo Rothen, *Jewish Treasury* (New York: Bantam Books, as cited by Jorge Bucay, *Recuentos Para Demion*, Buenos Aires: Editoiral del Nuevo Extremo S.A., 1997).
3. Janet and Stewart Farrar, *The Witches' Goddess* (Custer: Phoenix Publishing, 1987), p. 249.
4. Joseph Campbell, Mary Sue Flowers, ed., *The Power of Myth* (New York: Doubleday, 1988), p. 34.
5. Paraphrased from "The Charge of the Goddess" in *The Book of Shadows*, (New York: Gardnerian Rite Church, 1991).
6. Henri F. Ellenberger, *The Discovery of the Unconscious* (New York: Basic Books, 1970), p. 529.

CHAPTER VI

CHAOS

*From immediate experience
comes powerful knowledge.*

INVOCATION

The circle has been cast for the Celtic celebration of Samhain. We have gathered to remember friends and loved ones who have passed into the limitless void. Hermes stands facing the west. Other members begin whispering the names of the departed. Hermes holds a candle high and invites the ancient ancestors to our feast. I expect that he will turn back to the group and the rest of the ceremony will resume. Instead, the room falls into silence. The candle flames in the west of the circle seem to lengthen and grow brighter. A translucent, vaporous glow forms just outside of our sacred space. I can't believe what I see. I think to myself that it must be a hallucination, an optical illusion. I have many thoughts and emotions about what I think I see before me. Suddenly I remember a line from Shakespeare: "There are more things in heaven and earth than are dreamt of in your philosophy..." The vapor in the west fades.

Hermes walks the perimeter of the circle, invoking:

> Out of the primal mists we evoke thee O Great One! Vast, swirling, vaporous is thy body and the void at the center of all things. Come to us, mighty god of that which is not yet known. We seek thy ways and look for the path that is hidden. Bring forth thy power and bless us with your ancient words. You who teach us that thought is not the end, open the boundaries of time and space. Grant us the bounty of your possibilities.

THE TALE—*The Shaman's Knowledge*

Once there was a shaman, a holy woman, who lived in a small village. The villagers gossiped to one another of her great power and knowledge. One day, a villager came to the shaman and said, "Teacher, tell me what will happen when mortals die." The shaman turned slowly to the man and replied, "I cannot tell you." The man was outraged. "Why can't you tell me? You possess great wisdom and power. You are selfish with this gift, old woman!" The woman replied, "I cannot tell you because I am not yet dead."

MAGICAL LAW — *From immediate experience comes powerful knowledge.*

Chaos' Law

"There was a jolt and a sudden, early-morning 'boom' which threw me to the floor." That was how I remembered the 1971 earthquake in southern California. I was eight years old and this was my first experience with a quake.

The elder named Chaos was seated across from me in the temple room of his house looking out the window with no facial expression. *Is he paying attention?* I wondered.

I continued to speak: "I remember then that the ground beneath me started to shake with tremendous force and deep, rumbling violence. The inside of the house appeared to twist with the ground movements. The furniture took on a life of its own and danced and dipped across the floor. The splintering and straining of the house's wooden frame against its lath and plaster encasement gave the entire event an almost supernatural effect. Walls were fractured, windows were crackled into mosaics. It was a horrifying experience."

Two years had passed since I had begun my elder's training and it was time for me to be tested. In order for me to achieve the status of elder and teacher, wisdom, magic, and power had to flow easily through me. Chaos was our lead teacher and he was assigned the task of assessing my wisdom.

His first question was regarding my knowledge of the element of earth. I had gotten sidetracked in all of my thoughts. I was distracted by the fact that Chaos did not appear to be following the conversation. Instead of sticking to the point, I had started talking about my own experience from childhood with an earthquake. Once I realized my mistake, I shut my mouth before I proceeded further away from the point. Once I stopped talking, Chaos turned his head back to me. "Huh?" he asked, "Oh yeah. That must have been something."

Chaos was a man in his early forties. He might have been older. He had wavy, loose, shoulder length brown and gray hair, a short, manicured white beard that outlined his broad jaw and dark brown eyebrows. He was a striking man, quietly magnificent. He was warm, yet at the same time he could be cutting. He was well known among my fellow students as a trickster-teacher. He sat across from me in a comfortable plush chair. Suddenly he picked up a goblet-shaped drum that was lying on the floor near his foot and he began to pound out a beat. *Doum tek a tek a tek a.*

"And what would you do if there was an earthquake right now?" Chaos asked while drumming. He stood up, shut his eyes, and started drumming harder. *Doum tek a tek a tek a.*

I was distracted by his unusual behavior and surprised by his question. He was drumming so loudly that I had to shout my answer. "I think I would run." I was sure he didn't hear me.

"What?" Chaos asked. His drumming became more ecstatic as he pulsed out a Mediterranean sounding beat. Then he started to dance in a circle across the wooden floor.

His behavior was outrageous. I had to shout over the drumming again, "I said, I would run!" But there was no way he could hear anything above the pounding on his drum. Suddenly he stopped.

Chaos looked at me as though he was truly mystified. "Run where? Where is there to go?"

I was dumbfounded. I knew Chaos was a bit eccentric, but how was he supposed to find out anything about me acting this way? I sat without saying a thing. He stopped drumming. He made an exaggeratedly serious facial expression and asked the next question stiffly. "Tell me, Timothy, is the magic of the circle a manifestation of internal or external energy?" Then he placed his index finger on the side of his chin as though he were considering the question himself.

I was relieved that we seemed to be back on track with questions. Then Chaos began to drum once again. I tried to give his question some thought, but found it difficult to concentrate with the constant drumming. "External," I finally said. *Doum tek a tek a tek a.* The drumming intensified once more.

"What is the traditional wood used in making a wand?" Chaos asked.

Why was he acting this way? I felt foolish. I considered my options. I could either walk away or reply and continue with the interview. I watched Chaos continue drumming and I replied, "Hazel." The pulse got wilder and faster now as Chaos began to freely dance to the tempo.

Chaos shouted, "What is one plus one?"

I felt insulted now. "Two," I tried to say, not knowing what else to say, but my voice was drowned out by the noise.

Without warning, Chaos stopped playing the drum, set it down, and started to walk out of the room.

"Where are you going? Am I supposed to go somewhere with you?" I asked.

"No. We're finished," he replied without looking at me.

I wasn't sure whether to ask how the interview went, but I felt compelled to say something. "Chaos, you haven't given me a chance to talk about what I know. You were supposed to determine whether or not wisdom flows through me yet."

He stopped at the doorway and turned back around. Without hesitation he said, "No, it does not." I felt a tingling like an electric shock throughout my body. I was stunned.

"But Chaos, all of the other elders have worked to teach me that wisdom flows through all things. It even flows through animals, plants, rocks, and streams," I said feeling confused.

"Yes, wisdom flows through all these things," Chaos said, making a low-sweeping gesture with his hand, "but it doesn't flow through you." He turned back to exit the room.

This was ridiculous. "Why not, Chaos?" I asked in a loud voice. I realized that I was getting annoyed.

Chaos sighed. He brought his drum close to my chair and sat on it so that his face was inches from me. "It does not flow through you because you ask this question," he said. "You need to go now. Another student comes soon." He patted my knee twice. Then we were silent.

"I don't know what you mean," I finally said.

"You *do* know," Chaos insisted. "And this is the problem. You know too much. How can you expect to learn the path of magic when you are filled with knowing? Wisdom cannot flow through you until you begin to not-know the world."

"But Chaos, you asked me questions about theories and facts," I said in my defense. "I gave you appropriate answers in response to each question."

"That's too bad," Chaos replied in a sad voice. He was sitting uncomfortably close to me, but I chose not to react. He looked at me for a while before he said, "May I ask how knowing has served you?"

What kind of a question was that? I was pulled in two directions. I wanted to stump this man with a plain, logical argument, but I also wanted him to teach me. My pride won the battle and I decided to put Chaos in his place. "Well, with rational thinking, I can at least manage to get through my everyday life. I can work. I can articulate my needs. I can make sense of my life all with knowing," I replied in a blunt, matter-of-fact tone.

Chaos laughed so hard he doubled over. "If that's your criteria for the kind of life you want, then by all means continue as you have. If you wish to explore the possibilities, to open to the wonder of it all, then you might try another route." There was a hint of mischief in his voice.

I was tired of his mysterious behavior. I wanted him to give me some real answers. "But what about facts like one plus one equals two? Aren't facts important?" I asked.

"Yes, but what you haven't considered is that it is only within the dimension of gross forms that one plus one is two. There are other realities. One such reality is unity. One plus one is one. You and that flower, and the man on the street corner pushing the shopping cart, and that new solar system being created this second, are all one. Not-knowing allows you to see the myriad of possibilities present in each moment."

I was feeling impatient with this nonsense. I didn't care if I became an elder or not. None of this made any sense. "That sounds nice and poetic," I said, "but how will that help me live my real life in a real world where one plus one is two?" I hoped that my question would stop this foolishness once and for all. But it didn't.

Chaos replied immediately, "That is the very point. Life is poetic. Can't you see? When you lose the poetry, the fluid movement of possibility, the 'verse' of life, then it becomes dull. Life without poetry is no life at all. It is empty movement. Yes, it is important to know how to do your job and purchase things at the grocery store, but it is also important to put these things into perspective. The grocery store, your job, are not the final word on life. Life has been around a lot longer than your job or the grocery store or you. It has much more in it than you could ever hope to know. Knowing is not the point of living. Knowing will only take you so far, and then what? What will all of your knowing do for you in the end? It isn't going to save you."

What he said changed me. I was no longer annoyed. In fact, he moved me to such a degree I began to question myself. Maybe I did function in my life with rational thinking leading the way. "What do you suggest?" I asked hesitantly.

Chaos got off of his drum and lay on the floor. "I suggest nothing," he said. He started to stretch and twist his back. Suddenly he sprang to his feet so swiftly that it startled me. Then he towered over me and stared at me with an intensity I had not seen in him before. It frightened me a little. "Suggestions mean that there might be alternatives. What I am saying is that there really is no other way to live. If you live your life from knowing, you have wasted a life. When life boils down to living within the limits of thought, you are merely existing. It's too bad that you choose to live in such a constricted way when it is you who is responsible for that constriction. Life has much more to offer than what you've allowed into your knowing mind. Getting into the heart of life, living by experience is the only way to be truly alive. It is from this experience that you gain wisdom. Take the risk and open to the vast life before you."

His words impressed me. Could it be that I had wasted a good portion of my life trying to know and understand the world? What good did all of my thinking finally do me? I felt an enormous knot in my throat. "Yes. I can see your point," I managed to say to Chaos, trying to stay focused on the moment, "but I am afraid that if I live without knowing, I will become lost."

Chaos placed a kind, warm hand on mine and said, "Knowing is what asked this question. I can see it." He closed his eyes to see a vision. "It is aligning with fear so that you will not venture into your life without it. Knowing senses that it may be cut off! Tell your knowing that it does not have to allow you to live. Life is fine on its own. You are entitled to do what you please with what little time you have while your heart still beats and your lungs still draw in air. However, you might as well be in a hospital bed on life support systems. Tell your knowing that life has greater vital signs than a heartbeat and breathing."

I sat motionless. My mouth was open. Chaos opened his eyes, winked, and then squeezed my hand. I collected my thoughts and asked, "Chaos, how does someone not-know the world?"

"You not-know the world by hooking your mind onto nothing." Then he taught me a method that consisted of sitting very still and counting each of my exhalations in rhythm to a soft drumbeat. He told me to empty my mind of thoughts for as long as I could during the exercise. "At first you will not be able to practice this for long," Chaos told me. "With effort, you might be able to hook your mind onto nothing for fifteen or twenty minutes at a time." He told me to practice this magical technique until I entered into a state of not-knowing. I asked him how I might recognize when I had entered into that realm. Chaos just laughed and said, "You cannot miss it."

Every day I practiced hooking my mind onto nothing. Nothing was all I got. I practiced this technique with no effect for several months. I had no idea what was supposed to be happening and I was starting to become frustrated. I certainly enjoyed the peaceful activity of emptying my mind each day. It was a soothing technique, if nothing else. My main concern was that I did not seem to progress. In fact after each session of hooking my mind onto nothing, it seemed as though I would return to my usual way of thinking and knowing. I was just about ready to give up and tell Chaos that I was hopelessly attached to my knowing when one day I had an amazing experience.

It was a Saturday afternoon and I decided to take a short nap after practicing hooking my mind onto nothing. I entered into a deep, dreamless state of consciousness. After some time, I awakened with a start. *I am nothing*, I realized with a gasp.

I realized that I still existed in that empty, thought-less, knowing-less state. I had truly entered into the void and found that the void was who I really was. Beneath all of my thinking and knowing and understanding there was still existence. Knowing was not necessary to exist. Knowing did not change what was at the core of life. I had a horrifying moment realizing that I had wasted time protecting myself with knowing over the years.

Soon, I arranged to return to Chaos' magical temple room and I delivered my news in person. After I related all that had happened, Chaos took a deep breath and pointed to the floor of the temple room in his home, "Lie there and close your eyes." I didn't know what he was planning, but I cooperated. I heard the uncorking of a bottle and soon I smelled something like cedar and eucalyptus. Before I knew it, I felt his fingertips on the base of my throat. He seemed to be applying the pungent ointment there. It tickled a little after he rubbed it in. Then he repeated the same process on the back side of my knees and in my armpits. I started to feel strange. The room seemed to be spinning. I opened my eyes and started to sit up. "What did you put on me, Chaos?" I asked in a louder tone of voice than I had anticipated.

"Shhh," Chaos hissed at me and he pressed my shoulders back to the floor. His strength was amazing. "This is teaching medicine. You must remain silent."

Without warning, Chaos began to drum again on his clay drum. *Doum tek a tek a tek a.* But this time, the drum sounded more resonant than before. Soon, I had the sensation that I was in two places at once. I was in Chaos' temple room, but at the same time I was back in my bedroom in 1971 Northridge. The sound of the drumming was deep and reverberating. It felt as though the beat was causing the ground beneath me to shake. Before I knew it, the whole room rumbled. It felt like an earthquake. I could see the same images of my childhood home during the earthquake. Walls were twisting and I could hear the sound of glass breaking.

"What will you do?" Chaos asked.

I did not think. I did not react, and this surprised me. "I don't *know*," I said.

The rumbling and the drumming stopped. "That's it!" Chaos shouted. "Just don't know—that's good." He laughed and helped me to my feet. Then we drummed and danced together long into the night.

Since that day, I've worked to release my reliance on knowledge. In magic, thinking, knowing, and rationality do not hold much power. Knowing has its limits that keep ordinary people from ever reaching the extraordinary realm of magical power. The laws of your own thinking determine the limits of your reality. As one mystic put it, "Your mind is wonderful, so the whole world is wonderful."[1]

Unfortunately, the converse can also be true.

The contents of your mind do not have the ability to take you into the extraordinary realm of magic and empowerment. Logic is the way of rational thinking, and logic can take the ordinary mind only so far.[2] Thinking is stuck in the realm of "facts" which exist in time and space.

Our Aristotelian heritage in the West is a major contributor to our being trapped by the limits of "facts" and rational cogitation.[3] In our culture, a "fact" is the name we give to a thought, an opinion that we hold up as established truth. It is a thought or opinion that someone externalizes and passes along to others. For example, one "fact" is that when you place the words you know into a certain order they convey meaning. It is also "fact" that history happened in a certain way. The problem with facts is that they are trapped, frozen in time and space. They are therefore subject to the laws of time and space. Because of this, facts do not age gracefully or travel well. From culture to culture and across history, the "facts" vary. The words that you know and maintain in a certain order have no meaning whatsoever for someone of a different language system. The proud history of one society is a dark time of despair for another. Although we like to snuggle up to the comforting thought that there is absolute truth in facts, it just is not so. A fact is only a snapshot of one possible reality, not the totality of life and experience.[4] It is an opinion dressed up as absolute truth.

Within the limits of the knowing-mind, you develop theories, concepts, and beliefs about whatever it is that you see in the world. For example, you can theorize that the world is flat, or that it is carried on the back of a giant turtle, or that it is the center of the universe. Nevertheless, reality is something different from any of these theories, concepts, and thoughts. The world is none of these references of the rational mind, and it might not even be whatever scientists think it is today. Because thinking has so many restrictions, magical people spend little time within the confines of this state of mind. Instead, powerful people focus on the not-knowing state of mind, which is purely experiential.

Experiencing is a holistic, extraordinary state of awareness which blends certain basic, functional kinds of mental processes with immediate sensory input. The experience of each moment is what results from Chaos' law of *not-knowing*. The power behind not-knowing is intuition and spontaneity. While knowing would have you hold on to "established facts" about the world, not-knowing keeps you fluidly perceiving the world and everything in it. When you not-know the world, you keep in mind the great cosmic joke that facts can rarely remain "established" or stable.

Human beings like to think that they have everything under control with facts and knowing, but what lies beyond our little dimly lit campsite is great and vast. People who follow the law of not-knowing consciously decide to abandon their assumptions, beliefs, and opinions that go along with knowing, and they open up to the ever-changing wonder of life.

Rational thinking has a place in ordinary life. Some forms of rational thinking and knowing are helpful because you exist within the context of time and space. It is important for each of us to understand how to exist within the limits of our context. For example, it is useful to keep in mind the danger of stepping in front of a moving bus. It is useful to remember not to jam a fork into an electric wall outlet. It is useful to be skilled with numbers in order to keep a bank book or to pay bills. It is a good idea to know about cause and effect. But using rational thought as a tool to help you exist in time and space is different from depending on knowing to be the totality of your existence. The first approach results in functional knowing; the other results in dysfunctional knowing.

Dysfunctional knowing is an abuse of the limited rational thought processes. Instead of using rational thought to assist you with your existence in the world, dysfunctional knowing is reliance on established rules and predetermined facts. If you know dysfunctionally, you become as rigid as your assumptions. For example, you may "know" that people who read the Bible are good people. You may "know" that people with money are happy. Or you may dysfunctionally know that family members always have your best interests in mind. Each of these rigid thoughts keep you from venturing beyond their limits and coping with reality. Moment to moment reality varies; it changes in its shape, color, texture, and taste before your eyes. That means that only sometimes will your dysfunctional knowing ever be true. At other times knowing the world fails miserably. When you are trapped within the confines of dysfunctional knowing, you eventually stir up your emotions.

Emotional, dysfunctional knowing creates discomfort, confusion, misery, and separation from reality and immediate experience. Functional knowing is linked with your present reality and does not generate emotional turmoil. For example, I need functional knowledge in order to make dinner tonight. In order to make dinner, I need to know how to turn on the stove, boil water, and cook rice. I don't need to add any more thought into these activities.

Dysfunctional knowing would enter if I rigidly thought, "Men are not good in the kitchen. Cooking is frustrating. I can't make anything else but rice." The rigidity of these thoughts not only causes me to separate from my task at hand, but it keeps me from knowing any other possibility. All I have left when I dysfunctionally know is my predetermined, internal script. Then making dinner *becomes* frustrating. All mental constrictions like this usually result in discomfort and disempowerment.

Meanwhile reality, the realm of empowerment, exists just outside of the membrane of my knowing. When I cut through the membrane to experiencing that reality, I open myself to empowerment. I do not need to know about life in order to fully experience it. A dog doesn't need this sort of knowing either, yet it is more actively engaged with experiencing life than ordinary people who dysfunctionally know their way through it.

Not knowing is when you keep in mind that the brain is not the sole source of consciousness. Every muscle, every fiber of your body is made up of consciousness. It is the power that is the source of all consciousness that magical people seek. To magical folk, the source of consciousness is deity, nature in the here and now.

Power is a state of being, not a state of thought. Power is an experience that cannot be contained within the limits of thoughts. When we think about it, it becomes a concept. Once it is a concept, power is lost.[5] You cannot think or conceptualize your way to power. In fact, conceptualizing keeps you locked up in your head away from direct contact.

The person who seeks power learns to see through the trap of linear, unidirectional knowing. When you spend your life in the ordinary realm of knowing, you waste your time supporting the illusion of order. When you move into the consciousness of power, when you experience the world, you intuit it and sense it. This allows for a fluid, whole, multidirectional experience. There is no such thing as order in intuition and sensing. In the realm of experience you only find Chaos.

In mythology, Chaos is the Greek god who personifies "the limitless void out of which the universe emerged."[6] Chaos is the power behind spontaneity. He brings forth creativity and unique outcomes to unique life circumstances. Within Chaos are all of the possibilities — ones that we dare imagine and others that we'd rather not. But they are all there, not only within Chaos, but within ourselves.

When you were a child the world was an open book. You believed that anything could happen. Even though your parents and teachers might have insisted on a world in which one plus one equals two, you were open to the possibility that it could be something else. "Cow" might have been a perfectly acceptable answer to you before someone showed you the knowing answer. Before you knew anything, you lived in a constant state of Chaos. Not-knowing is your natural, primal state. It is an open, flexible stance for your mind and all of its processes. This is the frame of mind of the beginner. From the perspective of Chaos, everything in life, each moment, each footstep, each breath you take is something new.[7] One mystic put it this way: "In the beginner's mind there are many possibilities. In the expert's mind there are few."

The power of Chaos' magical law comes when you become consciously aware of the spinning of your thinking. It comes when you recognize your "expert's mind." This power comes gradually as you keep track of the knowing that comes into your head and pushes you around.[8] The power of living by the law of not-knowing comes when you are able to match up your internal reality with external events. If you are driving, just drive. If you are making dinner, just make dinner. There is nothing to know. Chaos' magical law is a return to a plain, simple mind. In turn, this frame of mind simplifies life.

The perspective of Chaos, of not-knowing, is like a scientist who is curious about the results of an experiment. The scientist does not have a particular opinion about which way the experiment may go. He simply witnesses the unfolding of whatever may happen. Similarly, Chaos' law opens you up to curiosity about the grand experiment, which is your life. Each moment is experimental. The reality of life is much more than whatever you know or conceive it to be. Once you align with Chaos and gradually dispose of dysfunctional knowing, you open to a full and real life. When you arrive at this consciousness, your everyday life transforms into a miracle. Every word you speak becomes a poem. Every step you take is a wonder. Chaos' magical law helps you see that knowing keeps you living among people and things rather than miracles.

THE ENCHANTMENTS

Aligning with Chaos

When you are aligned with Chaos, your mind is functional, focused, and directed toward some aspect of reality. When thinking is misaligned from Chaos, it becomes emotional and habitual. When you sense a misalignment, that is the time to invoke the powers of Chaos. To begin this ritual, it is important to assess which aspect of thinking appears to be misaligned. Chaos rules the four elements, because it is from him that all forms proceed. Determine your areas of misalignment based on the elements below.

Misaligned Air—Constant or intrusive thoughts regarding facts, academic subjects, personal identity, fantasy, reputation, wandering thoughts without direction, or a jumble of racing thoughts without any particular form.

Misaligned Fire—Constant or intrusive thoughts of power, achievement or sexuality, sports activities, angry or aggressive thoughts, war, personal battles, gossip, health, the physical body, new enterprises, ego, fame.

Misaligned Water—Constant or intrusive thoughts of love, romance, relationships, marriage, divorce, family, death, physical appearance, the past, heritage, heredity, ancestry, psychological health, religion, secrets, the occult, friendships, or spirituality.

Misaligned Earth—Constant or intrusive thoughts of money, gain or loss, wealth, finances, investments, earning power, resources, values, pleasures, amusements, pregnancy, employment, status, promotion, suffering or limitation, eating, weight gain or loss.

Once you know your particular misalignment, you can try one of the corresponding ceremonies to help you release habitual thought in air, fire, water, or earth.

Air Charm

What you'll need:

- White sage, dried
- A large, white feather
- Yellow acrylic paint or fabric paint[9] and a fine-pointed paint-brush
- An essential oil with a light, airy feel, like lavender, lemon, or pine

Create this charm during one of the three nights of the new moon.

Begin by creating sacred space. After you have completed this, use your paint and paintbrush to copy the rune known as Birca from this page onto one side of the feather. On the other side

The rune Birca

of it, paint your name and a word that best describes your type of misaligned thinking.

Light the white sage, blow out the flames, and allow the herb to smolder for a moment. Hold the feather so that the sage smoke can waft over it. This imbues the charm with the symbolic quality of air. Next, take a dab of the essential oil on your finger and run it along the edge of the feather, moving in a clockwise direction. Make sure that the oil goes completely around the charm's edge. While you do this say:

This I create in the name of Chaos.

Keeping all other thoughts from entering your mind, face the east, hold the feather in your left hand, and blow on it three times. After each breath recite the following words of power:

When the wind blows, who knows?
A breath from the east says not.
Hurricane's gale, come alter the tale,
I summon you, come change my thought!

The charm is complete. Place the charm where it is always within easy reach. Whenever you catch yourself in an imbalance of "air" thought, take out the charm and hold it in your left hand. Blow on it three times and repeat the words of power. Then focus your attention on the charm, keeping all other thoughts out of your mind. Continue with this until your thoughts subside.

Fire Charm
What you'll need:

- A large, white, "pillar" style candle
- An essential oil with a sharp fiery feel, like cinnamon, clove, or rosemary

Create this charm during one of the three nights of the new moon.

Begin by creating sacred space. After you have completed this, use a pin or a small, sharp knife to inscribe the design of the rune known as Sig from this page onto your candle. Then, on the bottom of the candle, use the pin or knife to inscribe both your name and a word that best describes your misaligned thoughts in the fire category.

The rune Sig

Next, put a small amount of the essential oil on your finger and smear it into the designs you have etched into your candle. While you do this say:

This I create in the name of Chaos.

Face the south, hold the candle in your left hand, and light it. While keeping all other thoughts from entering your mind, recite the following words of power:

*When flame rages, I summon the sages
To pacify passion and yearning.*

Source of the fire, come alter desire,
Bring forth your sacred unlearning!

The charm is completed. Place the candle where it is always within easy reach. Whenever you catch yourself in an imbalance of "fire" thought, take out the candle and hold it in your left hand. Light the candle and repeat the words of power. Then focus your attention on the candle, keeping all other thoughts out of your mind. Continue with this until you extinguish all thoughts.

Water Charm
What you'll need:

- A large seashell
- A small container of spring water
- Blue acrylic paint[10] and a fine-pointed paintbrush
- An essential oil with a soft, watery feel, like chamomile, rose, or sandalwood

Before you begin, clean the seashell thoroughly on both sides. You will use the shell to drink sacred water, so I would suggest using a broad, flat variety, such as an abalone shell. Create this charm during one of the three nights of the new moon.

Create sacred space. Copy the rune known as Lagu, that follows, onto the concave side of the seashell. On the convex side, paint your name and also a word that best describes the type of thinking that represents your misalignment.

The rune Lagu

Allow the paint to dry thoroughly. Next, take a dab of the "watery" essential oil on your finger and smear it across the concave or "bottom" part of the shell. While you do this say:

This I create in the name of Chaos.

Hold the shell in your left hand as you face the west. Fill the shell with clean spring water and while you keep all thoughts from entering your mind, recite the following words of power:

> *When the oceans arise, I shall not surmise.*
> *O calm, thou turbulent sea.*
> *From now to my grave, I summon the wave,*
> *Bring forth your tranquility!*

The charm is completed. Place the shell where it is always within easy reach. Whenever you catch yourself in an imbalance of "water" thought, take out the shell and hold it in your left hand. Fill the shell with water and repeat the words of power. Drink the water and the focus your attention on the magical design on the inside of the shell, keeping all other thoughts out of your mind. Continue with this until your thoughts abate.

Earth Charm

What you'll need:

- A flat, smooth, river stone
- A bright green shade of paint and a fine-pointed paintbrush
- An essential oil with an earthy scent, like patchouli, musk, or oak moss

Create this charm during one of the three nights of the new moon. Before you begin, clean the river stone thoroughly on both sides.

Create sacred space. After you are finished, copy the rune known as Feoh from this page onto one side of the river stone with the green paint. On the opposite side, paint your name and also a word that best describes your misaligned thinking.

The rune Feoh

Allow the paint to dry. Next, take a dab of the "earthy" essential oil on your finger and smear it along the edge of the river stone, going clockwise. While you do this say:

This I create in the name of Chaos.

Hold the stone in your left hand[11] as you face the north.

While keeping all other thoughts from entering your mind, recite the following words of power:

In the silence of stones, I am nothing but bones.
The hush of the hill opens wide.
Salt of the tear, I turn from my fear,
Bring forth your silence, my guide!

The magic is complete. Place the stone where it is always within easy reach. Whenever you catch yourself in an imbalance of "earth" thought, take out the stone and hold it in your left hand and repeat the incantation. Then focus your attention on the design of the magical seal, keeping all other thoughts out of your mind. Continue with this until you still all thought.

Changing Perspective

For this exercise, you will need a pen and two pieces of paper.

Begin by recalling a difficult situation that involved you and another person, such as an argument or a disagreement. Close your eyes for a moment and see the situation. See the other person in the situation with you. As you see it allow whatever feelings you might have to surface. Open your eyes and begin writing by putting a heading at the top of the page. The heading should read "me." Next, write about the problem on the "me" page. Write everything you know about what happened and how you felt about it.

When you are finished with the "me" page, close your eyes again. Use your imagination to see the same event from the perspective of the other person. View how you looked and sounded to the person with whom you had the disagreement. How did you sound? What did your face look like? What are you thinking and feeling as the other person in this situation? When you see the situation from this other perspective, open your eyes and begin to write about the event from this perspective. Start by labeling the page with the name of the other person. Write about how you felt as the other person in this experience. If you get good at this, you can apply the technique in any circumstance and you will soon be opening to a broader sense of experience.

1. Stephen Mitchell, ed., *Dropping Ashes on the Buddha*, (New York: Grove Press, 1976), p. 19.
2. See, e.g., Arnold Joseph Toynbee, *Choose Life*, section 3; "Limits of the Scientific Intellect" (New York: Oxford University Press, 1976).
3. Joseph Campbell, *Transformations of Myth Through Time* (New York: Harper & Row, 1990), p. 124.
4. Jennifer C. Freeman and Dean Lobovits, "The Turtle with Wings" in Steven Friedman, ed., *The New Language of Change* (New York: Guilford Press, 1993), p. 193.
5. Thich Nhat Hanh, *Zen Keys* (New York: Doubleday, 1995), p. 111.
6. Janet and Stewart Farrarr, *The Witches' God* (Custer: Phoenix Publishing, 1989), p. 167.
7. Shunryu Suzuki, *Zen Mind, Beginner's Mind* (New York: Weatherhill, 1970), p. 21–22.
8. Charlotte Joko Beck, *Everyday Zen* (New York: HarperCollins, 1989), p. 6.
9. You can find these paints in either craft shops or art supply stores.
10. This paint is found at art supply shops. I suggest an acrylic because it dries to a hard finish and will not reabsorb moisture. This is important because you will be drinking water that has touched the magical seal design.
11. Instead of holding the stone in their hand, some students hold it to the center of their brow. Some of them claim that holding the stone there helps them center their minds.

CHAPTER VII

PANDORA

*Led by vain hopes and wishes,
one always arrives at destruction.*

INVOCATION

Ten of us sit within sacred space. We have met on the evening of the new moon. We have gathered to grind the sacred herbs together that are known to bring on "the sight," or magical vision. A heavy-set woman sits in the center of the room with a flat, stone bowl before her. With a grinding pestle the woman powders four dried herbs, each one separately. She grinds a fistful of yohimbe, sage, white oak bark, and copal, placing each one in a separate bowl. The rest of us chant and light the coals of the brazier as she mixes the herbs together. When she has finished, she tosses a handful of the mixture onto the white-hot coals.

Hermes raises his hands to the sky and invokes:

> *We summon thee, O Lady. We seek to know what must be known. Open the great box of life, and give us the gift of sight. You, who teach that life is perfect as it is, show us the sacredness of each moment. Teach us to see deeply into our own lives.*

Before Hermes finishes his invocation, the magic circle is engulfed in a thick, white smoke. It is uncomfortable and difficult to breathe at first. It feels as though I am choking, but soon the smoke parts before my eyes. The clarity of my vision is unparalleled.

THE TALE—A *Golden Reward*

Once there was a poor farmer who lived with his two daughters. The elder daughter was vain and greedy, the younger was simple and sought no favor. When the two girls were grown up, their father fell quite ill. The cruel daughter would not tend to her father as he lay dying, but the simple daughter cared for his every need. One day, as he neared death, he called his daughters before him. "Daughters," he said, "I am not long for living and I wish to give you what I have left in the world."

He bade them to lift the floorboard beneath his bed and there his daughters found two boxes. One box was made of sparkling gold and the other of old wood. When the sisters saw this, the cruel elder one said, "Let us see what our father has given to us and we will divide it evenly." Within the golden box, there lay a sack of cornmeal and the wooden box was filled with hundreds of gold pieces.

The meek sister said to her father, "How shall we divide this?" But before he could answer he died. The cruel sister snatched the wooden box filled with gold pieces and said, "This is how we shall divide it, dolt! One box for me and one for you. In any case, what good would a poor farm maid like you find for such treasure as this?" With the wooden box under her arm, the cruel sister marched out the door.

The younger sister was left to bury her father, and to do this she had to sell the old farm house. Now she had nothing left in the world except some hay in the chicken coop on which to sleep and the box with the sack of cornmeal. But when she saw that the chickens had nothing to eat, she sprinkled half of the cornmeal on the ground for them and cried herself to sleep.

The next morning she saw that all of the chickens who had eaten of the cornmeal had turned to gold. These golden chickens were also laying golden eggs. So she gathered as many gold eggs as she could and went to market to sell them. Within a short length of time, the younger sister had regained the farm and had enough wealth to live quite comfortably.

Meanwhile the cruel sister who had stolen the box of gold coins soon ran through all of her money. So she decided to pay her sister a visit to see what else she might gain. When the older sister saw how well the old farm looked she was amazed. She hid around a corner of the house and peered through a window and saw the finest furniture and softest bed she had ever seen. Truly these were the belongings of a queen. Then, when she saw her sister dressed in fine silks and satins, she flew into a jealous rage and could not contain herself any longer.

The cruel sister burst through the door and said, "How is it that you have such fine things? You are nothing but a poor farm maid who must feed the chickens and slop the pigs!" The younger sister, not knowing any better, told the cruel one the truth. "I have fed the chickens with this cornmeal and they have turned to gold!" "Then I must have some too," said the eldest. And she snatched the bag away that held the remaining cornmeal. "Shall I feed it to the hogs? Shall I feed it to the cows? No!" she exclaimed, "This magic is too good for mere beasts."

Soon she began to pull out bowls and she turned the cornmeal into cakes. "I shall eat these cakes myself and I shall become my own treasure!" said the cruel sister. She ate the cornmeal cakes and soon she turned to solid gold. "Ha!" said the cruel sister, "now I shall want for anything! My wealth is that of an entire kingdom." With that she flounced out the door and hurried to show herself at market.

When she arrived, she first stopped at a fine rug merchant. "Would you sell me that carpet?" the cruel sister asked. The merchant said, "Perhaps I shall for one of your golden fingers or toes." The cruel sister was outraged, but she went on asking other merchants. The answer was the same. Every merchant wanted to have a finger or toe, or for even finer things they might ask for a whole foot or hand. Soon the elder sister became fearful, for she did not wish to lose parts of her body. Not knowing what to do she ran from the market. As she fled, a band of thieves spied the woman made of solid gold. Secretly they followed her and when she was quite alone they attacked her, cut her into pieces, and divided the golden parts among themselves.

MAGICAL LAW — *Led by vain hopes and wishes, one always arrives at destruction.*

Pandora's Law

July 5, 1993

Dear Pandora,

I've been thinking of you often. I hope that "magical vision" serves you well and gives you power during this difficult time. I wish you were feeling better and were able to be here with us in the circle. I'm hoping that things will turn out all right for you. You're a real fighter! I will light a candle for you and offer a prayer to the moon for your health.

Blessings,
Timothy

July 15, 1993

Dear Timothy,

I was glad to hear from you. It sounds as though you're not doing too well with our lessons though. From your last letter I sensed your concern and I want you to remember not to wish anything for me—or for you. Things have already turned out all right (for both of us). They were never wrong in the first place. "Feeling better" does not change life, my dear. Death is near me. And so? Practice with the magic mirror has shown me that this is how it is—and I am fine with what is. Reality is the source from which both you and I will find power in this moment. My sacred envisioning reveals to me that death or no death, illness or no illness, it is all the same in the ways of the universe. Hoping and wishing destroys any fragment of power lent to you by the mirror. Don't lean on hope. Only envision. See what is real. Remember to stay focused on the reflection in the magic mirror and release yourself from any expectations you may have. Envisioning will surely come.

Although I am not in the magic circle of California, I am in a larger one with you even in this moment.

Yours in the Vision,
Pandora

August 2, 1993

Dear Pandora,

Happy Lughnassadh! Thanks for your wonderful letter. Your words have helped me to move closer toward envisioning. In reading your letter I felt such a sense of loss and powerlessness. I hope you have not resigned yourself to cancer.

The reason for my writing is to share with you something I recently saw on PBS that reminded me of your teachings. It was a documentary that examined the lives of religious individuals who hold poisonous snakes in their hands as a demonstration of deity's power in their lives. The danger of being bitten is real and sometimes people who handle the snakes end up with injuries or fatalities. During this documentary, one man said, "If I die because of this, that's fine. If I live because of this, fine. If I get hurt, that's fine too." From this, I could see what you meant by maintaining a frame of mind that does not cling to hope. This man had no hope that the snake would fall asleep in his hands, or that he would somehow be protected from danger. He simply envisioned whatever was.

Even though I grasp this concept in theory, I struggle with using the magic mirror. I have difficulty releasing hope. As a result, my envisioning is not very powerful. Please understand that from what I see everywhere around me, people live on their hopes and dreams. We are immersed in a *culture that tells us it is important to have a dream, a hope of some kind. How can everyone be wrong?*

I am feeling a bit cornered by this magical practice. Please let me know how to move forward from this difficult place.

I am eager to hear from you.

Blessings,
Timothy

August 10, 1993

Dear Timothy,

I received your letter the other day. I can see that we still have some work to do in gaining the power of envisioning. I am glad that you saw the documentary on snake handlers. It shows that you are still working out your understanding of this power.

You said you feel cornered. That sounds helpful. It is important for you to know that each corner is of your own making, Timothy. Feeling cornered is not useless; it can wake you up. If you cannot take action, then you must be asleep. If you are awake, then it is time to release this foolish and stagnant activity of hoping and get on with action in this moment.

You asked me if having hope is something wrong. I cannot say what is wrong or right. That you must envision. I can only tell you what is powerful and what is not. Power comes from learning to live outside of the biases that come with such things as culture. Tell me, Timothy, when was the last time you had a fantasy that made your life in the moment—in actuality— something fulfilling? It cannot. It opens the bag of worms called anxiety, and frustration. So what happens when you can't achieve the big hopes and dreams you've planned and toward which you have worked? You become sad or angry. You wonder why life is so unfair.

Hoping and dreaming are not bad in and of themselves, but when you insist on realizing your hopes, when you force the world to move as you command, then you are asking for trouble. Much like the magic mirror, life refuses to cater to any of our individual fantasies, hopes, or dreams. It just continues to flow impersonally. When you insist on the dream, you move against the flow of life, of nature, of deity. Action comes from what the moment requires, and the moment changes continually. Life is never fixed and stationary. It cannot be held to the strict guidelines that you set forth simply because you have a dream or a hope.

Merely by holding hopes in your mind, you carry excess baggage. They keep you from making quick, liquid movement, which are the movements of power. The excess baggage of hope makes you clumsy and heavy. When your hands are full of this kind of baggage, you have no room left in your hands for reality or for doing whatever is needed.

Continue to gaze into the mirror, remember these thoughts, and envision. Write soon and let me know how you progress.

Yours in the Vision,
Pandora

August 15, 1993

Dear Pandora,

I got your letter the other day. I really enjoyed your words of encouragement and I have begun to take steps in releasing myself to life. I am growing in my magical vision now. The magic mirror brings me some empowerment. However, as a result of this practice, I have experienced some sadness, which I assume would be natural, given this difficult task. It seems that hope would be helpful for me once in a while. In fact, wouldn't hope be useful for anyone when they feel sad?

I trust your vision and I will continue with my magic mirror practices. Please write soon and let me know what I must do at this point.

Blessings,
Timothy

Dear Timothy,

I received your letter and I must say that I am concerned about your feeling sad. You said in your letter that releasing hope has caused depression and that hope would be helpful for you when you feel sad. This makes me wonder what gives you the impression that the cure for feeling sad is hope? When you are depressed, it is a time for doing, for action. It is not appropriate to sit around hoping and dreaming for a change to come and be all-transforming. That is lying to yourself and will make things worse.

Understand that sadness is of your own making. Sadness means you feel some loss. But what have you lost? You only have whatever is right here, right now. Hopes and dreams are only fantasies of what might be. That is why hopes have never lent anyone power.

Of course, it is important to know that sadness moves in cycles. Sometimes sadness comes; sometimes it doesn't. Knowing that a cycle eventually ends can be helpful. But knowledge is not the same as hope. Having knowledge is not the same as dreaming for a guide while you are in the midst of the dark woods.

When you gaze into the mirror and release your grip on fantasies, you start to become flexible. You gain a mindset that operates in your everyday life, allowing you to move in any direction. Flexibility can come only to those who have no more clinging thoughts, wishes, or demands. Once you are flexible, you will find yourself taking action, appropriate action.

When you embrace the power of the mirror in its entirety, you will finally see clearly that using hope as a tool to resolve things is useless. The real magic of the mirror is that it motivates you to take action in each moment.

I have a story for you. Once in a far off village, there was a young, unwed girl who became pregnant, much to her family's embarrassment. Her family members demanded to know the name of the father so that he would be held responsible. In order to spare the real father, the girl named the village wise man.

The family visited the village wise man and confronted him with their daughter's story. The wise man's only response was, "Is that so?" When the girl finally gave birth, the family brought the baby to the wise man and said it was now his to raise. "Is that so?" was his only response. The wise man took the baby in and raised it as he would his own child.

One year later, the child's mother finally confessed that the wise man was not the father, but rather a poor boy who worked in a nearby farm. The family went to the wise man once more to beg his forgiveness and ask for the child back again. The wise man yielded the child to the family saying only, "Is that so?"[2]

You are sad. Is that so? You are happy. Is that so? Death is coming to me. Is that so? Each moment is something new and wonderful. You won't ever envision it through a veil of dreaming and wishing.

Continue with your gazing practice. I look forward to hearing from you.

Yours in the Vision,

Pandora

I have a little box of letters that I keep near my magic mirror. I used to read the letters over and over and then I would gaze into the sheet of flat, black glass encased in an antique, cherrywood frame, hoping I would see something that I did not see before. All I see now is what is before me, so I have learned not to cling to my hopes any longer. Pandora would have loved the irony in the fact that her lessons finally sank in after her death. These days, I just keep the letters in a neat little box tied with a black ribbon that came from a floral funeral arrangement.

I recall the day that news came about Pandora's death. I spent many hours looking into the magic mirror that day and for weeks after that. I suppose I was searching for one last lesson. I hoped for one last penetrating word of insight from her. In those days when I would look into the mirror, I would often conjure her image. She was a gentle, petite woman who always wore a blue paisley handkerchief wrapped around her head. She had a laugh you could recognize with your eyes closed. She smiled a lot. She was young; I believe she was only twenty-eight years old, but she had wisdom and power beyond her years.

"The mirror never lies, Timothy. It only sees." That's what I remember Pandora saying when she taught me to use this magical tool. I know that I haven't completely given up looking for Pandora. I still gaze into that reflective black surface upon occasion and hope to see her. Pandora wouldn't want me to do this. To that end, I must admit that I have misused the mirror terribly. "The mirror does not offer illusions of hope. It only shows what is," she would have said to me. "You must learn to become the mirror."

Although years have passed, Pandora's lessons in the magical law of envisioning are as clear as though she had taught them to me today.

Pandora's law was developing clear magical vision. Pandora taught that there are only two kinds of sight for human beings. The ordinary, non-magical way of sight she called "looking." "Looking is the ability to see the surfaces of people, things, and events," she said. "When you only look, you filter what you see through the veil of the mind, which usually sees what it wants, hopes, and wishes to see — not what actually is." She insisted that looking was a rigid kind of vision that did not allow for the fluidity of the moment.

"When looking at the world, the critical mind is a prism made of stained glass, through which the light of reality must pass," she said. She saw that, for people who looked at the world, the purity of the moment was always tainted by the stained glass panels of wishing, wanting, and hoping. When using only the ability of looking, people place their inner reference, the contents of their critical minds, onto whatever really is. That is when reality turns into fantasy. By living in fantasy, one is living in discord with reality, nature, the divine. Looking is a self-centered kind of sight, which is fueled by hopes and wishes.

According to Pandora, the other way of seeing is called *envisioning*. Envisioning is the ability to filter your sight through the open, spiritual mind. It allows you to bypass the chatter of the critical mind and see whatever really is, despite what you wish, want, or hope. When you have the ability of envisioning, you have developed insight. Magical vision only comes when you have the ability to see into the center of your own nature.[1]

In teaching me to use the magic mirror Pandora once said, "When you see the hopes and fantasies of your critical mind, with practice you can strain these out. As a result you can see into the nature of reality. That is your true nature. Your power and vision are intertwined with reality."

Her lessons are still clear, but they weren't always that way. I struggled to develop magical vision for a long time. I know now that it was my own inability to let go of fantasies that hindered my progression. I wasted so much precious time, and before I knew it, Pandora had moved far away. Her family lived in Maine, so she left to spend her last months in a hospice for cancer patients that was near her mother and sister. I am thankful that during that period, Pandora and I corresponded. Even in her final days she continued to teach me. I suppose she did what she envisioned was needed in each moment.

The letter dated August 21st was the last letter I would ever see from Pandora.

It was on the day of her funeral that I finally opened up to the power of envisioning. On my flight to Maine, I was looking out of the airplane window just as the sun was setting. The plane was skimming over the tops of wispy clouds that reflected the last rays of the sun. It was then that I suddenly realized my place in the universe.

Which part of this creation needs hope? I wondered. Does the sun need hope to produce its golden light? Does the earth need hope somewhere to keep spinning on its axis? Which of these clouds needs hope to form in the sky? I realized that there is no part of nature that relies on hope. Reality, nature, the universe itself continues to exist without a single hope.

Then I glanced across the airplane cabin. I looked at the people around me. Then it dawned on me that it was only human beings that used hope as a crutch to get them through life. It occurred to me that none of us were born hoping. It was something we learned. *There is no need for hope,* I finally understood. In that moment, my sadness disappeared and I began to envision.

All I have left of Pandora now is a little box of letters and a profound magical experience.

In further explorations of the power of envisioning, I realized that the story of Pandora from Greek mythology provided a clear message regarding the dangers of hope. Pandora was the heroine who was duped into opening a box full of trouble. Before she was born, Pandora was made of many gifts, virtues, and blessings of the world. When the gods completed her, they placed her on earth. Little did Pandora know that she was about to be caught in a web of intrigue. She did not know that Zeus had an ongoing grudge with Prometheus who, sometime earlier, had stolen fire from the heavens and had given it to humanity. In an act of revenge, Zeus fashioned a box and filled it with every difficulty, discomfort, and hardship that the other gods did not want to place in the world. He then gave this box as a gift to the unsuspecting Pandora. The other gods warned Pandora to be wary of Zeus' gifts. Nevertheless, Pandora was consumed with curiosity about the contents of the box, opened it, and released its effects. The myth goes on to say that at the bottom of the box, beneath all of the hardships, was hope.

When you understand the story from the perspective of looking, it is easy to identify your enemies in the box. Greed, anger, hostility, sadness, despair—it isn't hard to notice what you don't like. Nobody likes difficulties. From the position of looking, people can be fooled into believing that the final content of Pandora's box is something of great value. People without magical vision perceive hope as a virtue. To them, hope sounds like a promise; it is a glimmer, a prospect for something better to come along. People who can only look cling to hope as a possibility of an escape from the contents of Pandora's box.

But the box never shuts. There is no escape from the contents of Pandora's box, which is the mix of life. This can be too dreadful a thought for people who can only look. They would rather hear the sweet talk of hope. The promise that hope holds out is relief, or happiness, or a second chance, or simply anything other than what you have now. Without magical vision, it is easy to believe that an important aim in life is to feel good.[3]

People who can only look believe in the promise of their hopes and live their lives as slaves to feeling good. They will engage in destructive behaviors in the name of maintaining a "good feeling." They take drugs, spend past their limits, eat until they are obese, have extramarital affairs, or endlessly sit in front of the television trying to grasp at hope's elusive promise. They will even harm other people, harm the environment, or go to war if "feeling good" is in any way threatened.

Back in the realm of reality, you only get whatever this moment brings, whether it feels good or not. Dreaming is useless within the moment, just as a mirage is useless on the dunes of a desert. The mirage may look pretty, but when you reach it, it is never what you imagined. Envisioning allows you to see through the mirages of hope into whatever is right here, right now. There is no mirage, no hopeful promise that can place you in a position of empowerment. That is why people who envision know that hope is at the bottom of Pandora's box for a reason. Magical vision allows you to see that inertia is the true result of hoping. Hope takes you out of the field of immediate experience and immediate action. When you do not act in accord with reality, you open yourself to feeling the darker effects of Pandora's box. Without envisioning, you lead a life in the direction of misery.

The practice of envisioning does not offer a life without difficulties. But it offers a life free of misery and frustration. It offers this by pointing you in the direction of releasing your grip on hope and getting a grip on action. People who can only look at the surfaces of things worry that releasing hope also means embracing despair. Without deeper vision, it is difficult to see that despair is just as deceptive as hope. Being hopeless or hopeful are both foolish wastes of time and energy for the person of power. Both hope and hopelessness take you back into your critical mind, far away from appropriate physical action. When you are hoping or when you are hopeless, the action takes place only in your head. Regardless of whether you want to believe in the power of envisioning or the experience of everyday living, reality reveals that the box and its contents remain open regardless of whatever the critical mind may have to say about it. In other words, reality continues to be whatever it is despite your hopes or despairs.

A wall continues to exist as a wall independent of your fantasies, denials, wishes, hopes, and despairs. Reality does not mind you having feelings toward it, but your feelings never cause it to change. When you approach the wall with disempowered looking, you might hope for something else. You might wish that the wall were not there. You might cry about it. You might sit in front of it and pout. The wall doesn't mind at all. When you envision the reality of the wall, you don't bother with your feelings for it. You take appropriate action with the wall. You go around it, climb over it, or dig a hole to go beneath it. If you operate within your life minus the element of hope, then you are left with nothing except for the bare moment of whatever is happening right now. That is the vision of a magician, of a person of power.

People without magical vision also worry that without hope they cannot have goals. This is also the optical illusion of merely looking at the world. The difference between hoping and having goals is that true goals are based on reality, feasibility, and actions. I might set a goal to finish painting my house or to read a particular book. The goal is only a tool to get me moving in a particular direction. It is when I insist on the outcome of the goal that my activity becomes hoping, wishing, forcing. When I use magical vision, I agree with reality despite my goals and preferences for which way I think it should go.

THE ENCHANTMENTS

The Stone Circle

The Stone Circle is a form of divination. The word "divination" comes from the word "divine," which means "related to deity." Divination is a way of getting in touch with deity to determine a course of action in your life. Some popular forms of divination are tarot cards, runes, astrology, and numerology. The divination method of the Stone Circle is very different from these other methods. It relies solely on both your input and interpretation. The Stone Circle is not meant to look into the future, as is popular with other methods of divination. Rather, it is a magical tool meant to assist you in a decision-making process. It is grounded in the here and now.

What you'll need:

- Twelve flat river stones, each one no more than 4" in diameter
- A black, felt-tip, medium-point, permanent marker

When you have a big decision to make, take out the stones and the felt-tip marker. On six of the stones write single words that represent a potential positive outcome of making the decision. Write only one word on each stone. On the other six stones, write single words that represent a potential negative outcome of your decision. Again, write only one word on each stone.

Next, create sacred space. Place the six positive stones on the floor at equal intervals around half of your circle. Place the negative stones around the other half of the circle in the same way. Sit in the center of the Stone Circle and take one stone from each side — both a positive one and a negative one — and place them in front of you. Using your own magical sight, see how each of these outcomes says something about who *you* are. What does the positive outcome say about your desires? What does the negative outcome say about your fears? Continue with this process until you have finished with all of the stones. By the end of the process, you should have a clear idea of what motivates you in this decision-making process.

The final task of this magical working is to take action, to make a decision outside of your circle of hopes or fears. Resolve to take some form of appropriate action that is independent of your Stone Circle.

The Magic Mirror

Contemporary magical folk use a "magic mirror" as a form of divination. The magic mirror is either a flat or concave shiny, black surface into which a magical person gazes. In traditional lore, images, messages, and portents of the future will appear within the mirror. However, there is a deeper use for this extraordinary tool that goes beyond gazing at the shadows and images that one may see in the magic mirror. It is a tool to develop envisioning.

Magic Mirror Construction

There are several methods for constructing a magic mirror. Some people purchase a large photo frame, which usually comes with a piece of protective glass inside. Paint one side of the glass with a glossy, black paint.[4] When it has dried, place the glass back inside the frame with the painted part pressed against the back of the frame. All you should see in the frame is a shiny, black surface.

Another method is to purchase (or if possible, make) a shallow, black bowl. Fill the bowl with water, and the surface of the water should also suffice as a gazing tool. Some people also decorate the outside of either the bowl or the mirror with images and symbols of their own power that come to them through meditation or dreams.

The Practice of Envisioning

When you have your completed magic mirror, take it to a dimly lit but well-ventilated room. Place the mirror about two feet in front of you. Find a comfortable sitting position and simply gaze into the black surface. Hold no thoughts in your mind. Focus on your breathing as you gaze into the mirror. Focus on your bodily sensations as you maintain attention on the black surface. Listen to the sounds of the traffic going by.

Feel the air of the room and the clothes on your body. Stay present with your gazing.

Next, begin counting with each exhalation. Try not to force any unnatural rhythm of breathing, just breathe as you normally would. Count from one to ten, one count per breath. Inhale and then exhale, counting to yourself, "one." You inhale and then exhale, counting to yourself, "two." If you find that your thoughts drift from counting and breathing, start over again with "one." Once you make it all the way to ten without thoughts intruding, start over with "one."

It is a simple practice, but difficult to sustain. It takes a good deal of time to master this method. Practice time should be no more than fifteen minutes when you first begin this method. As you gain in your abilities to envision each moment, you can lengthen the practice to thirty minutes at a time. I would not suggest starting with thirty minutes of practice, because it is quite strenuous; you begin to have diminished returns after more than thirty minutes of this practice at a time. I call this a "practice" because this is literally practice or training for envisioning in everyday life. As with any magical practice, it is important to develop a routine and to engage in the practice on a daily basis.

1. Thich Nhat Hanh, *Zen Keys* (New York: Doubleday, 1995), p. 34.
2. In researching, I discovered that this is a retelling of "Is That So?" also found in Paul Reps, comp., *Zen Flesh, Zen Bones*, (New York: Anchor Books, 1989), pp. 7–8.
3. Charlotte Joko Beck, *Nothing Special* (San Francisco: HarperSanFrancisco, 1993), p. 19.
4. For a more traditional method of making a magic mirror, see e.g., Timothy Roderick, *Dark Moon Mysteries* (St. Paul: Llewellyn Publications, 1996).

CHAPTER VIII

SATURN

Where bias leads, trouble follows.

INVOCATION

▼ ▲ ▼

On one night of the dark moon, three apprentices gathered with Hermes to learn how to spiritually cleanse their homes. "When you are out of balance, your home assumes that condition," he whispered to the three of us as he looked out of the corner of his eye. "Here, take these," he said thrusting one black and one white candle into my hands. "And don't say a word," he continued, pressing a finger to his lips. "Focus, focus. Clear your mind." Hermes then directed us to form a line. The two other apprentices also held objects of power that they were told could clear a space of any unbalanced energies. One of them carried a flat, weathered stone topped with a powdered herb that smoldered and made a pleasant-smelling incense. The other apprentice held a bowl filled with warm water infused with dried hyssop. Then Hermes took the lead and walked, facing the walls. He looked back and signaled for me and the others to follow. "Whatever is in your mind, is in your house. It follows you just as a shadow follows your body. Evil mind, evil house; empty mind, empty house," he said to us. The apprentice with the flat stone was told to blow the smoke from the burning herb toward the walls. The other apprentice was instructed to sprinkle the hyssop water on the walls. As we walked through each room, keeping our minds empty we heard popping and creaking noises from every corner of the house. One particularly loud creak sent a jolt of fear through my body like a current of electricity.

At that moment Hermes called out:

> *Come, O ye noble giver of law! You who knows the secret ways of nature, bring forth Her empowerment. Great God of the universal decree, bless us with your balance. We who stand within this sacred space, call upon your magic. Be with us now and open us to your neutral ways. As above, so below, O Mighty One!*

THE TALE—*Initiation*

Long ago, the Queen Priestess of Tuatha de Dannan had two young novices who wished to become elder priestesses in their time. Both novices were quite vain and selfish. Despite the Queen Priestess' efforts to soften them, she could not. The two had gone through years of training and finally the day arrived when the Queen Priestess announced that the two novices were both to be formally initiated.

The two novices were thrilled and spent hours together planning how they might rule over others with their privileged priestess class. The Queen Priestess soon gathered the two young women and marched them to the boat docks. To the boatkeeper she announced, "These two novices must be taken to the Isle of Priestesses, for they are both to be initiated." The boatkeeper, recognizing the Queen Priestess, bowed deeply saying, "My Lady, I have only two boats left in my docks. The others are out with fishermen." The Queen Priestess turned on her heels and said, "Very well, I trust you to work it out with my novices," and she marched away.

The boatkeeper told the two selfish novices that both his boats were capable of journeying to the Isle of Priestesses, which was three days' journey. However, neither boat would have the best of accommodations. "The green vessel has lovely living quarters, soft beds, and the food is excellent. The only problem is that it rides roughly through the waves and its deck is too narrow. You can't move about the boat. The blue vessel has only a hammock in which to sleep, the food is not very good, but the deck is wide and the boat rides smoothly and evenly through the waves. You must choose between you which boat to take."

The two novices could not decide which boat would be best. "I must have a good night's sleep," said one, "so we must take the green vessel." The other would snap back angrily, "I become ill in boats that ride roughly. We must take the blue vessel." On and on the two novices bickered until the boatkeeper, weary from such a display, suggested that they take both boats—one novice to each vessel. The novices agreed, each boarding one boat, and side by side the boats sailed off to the Isle of Priestesses.

During the first day, all seemed well for both of the novices. But when night came, the swells of the sea became strong, tossing the green boat about. The novice aboard was served a sumptuous meal, but she could not manage to choke down a bit of the food because of seasickness. She began to bemoan her choice and dreamt about the smoothness of the ride aboard the blue boat. She imagined a calm journey and envied the other novice for having made the choice to be aboard that vessel.

Meanwhile, the novice aboard the blue boat felt not a ripple upon the sea. However, when mealtime came, she was given stale, dry beans to chew and a cup of rusty water to drink. She was miserable and began to imagine the wonderful food that must be served aboard the green vessel. She too became jealous of the other novice's choice. She climbed into her hammock and had many dreams of glorious meals served to her on the other boat.

The next day, the novice on the green boat was still suffering from the rough sea and could not eat the sumptuous meals placed before her. She attempted to walk about the decks for air, but they proved to be too narrow to walk upon. Again she wished she were aboard the other boat with its lovely wide decks and its smooth ride. She imagined the other novice was enjoying her voyage to the Isle of Priestesses. She became enraged that she had not chosen the other vessel. She imagined that the other boat was more becoming to a woman who would soon be a Priestess.

As she looked out across the short space between her boat and the next she plotted a way to board the other boat. "Surely just a few strokes away and I will be able to reach the other vessel. Then I will have a more dignified journey to the Isle of Priestesses." With that, she threw herself into the sea and began paddling toward the blue boat. What she did not know is that the sea upon which they journeyed was inhabited by sea monsters avid for human flesh. Before she knew it, the novice felt a tug at her foot and shortly thereafter she was dragged to the bottom of the sea.

Meanwhile, the priestess aboard the blue vessel was served the dried beans and rusted water for both breakfast and lunch. She envied the other novice aboard the green vessel and continued fantasizing about delicious meals served to her in the fashion appropriate to a Priestess of the Holy Isle. She wanted to walk upon the large, lonely decks of the boat to pass the time and quell her hunger. But she was too sore from a night spent in a hammock and her back ached so that a walk was impossible. She imagined the soft comfortable mattresses, filled with goose down, that the other novice must have enjoyed upon the green vessel. Suddenly she realized that the green vessel was just a few short strokes away from her own boat. Without much thought upon the matter, she flung herself into the sea and began to swim toward the other boat. Shortly, she too felt a tug at her foot and thereafter she was dragged to the bottom of the sea.

On the third day, the boats arrived at the Isle of Priestesses. The Queen Priestess of Tuatha de Dannan waited on the shore watching the boats land. When the boatsmen approached her, they reported what had become of the two novices. To this she said, "Their initiation is complete."

MAGICAL LAW — *Where bias leads, trouble follows.*

Saturn's Law

"He can heal with a touch of his hands," Hermes said to me. "He can free you of this problem." I remembered his words as I laid in the middle of Saturn's magic circle watching the flickering orange reflection of votive candlelight on the ceiling. Saturn stood behind me and rubbed his hands together briskly. He was a tall, thin man, and while I lay on my back looking up at him, he seemed to be a towering presence. He placed one hand on each side of my head near my temples and I closed my eyes.

I needed healing and I was willing to try anything. But neither traditional medical treatment nor alternative remedies seemed to fix my laryngitis. I could have had almost any other serious illness and I would have been less panicked, but a week without my voice left me desperate and anxious.

That week of silence gave me time for reflection and self-observation. Up until that point, I had never realized my emotional dependence on talking. I discovered that talking for me was more than a means of communication. It was a nervous habit. It was a drug. I was addicted to chatting. But now I couldn't say what I felt, what I needed, or what I thought. It was a shocking thought, but I recognized that I had created a lopsided level of participation in the world around me, and now my flimsy little structure was collapsing in around me. I wished I could restore balance to my life, but I didn't know where I might begin. Every day that I awakened without my voice, I would feel a helpless twinge or a kind of knot in the pit of my stomach.

But with Saturn's hands on my head, that usual discomfort was gone. It was replaced by something that felt like a low buzzing or vibration, which seemed to pass through my head. The vibration wasn't painful in any way. Instead I began to feel relaxed and a bit sleepy. Suddenly, Saturn removed his hands and the sleepy feeling dissipated. "You've got judging mind," he said.

I didn't anticipate his statement and I felt caught off guard. "What's wrong with me?" I managed to say in a hoarse whisper. "You have no voice because you are caught by a curse," he said in a matter of fact tone. This was unexpected. My heart leapt. I felt quick, deep thumping in my chest. I was scared. "Someone is cursing me?" I asked with a cough and then sat up quickly. "Curses aren't always what we expect," he said. "That is why they hold great influence." *What does he mean?* I thought. I made a helpless gesture, hoping he would explain more.

"Sometimes we curse ourselves," he said trying to lay me back down. "In this case, you are cursed because you have discarded your dreaming." The pain in my throat was unbearable, otherwise I might have had something to say. "Only your dreaming can help you now," he said. "I can help you find your dreaming and then you will be powerful again." I couldn't help myself any longer; I had to ask what he meant by "dreaming." I pantomimed writing in an exaggerated way and then Saturn allowed me to write my question to him.

I handed him the question scribbled on the back of an envelope. Saturn read it, then shook his head and chuckled. "Why must you know in order to act? Must you know how medicine works before you choose to take it? Instead, you seem to crave the very poison that has infected you." I stared at him with a blank expression. Saturn continued, "Judging mind is that poison. It is what has cursed you."

I grabbed the envelope again and wrote another question. "What do you mean by judging mind?" I asked.

Saturn said, "Judging mind is divided mind. It is the mind of bias."

I wrote another question: "How did I get judging mind?"

Saturn chucked again, evidently amused at my persistence in asking questions. "Judging mind takes two acts," he said. "The first is thinking. The second is talking. Thinking is troublesome when you use it to make differences. It is an improper use of thinking when you cling to your running opinions and distinctions. You curse yourself when you use thinking to differentiate between desirable and undesirable, better and worse, useful and not useful. Talking magnifies the trouble. It gives body to your judging mind. It turns your thinking into something tangible, into something that seems real. You curse others with judging when you engage in talking. In and of themselves, neither thinking nor talking are problematic. They are, in fact, necessary to live in the physical world. But when you are attached to thinking and talking they combine into the curse called judging."

Silence fell between us and I thought about what Saturn said. It seemed as though there were gaps in his logic. I wrote again. "Not everything in the world is equal. There are real differences between experiences and people. Judging is what helps people to see this and to possibly avoid trouble."

"The reason for your seeing inequity is that you have somehow lost reality," he said. "You participate in the unreal game of judging what is equal and unequal in the world. Once you start to play this game, you will see disparity everywhere. The sun is not equal to the moon. Is this unjust? Inequality is there for anyone who wishes to see it. Inequality exists only in the human mind. It keeps you worried that you need to balance things out, or make things right, or come to terms with whatever is in your life. At the baseline of existence, there is nothing to balance, no wrong to right. Nothing needs resolution. Inequality is only as real as you believe it to be. It is real as long as you cooperate with judging mind."

I wrote back quickly, "But there are many people who experience inequality and prejudice every day of their lives. That is very real inequality."

"Yes," Saturn said, "the harm someone suffers because of inequalities is real. Pain is real. Ugliness is real. Each of these arises when the judging minds of individuals or of a society arbitrarily superimposes value on reality in one way or another. That one kind of person is better than another is foolishness. That one group is better than another—it cannot be. The essence of life is a state of equality, balance, and neutrality. When you see through the masquerade of the judging mind then you can cut through prejudice, blame, and condemnation. Gold has value simply because someone says it does. Does it have value in the vastness of space? Does it have worth when death comes to you? Does it hold some advantage for a butterfly? No, value is arbitrary. It depends in which seat you are sitting and when. If someone has something you want, your judging mind may see inequity. Does the thing you want have value above other things? It cannot be true. Did any inequality exist? In your mind, perhaps, but in reality, no. You must gain the power to see through this and recognize that judging robs you of the power that already is. Timothy, you have lost your voice because you are an apprentice to power. Deity is giving you a chance to uncover your dreaming."

I wrote again, asking Saturn to explain dreaming once again. "This is only words," he replied. "Don't try to gather too much from my useless words. I've said too much already. Words mislead and distract from the main event, Timothy. Power has nothing to do with anyone's words. You must experience the mind free of judgment for yourself," he said. "I can lead you to the power of your dreaming, but once you recognize it, you need to release my words."

Despite what he said, I felt as though his words held great importance. They caused me to become acutely aware of my thinking. As I observed my thoughts, I noticed that much of what I judged to be reality were thoughts that came from someone else. I was full of conditioned thinking, and I had simply taken it for granted for most of my life. I felt an oppressive sadness begin to overcome me. I felt it first as a lump in my throat that was filled with tension and pain. Before I could think or feel for too long, Saturn once again laid me back on the floor of his magic circle. "Now you have an appointment with your dreaming," he said. "It is time." He rubbed his warm hands together and once again placed them on either side of my head. Soon I felt the familiar internal vibration.

I waited for something to happen. The next thing I knew, I found myself standing outside of the New York City Public Library looking at the two stone lions that crouch at the entrance. The colors and clarity of what I saw made the vision seem real. I would have sworn that I was actually standing in New York. Suddenly one of the lions moved. Without a sound, the cold, gray animal on the right stood up and shook its head from side to side. As I watched, the lion began to transform. Soon it had the head of a zebra and the hindquarters of an ox. Then, as quickly as I had drifted into a deep dream state, I snapped back into full waking consciousness. I opened my eyes and found myself back in Saturn's magic circle.

I shrugged in apology for evidently falling asleep. Saturn only laughed. Then he asked, "Did you dream?" I nodded. "Close your eyes now and bring the dream to mind. Tell me what strikes you the most about this dream as you watch it."

I contemplated the short dream for a few moments and then I had an unusual insight. I found it odd that I wasn't surprised at the statue coming to life. I wasn't amazed or frightened by this sight given the fact that everything appeared vivid and real. I wondered how I could simply accept the fact that what was once stone was now animated. I wrote down my observations and passed them to Saturn.

He beamed with pleasure as he read the note. "This is the true way of dreaming. In dreaming, differences disappear. Strange is not strange. Stone can move when you do not inhibit it with your judging. In dreaming, reality is whatever presents itself in each moment. Most people leave their dreaming in bed, so they have no power. You must learn to stretch the power of dreaming across your entire life. This is the way of true balance."

Then Saturn asked, "How is your voice now?"

I cleared a thin layer of mucus that had accumulated in my throat and then, after a week of pain and silence, I actually spoke. The pain was gone. I spoke clearly and resonantly. I would have been astonished, but I remembered to keep centered in my dreaming and I accepted this small miracle without judgment or critique.

I understood now. For me, dreaming was the power of balance, of natural justice. In nature, justice is a restoration and maintenance of neutrality and impartiality. Neutrality allows for many possibilities and fluid change. The justice of nature is the core of Saturn's magical law.

In ancient Roman religion and myth, Saturn was the deity who presided over natural justice, balance, and spiritual order in the world.[1] Annually, the ancient Romans celebrated this principle of balance in a feast called Saturnalia. During this festival, the usual roles of everyday life were reversed. For example, a wealthy landowner or person from the upper class might prepare a banquet for people of a lower class. Or a master might perform a servant's tasks. Likewise, the servants might take the role of the master for the feast day and indulge in his world of socially established privilege. The celebration and symbolism of Saturnalia made it clear to everyone of ancient Rome that distinctions such as class and wealth, or roles like master and servant, were arbitrary assignments. Saturn made them aware that these were human-created limitations, which held no power beyond the boundaries of their own society. They knew it was not deity, nature, or reality that assigned such roles or held distinctions between one being and another. It was the doing of ordinary people.

We don't celebrate natural Saturnine justice any longer; for the most part, people live their lives out of the mistaken belief that their distinctions about reality are reality itself. Ordinary judgment proceeds from this limited, constricted belief. The price of living by judgments is a loss of freedom and dreaming. Dreaming is the spiritual gift given to people who recognize power in neutrality and impartiality.

Nature is impartial. At the core of reality there are no real distinctions between such concepts as wealth and poverty, better and worse, desirable and undesirable. Distinctions, opposites, and judgments such as "better" or "worse" are only relevant in the lives of ordinary human beings. Reality and nature are independent of human judgments; the universe operates freely, impartially, and indifferent to human affairs.

If you do not travel the path of dreaming and you insist on living according to manmade distinctions, you live in the realm of bias. Bias indicates a mindset of favoritism. It means that you idealize and isolate some aspect of life. A biased mind shatters the whole of life into fragments—some of which are considered "good" and others "no good." There are things to like and things not to like from this perspective. Under the rules of bias, perhaps you might believe that red is nicer than blue. Or you might think that left is more valuable than right. Or perhaps one race of people is better than another. One god is holier than two; male is superior to female; happy feelings are more desirable than sad ones. When you guide your life by biases, the list of limitations and boundaries goes on indefinitely. You yourself are fragmented when you operate from biases and distinctions. You are not joined with the whole of life because you cling to one perspective and value it over others.

Bias is insidious. It cripples you without letting you know that you have lost any power at all. In fact, when you discriminate and favor one thing over another, it validates your fragmentation of the world. It gives body to the illusion that there are "right" choices that you can make and "valuable" ways to exist. A false sense of reality and human suffering both flourish from the ground of bias. Dominance, war, hate crimes, murder, rape, and abuse of all kinds arise from the fragmented human consciousness that values one way of life over another.

People of magic live by the whole—the neutral, underlying current of reality—instead of finding ways to validate fragmented lives or feel "right" or "good." You have begun your own journey toward magical living when you learn that there is neutral, interconnected unity in all living things. Power comes when you act from the knowledge that one part of the whole is not more valuable than another. In this sacred consciousness, you realize that ordinary distinctions are empty in the face of reality. The dreaming of Saturn is impervious to bias. While dreaming you assume a stance of power and are open to ingenious and unique options for living in each moment. Dreaming allows you to act appropriately in response to actual life circumstances—to whatever is happening right now.

Beings of power recognize that when you fight to hold on to some ideal—or any fragment of the whole—you lose your stance of power. Outside of Saturn's influence, you lean in one direction or another, hoping for something or averting something else. Judgments easily throw you off center. Life continues on despite your ideals, and when you live by fragments and judgments you can easily get knocked down. That is typical when you believe that life has been unfair and unjust to you.

From the fragmented world view, you demand fairness from life. More often than not, the ordinary idea of fair has something to do with things going your own way. For the magical, powerful being, freedom comes from the knowledge that life cannot deliver the brand of fairness that ordinary beings come to expect. Once you know that the ordinary concepts of "fair," "right," and "just" have nothing to do with reality, it is easy to claim power by simply releasing them.[2]

A cloud drifting by does not demand fairness. It does not have a particular bias for a certain shape or size. It is not more or less valuable when it produces rain. It is not angered when the sun and the wind work to destroy it. Neither do the sun nor the wind show bias by destroying the cloud. Each is simply doing its own job. An ant does not show animosity toward life when a bit of debris covers its dwelling. It does not race to thoughts about how difficult the debris has made things. It does not try to find the culprit who caused the harm. It simply moves into action to clear away the debris without complaint. It does what is needed. Because of its nonjudgmental action, an ant demonstrates a greater range of magical power than do the people who live in the realm of bias.

According to ordinary standards, the cloud and the ant should both seek angry, self-righteous justice. They should demand repayment for the "harm" they have suffered. They need a good lawyer. According to magical standards, the life of the cloud or the ant demonstrates that true justice is an escape from the *need* for justice. It is doing whatever needs to be done moment by moment without judgment or bias. When the moment requires action, then it is time to act; when it requires nonaction, then do not act. How do you know when it is time for each? When you let go of judging, you open to existing in the here and now. Once you are present, life itself instructs you on what to do. This is the power of dreaming.

The dreaming mind simplifies life. Where the judging mind understands struggles, the dreaming mind sees only existence—things just as they are.

The first step in gaining Saturn's power is to notice whenever you engage the judging mind. Each of us slips into judgments hundreds of times each day. You slip into judgments whenever you think you are right, whenever you criticize, worry, or rationalize. Whenever you feel sad, angry, or disappointed, it is time to understand that you have placed life in a hierarchy and have judged one aspect to be better than another. The key to freeing yourself from the judging mind is recognizing it when it first appears and then tracking and observing the influence of any judgments you make.

Tracking your judgments and remaining neutral is critical, but it can be a bit tricky because it requires careful observation of your mind's contents. You might be able to pick out your most obvious judgments from the start. "I don't like that," or "this is great," are a couple of glaring examples. Over time, you might discover that the judging mind hides out in the middle of your usual, day-to-day thoughts. These are often too subtle to catch immediately. An overall rule of thumb is to notice whenever you feel tense or emotional. The body never lies and when you feel tension, it is usually a sign that the judging mind is somewhere close by, manipulating your life. Perhaps judgment is telling you that you must hold a certain type of job, or that you need to look a certain way. Whatever the case, start by following each judgment as you discover it. Take note of the effect it has on the rest of your thinking. Try making a list of the biases you have tracked. Keep the list in a place that you can see often. As the list grows, you can have a visual reminder of bias' intrusion in your life.

Sometimes judgments may try to trick you into judging yourself for even having a biased mind. You are neither right, wrong, good, or bad for having ordinary thoughts. Everyone has a judging mind. But not everyone allows it to drain them of power. It is only the magically minded individual who develops the tenacity to pursue these thoughts and gain dreaming.

THE ENCHANTMENTS

The Astrology of Saturn

In contemporary astrology, the planet Saturn reflects one's "karma." Most people seem to be familiar with the term karma, since it has entered into popular vernacular. Although most people have heard the word, many do not know its specific reference. In the popular imagination, karma is simply payback for the deeds you have done. It makes you suffer for the wrongs you have committed or it creates joy in return for your good deeds.

Actually, karma is a Sanskrit word that means action. It is not a mysterious force. It is a simple matter of cause and effect. Natural consequences arise from any kind of action. If your actions reflect a mind of judgment, then your life moves in one direction that will yield one set of natural consequences. If your actions come from dreaming and natural justice, then a different set of possibilities and consequences opens for you. Each sign through which Saturn passes in the astrological chart indicates these two potentials. In knowing each path, Saturn can become the herald of your greatest potential for natural balance.

The exact location of Saturn in the birth chart (the chart of the celestial bodies' positions at the time of your birth) can tell you even more. For our purposes, we shall look at trends for each sign in which Saturn falls. Saturn passes through approximately one sign every two years. It takes about 28 years for Saturn to pass through all twelve of the zodiacal signs.

For this exercise, consult the appendices in the back of the book to find Saturn's placement in the year you were born. I have listed in the following pages the possible trends of action for people born with

Saturn in each sign. The first listing is for people who live in alignment with natural justice. The second listing is the trend should you find yourself living in ordinary ways and acting through your judgments.

Saturn in the Signs

Saturn in Aries

This indicates a trend toward initiative and persistence. Inventiveness might also be a part of your nature. If it is, you most likely direct your ingenuity in ways that can benefit everyone around you. Another trend for Saturn in this sign is strong reasoning abilities. People with Saturn in Aries can find themselves in leadership roles. In its most natural expression, your leadership is one that relies on other people for direction. You have learned neutrality, to overcome any insensitivity toward other people that you may have had in your youth.

OR: Without coming to terms with your neutral, natural side, Saturn in Aries can indicate difficulty in maintaining motivation in many activities of your life. It might also indicate that you have learned insensitivity in your youth. Without gaining the powers of neutrality, your learned insensitivity can be an instrument of pain in other people's lives. With Saturn in Aries, you might not even notice that you have caused pain in anyone else's life. When you are outside of your own power, Saturn in Aries can indicate a trend toward impatience.

Saturn in Taurus

People with Saturn in Taurus have a tendency to base their self-esteem on their finances. However, once you have learned the lesson of neutrality, you learn that satisfaction in your life has little to do with financial security. In your power, you are released from any drive toward gaining money or desirable things. This aspect can lend you skills in establishing order out of chaotic circumstances. Perhaps you feel best when you can teach other people how to come into their own natural order.

OR: Without gaining the natural freedom of Saturn, this aspect can indicate feelings of possessiveness. People born with Saturn in Taurus tend to have a strong ego dependence on money and material things. They can find themselves on an emotional roller coaster based on their financial outlook. Be very cautious that you don't slip into miserliness. With Saturn in Taurus, you might also find yourself depending on order around you. Outside of their power, people with Saturn in Taurus can have real difficulties functioning and thinking if they don't have order in their immediate physical environment.

Saturn in Gemini
With Saturn in the sign of Gemini, you might have a tendency to be very logically minded. When you stand in your power, you do not rely on logic to solve all matters of your life. Perhaps you have learned to balance your logic with compassion. Anything that stimulates the mind might be of interest to you, but once you've learned the lessons of neutrality, you know that experiencing life in ways beyond the mind is important. With Saturn in Gemini, you are always ready to learn new things and higher education can interest you.

OR: If you stand outside of your power, Saturn in Gemini indicates that you rely on your intellect. Because of this lopsided reliance on the critical mind, you can have difficulty in detaching from your mental processes in order to experience each moment. People with Saturn in Gemini can tend toward cynicism and doubt of other people—so this is something to keep in check. It is important for you to remember that if you rely on your thinking too much, you can overtax your mental processes. If you are someone who often relies on the intellect, you might try to develop techniques for handling any tension or nervousness that can arise from neglecting your emotions.

Saturn in Cancer

People with Saturn in Cancer tend to have strong connections to their families and their homes. They also see the influence of their family on the greater community and they hope to foster socially responsible family and community members. If you are someone with Saturn in Cancer, most likely you have a very good memory. People with this aspect tend to have the ability to recall their past in great detail. If you have found your power inside of Saturn's neutrality, then you have learned the valuable lesson of not dwelling on the past. You have learned not to allow the past to influence you in the present. Saturn in Cancer can indicate sensitivity toward the feelings of other people. When you claim the power of nature, you can turn this sensitivity into empathy and the ability to act on behalf of other people.

OR: Saturn in Cancer tends to create sensitivity. People who live ordinarily can go to great lengths to either hide this sensitivity or to defend themselves in one way or another. People with this aspect sometimes try to protect themselves by gaining the approval of the people around them. Another strategy of the Saturn in Cancer person is to emotionally block out the rest of the world. If you have Saturn in Cancer in your birth chart and you choose either one of these tactics, don't be surprised if you find yourself feeling sad, weepy, or alienated from the rest of the world. Outside of your neutral stance, with Saturn in Cancer you tend to dwell on the past and this rumination often influences your actions and decision making in the present.

Saturn in Leo

People with Saturn in Leo have natural leadership. If you claim the power of neutrality, you recognize that your leadership can influence many other people, so you are circumspect and evenhanded in your leadership choices. With this aspect, you find ways to share your leadership and powerful influence with other people, and you inspire the people around you to find their own inner strength. With Saturn in Leo, you are naturally even-tempered, and this helps in your process of sharing power and influence. People with this aspect often have learned how to combine the serious self-discipline of Saturn with the sense of fun and enjoyment of the Sun (which is the ruler of Leo).

OR: With Saturn in Leo, there is no doubt that you can land yourself in a leadership position. But you should be careful in your leadership role that you don't claim power over other people. If you do not claim the power of neutrality, you may rely on hierarchical models of power and use your influence to establish a "pecking order" and place yourself at the top. Before this happens, try to determine any internal, emotional influences that may be leading you to establish such a hierarchy. Ask yourself why it is important to be in charge or to have control over other people. Keep in mind that when you bypass your neutral, natural power, you might also find it difficult to share power within your friendships, family, and romantic relationships.

Saturn in Virgo

If you have Saturn in Virgo as well as the power of neutrality on your side, you find it easy to determine what is most important for you in life. When you have neutral power, you can help other people to discriminate between their own powerful or not powerful options. Sometimes people with this aspect have an iron will. If this pertains to you, most likely you can use this internal fortitude to overcome any personal biases or judgments. With Saturn in Virgo, you can have a natural inclination to place practicality above any other objective. When in your power, you can use this ability to apply spiritual matters to everyday situations with ease.

OR: If you have Saturn in Virgo and you do not claim the power of neutrality, it is important to keep in check any impulse to voice critical or judgmental opinions. With this aspect, you love practicality, but without neutral power, this practicality can override any natural pleasure and joy that can come from simply being alive. Try not to buy into any rigid or pessimistic thinking that may try to influence you. If you find it difficult to make friends, it might be because Saturn in Virgo people can appear to be cold or distant when they lead their lives outside of neutrality.

Saturn in Libra
If you claim the power of neutrality, the aspect of Saturn in Libra can lend you a strong sense of social awareness. Perhaps you take less fortunate people into consideration, donate regularly to charities, or involve yourself with social causes. With Saturn in Libra, you can find yourself working to mediate the problems that arise between friends and co-workers. When you claim the power of neutrality, your powers of diplomacy come from your ability to understand and empathize with all sides of an issue. With Saturn in Libra, you can be a model of cooperative effort.

OR: If you do not claim the power of neutrality, Saturn in Libra can still lend the power of diplomacy. However, it is important for you to understand any psychological or emotional motivations for your diplomacy. Are you uncomfortable with anger? Are you trying to please everyone? Watch for helping other people at the expense of your own well-being. It is important for you to remember that giving of yourself out of a sense of low self-worth cannot occur without taking a toll on you. If you are not careful, perhaps you might have flashes of anger or intolerance in more private moments.

Saturn in Scorpio
This aspect indicates that you are a person who has strength of character—especially when this falls in the chart of people who have claimed their magical power. If this applies to you, then most likely you have the ability to see through the veil of the physical realm into the emptiness of such things as money and prestige. Once you align with your magical abilities, you can develop strong psychic senses. With Saturn in Scorpio secretiveness can be a possible trap for you. However, in your power, you see that there is no secret that you must keep and you open yourself to the incoming and outgoing of truth.

OR: Saturn in Scorpio always indicates strength of character. However, if you live ordinarily, you can overwhelm other people with your bold personality. Outside of neutrality, you won't have as much ability to resist feeling dazzled by the world of money and prestige. These could even become a focus for you if you do not keep this in careful check. If you do not live within your magical abilities, any psychic flashes you have can be sporadic and sometimes illusory. Watch out for any tendencies to be secretive. Ask yourself why it is important to hold on to secrets and who those secrets serve.

Saturn in Sagittarius
There is a tendency for those born with Saturn in Sagittarius to have interest in religion or philosophy. Even if you do not think of yourself

as either religious or philosophical, you might find yourself intrigued by the concepts of these disciplines. Another expression of Saturn in Sagittarius is independence of thought and action. If you are someone aligned with neutrality, then this aspect helps you to be independent of culture, time, space, family, and other potentially inhibiting factors. Saturn in Sagittarius people are often generous, and once aligned with their power they can give what is needed in each moment.

OR: Saturn in Sagittarius often leads to interest in religion or philosophy. However, once you step out of neutrality, this interest can wind up in rigid or moralistic thinking. Although Saturn in Sagittarius usually signifies independence of thought and action, outside of a neutral frame of mind you should guard against becoming independent to the point of having no connection to anyone or anything else. When you live in ordinary ways and have Saturn in Sagittarius, it is a good idea to arrive at an understanding of what motivates your feelings of generosity. There may be an agenda beneath your actions that you did not initially suspect. Many people with this aspect can benefit from meditation.

Saturn in Capricorn
Saturn in Capricorn people are almost always hard workers. When they are of a neutral frame of mind, they do not let their usual work concerns override their enjoyment and fulfillment. They can have an innate sense that the ultimate aim in life is not "happiness." They understand that "feeling good" will not lead them to their ultimate goals. In the highest expression of this aspect, they can manifest their lofty ambitions for the benefit of everyone. Saturn in Capricorn people have learned to take responsibility for their actions and promote self-reliance in other people.

OR: Saturn in Capricorn people can be hard workers. Outside of neutrality, however, their sense of work becomes imbalanced. Sometimes people with this aspect have difficulty "letting go" and just having fun. People who have Saturn in Capricorn can dismiss personal enjoyment as a luxury if they live outside of power. In this state they can have high ambitions, but these might be personally motivated. You must guard against taking life too seriously. Adopt the habit of asking yourself what is serious about this moment and what is not.

Saturn in Aquarius
Saturn in Aquarius can lend a common sense attitude to people who claim the power of natural neutrality. If this pertains to you, most likely you have a practical approach to many things. Within this unique power you can find a mysterious source of internal strength that aids you in completing long or even complex tasks. In the neutral aspect of Saturn in Aquarius, you have learned to appreciate the goals of other people. You have developed patience and forgiveness because your awareness of reality allows you to see that there is no cause for anxiety; there is no one to blame for the way life is.

OR: Saturn in Aquarius can instill a common sense attitude in your approach to life. Outside of your power, you may not have tolerance for people who do things impractically. You might like to plan things out for your life, but it is important to remember that clinging to personal goals creates stress, anxiety, and a loss of magical balance. Outside of the neutral aspect of Saturn in Aquarius, you can have difficulty appreciating the goals of other people. This aspect can sometimes indicate that you are restoring karmic balance from a long history of self-centered encounters with other people. In this case, it is wise to accept other people for who they are and allow them their self-expression without your quick judgments and impatience.

Saturn in Pisces
Saturn in Pisces can lend you a strong sense of intuition if you align with the power of neutrality. You can also be sympathetic and sensitive to other people. You can have a natural inclination to self-sacrifice so that other people will benefit. However, in a powerful stance you have learned the value of allowing people the space to come to power and enlightenment on their own terms. In your power you have learned to persevere and to overcome obstacles that stand in the way of achieving idealistic goals. You have learned to overcome any knee-jerk, emotional reactions you may have once had before you claimed your power. You have learned to quell old feelings of sorrow and because of this you can be a great example or a teacher for other people.

OR: Although Saturn in Pisces can lend you a strong sense of sympathy and sensitivity to other people, outside of neutrality this can cause difficulties. For example, your sensitivity might lead to feelings of moodiness or indecision. Be careful not to self-sacrifice to the point of losing yourself to the needs of other people. It is important for you to keep in mind that you have needs too. Without the power of neutrality, you may not have learned that the value of perseverance is not always in the achievement of a particular goal. To the person of a neutral mind, perseverance may be what is needed in the moment. It has inherent value. Saturn in Pisces people who live ordinarily can also find that they become depressive. When dealing with other people, be careful not to allow emotional, knee-jerk reactions to control you.

Neutral Space Ritual

The purpose of this ritual is to neutralize any imbalancing influences in any space you choose: your home, office, car, etc. Historically, magical people have used this ritual to cleanse their homes of negative forces and "evil spirits." In contemporary practice, you will find that this ritual not only neutralizes your environment, but also assists you in attaining a state of neutrality. Whenever you feel that your life is imbalanced, it is a good time to summon the forces of neutrality through this ritual.

What you'll need:

- One black candle
- One white candle
- A dish of salt (I find coarse kosher salt aesthetically pleasing for a rite like this)
- A dish of water
- Dried white sage
- An essential oil—preferably rosemary or lavender

Start at the front door of your home or office and light your black and white candles. Hold one candle in each hand and begin walking along the walls, going clockwise inside of the space. Go from room to room, finally making a full circle inside of your home or office and ending back at the front door. If you perform this ritual in a multi-level space, start at the front door and work your way around clockwise on each level. As you walk holding the candles, keep your mind clear of any thought. Since you have had plenty of practice to this point in maintaining a clear mind, you should not find it difficult to do. Simply pay close attention to what goes on inside of your mind. If a thought pops into your consciousness, stop where you are. Simply notice the thought and allow it to pass. Once it drifts by, continue walking the perimeter of each room. When you arrive back at the front door, set the candles in holders and let them burn there until this magical working is complete.

While the candles burn near the front door, gather together your dish of salt and your dish of water. Hold your hands over the salt and say:

> *I bless this sacred earth.*
> *This sacred earth blesses me.*
> *It shall ground cause and effect.*
> *It shall bring peace.*

Then hold your hands over the small bowl of water and say:

> *I bless this sacred water.*
> *This sacred water blesses me.*
> *It shall wash away cause and effect.*
> *It shall bring peace.*

Put the salt into the water and mix it together. Sprinkle the mixture of salt and water around each room, again going through the entire space clockwise. As you did with the candles, keep your mind clear during the sprinkling. If you have any thought, stop where you are, notice the thought, and let it pass through you. Continue around the space until you get back to the front door. Set the bowl of salt water there.

Next light the dried, white sage with one of the candles and say:

> *I bless this sacred fire.*
> *This sacred fire blesses me.*
> *It shall burn away cause and effect.*
> *It shall bring peace.*

Blow out the fire and allow the sage to smolder. As the smoke rises, say:

> *I bless this sacred air.*
> *This sacred air blesses me.*
> *It shall blow away cause and effect.*
> *It shall bring peace.*

As you did with the candles and the salt water, walk along the perimeter of each room, again moving clockwise until you reach the front door. Do this silently and without thought as best you can. When you return to the front door, set the sage in a container that will allow it to burn until you have completed this magical working.

Finally, take the lavender or rosemary essential oil out, put some on your finger, and anoint each doorway of your space with it. Again, complete this in a clockwise manner and monitor your mind for conscious thoughts. Focus on the anointing and allow no other thoughts to intrude. When you arrive at the front door again say:

> *This and that, beginning and ending,*
> *Time and timelessness, positives and negatives*
> *All shall leave this place.*
> *The rapture of this moment beyond moments shall remain.*

The magic is complete.

Spiritual Balancing Techniques

Here are some magical techniques to help anchor the experience of remaining neutral in your everyday life.

- Hyssop is a traditionally magical herb that people use for purification. The herb can also be used medicinally to purify and tone the body. At the end of each day, make a magical infusion of hyssop herb. Place two tablespoons of dried herb in one cup of boiling water. Let this steep for five minutes. When the infusion cools to room temperature, sprinkle yourself with it. Or pour the infusion into bath water and bathe in the soothing, balancing influences of hyssop.

- Some sources claim that the essence of lavender creates psychological and emotional balance. When you sense tension in your body, dab a bit of lavender essential oil onto your temples. Some people are sensitive to essential oils, so test a bit on your forearm prior to using it on your temples. If your skin feels irritated, you can dilute the essential oil with another, more neutral oil. Many herbalists use almond oil or grapeseed oil to decrease the potency of essential oils.

- To help keep your thoughts clear all day long, fill a sachet with patchouli herb and myrrh "tears." A sock cut in half and tied at the tip with ribbon or silk cord can always double for a sachet bag in a pinch. For added strength, place a fluorite stone in the bag and put a few drops of mimosa essential oil on the bag itself. Place the bag someplace close to you, where you can inhale the essences of the herbs throughout the day. Rub the bag between the palms of your hands to help clear your thoughts in especially difficult circumstances.

The Magical Mandrake

This is another traditional Celtic technique that magical folk use to create balance.

What you'll need:

- A mandrake root (whole is preferable)
- One to two feet of black thread
- A chalice or cup filled with water
- Salt

Mandrake is an exotic herb that you will only be able to find in an herb store. This herb is so exotic that you may even have to special order it. Though it is difficult to procure, it is well worth the trouble it takes to find it. When you buy a mandrake root, try to find a full-length one.

Begin by stating aloud any of your biases. As you say each bias, wrap the mandrake root once with the black thread. Imagine that you are tying each bias to the root with the thread. When you are finished, wrap the rest of the thread around the mandrake root.

Next, take out your chalice or a cup and fill it with water. Mix a bit of salt into the water. Place the mandrake root in this cup. Set the cup where it can be exposed to the light of the moon for a full cycle (full moon to full moon). Take the cup out of the light of the sun during the day. When you move the cup out of the daylight, notice the water level. Over the next few weeks the water should begin to evaporate and the water level should decrease considerably. While you are setting the cup aside, take a moment to remember the biases that you bound to the root. At the end of the lunar cycle, bury the mandrake root and pour any remains of the salt water onto it. The magic is complete. Your biases and judgments should be decreased.

1. Thomas Bullfinch, *Bullfinch's Mythology* (New York: Avenel Books, 1929), p. 10.
2. Joseph Campbell, Betty Sue Flowers, ed., *The Power of Myth* (New York: Doubleday, 1988), p. 67.

CHAPTER IX

DEMETER

You are part of the whole.
Live your life accordingly.

INVOCATION

I was supposed to meet Hermes at the seashore on a clear, brisk spring night. It was already midnight and I sat alone on the sand feeling foolish and somewhat self-conscious; I could have been at home in bed. I tried to clear my mind by listening to the crashing waves. Without warning, a raspy voice whispered in my ear, "I have something to show you." Hermes had a knack of appearing out of nowhere.

He pointed to the moon. "Look at that," he chuckled. I was incredulous. "You wanted to show me the moon?" I asked. "No. I wanted to show you the sun," he said suddenly stone-faced and somber. I saw that he held two smooth stones, one in each hand. "Look at that! The moon is nothing," he said. "Hermes, what are you holding?" I asked, feeling suddenly wary. Hermes acted without warning and swiftly pressed the two stones into my eyes. "What are you doing, Hermes? Stop it!" I shouted as I lost balance. I fell back onto the sand and Hermes shrieked with laughter. "Look at that," he said through gasps and laughter. He pointed to where I saw the moon just moments before; but it was now gone. I was astonished. He continued, "The moon is nothing. We cannot see her without her brother, the sun. Without grandmother moon, the earth is nothing; it is barren, lifeless, dead. If you want magic, you must know that you are nothing alone—just like the moon and the earth. It is your link to something else that gives you substance and power." We stood in silence for a long time looking at the dark sky.

Then he raised his arms and called out to the night:

O guardian of earth's treasures, we call upon you. Look favorably onto us. Guide us through your realms and teach us the mysteries of abundance. It is in union with all that life comes forth. You, who rule the cycles of the seasons, be with us as we learn to be one with the great all. Come, come, O Great Mother, and bestow upon us your treasures. For, devotion to you is devotion to all of life.

THE TALE–*The Oak Leaf*

Once in the beauty of spring, an oak leaf was born. It was the only leaf on a branch and so it enjoyed reaching out to drink from the spring rains and it loved basking in the warmth of the sun. As summer came, other leaves began to appear and they crowded in more and more. The branches began to thicken and they obstructed the sun and rain that the little oak leaf so enjoyed.

When the rains would come, the other leaves would take some of the little oak leaf's water and when the sun would shine, the other leaves would shield the little leaf, preventing it from warming itself. The oak leaf protested and tried to push the other leaves and branches aside. "This is my place in the world," it said. "This is my rain and my sunlight. The rest of you go away!" But the other leaves and the branches went on taking as much rain water and sunshine as they needed.

One dark night, the voice of the tree spoke to the oak leaf. The little leaf shivered because it had never known that there was a tree. "I am your mother," said the voice, "and you must come to know that you are not just a leaf, but a part of the whole of me. You cannot live without me or the branches or other leaves. What you are is me." When the leaf heard this, its life was changed.

MAGICAL LAW — *You are part of the whole. Live your life accordingly.*

DEMETER'S LAW

Demeter was the witch who lived next door. She was a kind, grand-motherly woman who I always saw working in her backyard garden. Whenever she was out in her yard, she wore a big, floppy straw hat and white garden gloves. One year I watched out my window as she planted a thriving, magical herb garden. She started planting seeds in the late spring. She waited until the days were long and warm. Every day I watched her from my kitchen window as she attentively tended to the soil and watered each group of seeds until they all began to sprout. She cultivated each seedling as though it were something spe-cial and unique. That year it seemed as though her garden came to life overnight of its own volition. Rue and basil, chamomile and lavender grew plush and intoxicatingly aromatic.

Her garden was utterly inspiring. I tried to plant a similar garden in my own backyard the following year, but the herbs just didn't grow like Demeter's. They were small, they didn't have much aroma, and they didn't live very long. My garden was a pitiful sight in comparison to Demeter's. One day I decided to ask her secret in gardening.

It was never Demeter's style to give short bits of advice. She was originally from Leeds, a small town not too far of London. She was a Witch Queen of etiquette and old world formality. This would ex-plain why she gave me a gardening lesson over tea and sandwiches.

"Relationships are the secret," she told me in a clipped British ac-cent. I loved listening to her speak. She poured a fragrant, spicy con-coction from an antique silver teapot. "They are the secret of all life. They are central to growing a garden and they are at the center of every form of power and magic." The simplicity of her statements amused me. I thought it was sweet how she could perceive magic in any activity. Yet she seemed genuine; she believed what she said.

I tried the tea, but it was a bit too strong for my taste. "Tell me more about what you mean about the secret of relationships," I said.

She looked at me curiously with her glassy blue eyes. "Nothing exists on its own, you know. Everything is in relationship." The folds of skin under her neck wobbled as she spoke, "The whole of life blends together. It is a lot like our tea. Some of the herbs in my cup are bitter, some are sweet, while another one adds some spice. But they relate. Which herb doesn't fit into the blend?" She laughed to herself. "They are really something special when they find unity. Do you want a garden? Then find out how to exist in unity with it."

I found her idea unusual. I knew that we weren't really talking about gardens anymore, but I didn't care. I was eager to hear more about her magical ideas. "Demeter, you say that magic comes from unity. But how would I ever benefit from that? I lead my life independent of you and I find power in my own way. Isn't that right?" I sipped at the edge of my cup. The flavor of the tea was starting to grow on me now.

"Your 'own' life?" she asked and then dried her lips with a cloth napkin. "When did you come to the misunderstanding that life was something that you owned?" she asked. She appeared to be disappointed by my comment. She looked down into her cup for a long time. Then she spoke, "When you approach life as though you owned any part of it, you soon believe that you must protect your 'belongings.' There is nothing to protect. There is nothing over which you must exert control. Nothing belongs to you solely. You are simply part of the mix. Your body may appear separate and may give the impression that you have something to protect. You might say the same about a single herb in a garden. It certainly appears to be a separate manifestation. But isn't it dependent on the soil? Doesn't it need the sky? How would it do without the rain and the sun? An herb is woven into the fabric of existence no less than you. It does not own its life, and neither do you."

The silence that fell between us made me feel awkward. I could hear my own exhalations and the gurgle in my throat as I swallowed more tea. I watched Demeter take another bite of a small sandwich, leaving a bright red lipstick stain on the edges. The grandfather clock down the hall chimed.

"I don't mean to be disagreeable, Demeter," I finally said in a gentle voice, "but what you are saying is difficult to accept. If my existence is not my own, whose is it then?"

"It is mine," she said. "It is life's. It belongs to all of the gods and goddesses throughout time. Once you release your hold on making boundaries for yourself, you will open up to simply being part of the flow that is life. You would learn to overlook the petty problems of living because you really join into the mix of things. In fact, those things that you thought were problems would just become part of the whole parade of life events once you live life as though you were one part of the whole garden of existence.

"Life offers no promises, but the more you attempt to separate yourself out and say, 'No, that isn't me. This can't happen to me. I am different. I am special. I can survive on my own,' the more you make yourself vulnerable to pain and powerlessness. A drop of water has no power in and of itself. If it were to attempt to separate itself out from a whole body of water and remain a special entity, it would eventually dry up. But when it joins the sea, it can move ships and wear away the face of a stone cliff. There is power in cultivating a relationship with life, which means joining in and losing the thing that separates you from everything else. That is when you truly begin to create magic."

I was astonished at the power of Demeter's persuasive argument.

It reminded me of a line from a chant that I once heard from my early magical training: *We all come from the goddess, and to her we shall return, like a drop of rain, flowing to the ocean.* I told Demeter my association and she nodded. She fingered her necklace of jagged bits of luminous amber and jet as she replied.

"Yes, except you do not have to flow to the ocean, you are already there. All you need to do is open your eyes and look around. Life does not change once you join into the mix, but you change. The same problems will be there waiting for you, but they become less significant, less damaging, less traumatic, and less earth-shaking when they are just part of the whole mix of life. Once you are settled into the mix of things, your understanding changes. A problem is no longer a problem; it is simply part of whatever is."

"I am blocked. I can't keep this in mind. If I meet someone who behaves in a mean or cruel way," I said in response. "I have a hard time seeing myself and this person as one, as part of the mix."

Demeter shook her head and pursed her lips. "And until you do see the two of you as the same energy, the same being, that person will never have the chance to be anything more than mean and cruel in your eyes," she said. "Mean and cruel is how you see that person from the limits of individual perspective. What you may not see is the damage, the vulnerability, the anger, and hurt behind what appear to be cruel or mean actions. Something else that you don't see here is that this person is not meeting your own self-centered needs and expectations. Ask yourself why it is that you need people to be kind or nice in order for you to accept them.

"Once you open to the big picture and allow that person in, then you open to true transformation. I am not saying that empathy is opening to other people at the expense of your own life. That is called foolishness. True empathy is a neutral state that allows you to commit to your relationship to whomever or whatever is around you in a natural give and take."

I thought about this for a moment and took another bite of my sandwich. "But sometimes I don't want to take that responsibility for empathy, especially for someone who seems to be mean or cruel."

Demeter leaned back in her chair. "A coyote traps a rabbit, kills it, and eats it. Is it cruel? Or is it living in some sort of harmony?" she asked. I wondered about that. "You are starving, so you kill a rabbit and eat it," she said and her eyes became wide. "Are you cruel? You cannot escape the inevitability of life itself trapping and eating you. Is life mean because you must die? If you open to what appears to be mean or cruel, then you might see, instead, an adaptive way of coexisting. That is not to say that there are not people who cause evil. There can be people who act out of their own sense of separateness and who thrash about wildly at the rest of the world. Empathy does not mean that you have to forgive someone for causing what appears to be harm. It does not mean that you feel sorry for them or justify their actions. It means that within certain parameters, you allow them the space to be. Evil action needs boundaries and you might need to draw the line in some way that is helpful. But you need to remember that something happens to people who live separately from the rest of life when they encounter someone like you who is open and accepting. They begin to see their evil actions reflected. It may not change them right away. It may take a lifetime, but it sinks in eventually and they change their tactics when they see that you are neutral in response to them."

She stood up and left the room. When she returned, she placed a single seed in the palm of my hand. "Now go find your relationship," she said with a knowing smile.

My tea with Demeter opened me up to a powerful lesson. If you want to master the secrets of living in a magical way, then plant a garden. It is there where you only have seeds, earth, water, and sun that you discover the mysteries of relationship. In a garden, you learn that without the soil, your seeds turn to dust. Without the seeds, the soil stands barren. Without water, the seeds cannot sprout within the soil. Without the right amount of sun in the proper season, the seeds cannot germinate, and they soon become food for the birds. The secret teaching of the garden is simplicity itself, yet it is the secret mastered only by the greatest of magical adepts. The garden's secret teaching is this: nothing in the universe can exist alone. Everything and everyone depends on their relationships to one another in order to thrive. The revelations you find in the garden are, in sum, the magical knowledge of the shaman.

You can work in a garden any way you want. There is no rule that says you must plant seeds in soil during any particular season. No one forces you to give the seeds water. In your garden, you can either combine the elements and allow them to create harmony and life or do as I did, which was almost nothing at all, and hope for the best. The garden is neutral about the whole thing. In fact, with the same garden you can either have a feast or a famine. The seed, the soil, and the water do not care how you use them. Neither does the power of magic.

Magic is also something neutral. It does not concern itself with how you use it. With the same power you can build or destroy, bless or curse. At every second you have the opportunity to use the life you have, your time, your energy in either direction. How you use your magic depends on whether or not you have learned the secrets of the garden. If you have mastered them, then you value your relationships to everything and everyone around you. In this state, you realize that you are only one part of a vast network of relationships that binds the universe together and causes it to operate as a whole. This in turn becomes the guide for your magic. This is the powerful magic of the shaman.

If you have not learned this lesson, you live without understanding the profound impact you make on everything and everyone around you. Without the lessons of the garden, it is easy to mistakenly believe that seeds can sprout without soil, water, or sun. This perspective is the basis for the deceptive and self-serving magic of the sorcerer. It leads to a life lived outside of commitment to magical relationships.

Most of us think of relationships in terms of people. Generally we define relationships on the basis of our family, friends, or romantic ties. Despite this, the reality of living is that you are in constant relationship to whatever is in your environment. You have a relationship to the book you hold in your hands. You are in relationship to the chair in which you sit, to the air you breathe, to the light around you right now. You live in a world of physical forms and you are constantly constructing your relationships to these forms moment by moment. You hear the sounds around you right now; you breathe in the aromas of your environment and you feel the weight of your body. From the magical perspective, there are only two ways to manage these relationships you form with life. You either embrace them in each moment or you reject them. There is no happy medium.

If you live as sorcerers do, by rejecting your relationships to the world around you, you close yourself off from the life force. Shamans know that it is impossible to obtain any real power when you exist in such a closed-off state. When you reject your relationship to the rest of life you begin to focus on your self at the expense of other people and things in order to create some *sensation* of empowerment. Sorcerers can feel powerful only when they manipulate the world and its inhabitants. In such a state, a sorcerer views everything and everyone as "the other," as an object to be used. Sorcerers do not value the world beyond its ability to be exploited. A life lived solely in the service of one's own interests is the most constricted option for living in a universe of infinite options. If you are unable to commit to life, you are of no use to life. Consequently, life cannot be committed to you. The path of the sorcerer is a life cut off from meaning, beauty, and community. The magics of the sorcerer are only limited to wounding, destroying, and cursing. Ultimately, the sorcerer pays a price for his or her self-serving actions. Disempowerment, isolation, depression, struggle, and dissatisfaction with life are only some of the price tags of sorcery.

The path of the sorcerer begins and ends with a feeling of dissatisfaction with life as it is. Sorcerers do not want to be inconvenienced with realities such as a seed's need for fresh water and the proper soil. A sorcerer plants seeds in the snow or scatters them among stones and commands them to grow. Acknowledgment of life's demands would make sorcerers face the reality that life is not about what they want or what they can get individually. So they run away from the life that is in front of them. They choose to live in their own reality, inside their heads. Consequently, when sorcerers sow their gardens, they reap a pitiful harvest.

On the other path, the path of the shaman, you learn to heal, build, and bless. You celebrate the world as well as each of your relationships. The shaman sees that there is no other way to live because relationships are the very essence of existence in the field of time and space. The universe functions as a whole and nothing can survive outside of the whole. When you commit to the whole, you commit to that which sustains the whole: the sky, earth, seas, sun, animals, plants, and, of course, other people.

Shamans generate magical power by taking actions based on this commitment. The actions of shamans look unusual to the average person. They are actions that demonstrate an openness to the forces of life. Shamans know the lesson of the garden, which is to commit to nature on its own terms. Once you master this lesson, nature gives everything it has to offer.

The more you commit to life and the world around you, the less you focus on self-centered interests and actions. You take actions that benefit the whole. In this frame of mind, you act as nature directs you. On this path, you do not hesitate to blend with the immense tide of life as it is. When you connect to this tide, you plug into a vast stream of power. Just as the sorcerer yields a result for his or her choices, so does the shaman. The result of committing to your relationships is empowerment, satisfaction, ease, and functional living.

The world's religions reflect both paths—that of living closed off from relationships and that of building relationships. For example, Jainism in the East and Christianity in the West both generally center their beliefs on the principle that there is nothing particularly sacred about the world and life within it. Neither path fosters relating to the world of forms.

In the Jain tradition, the goal is to end physical action in the world. The Jain's mythology tells them that action causes the spirit to become blackened and heavy.[1] The spiritual practices of Jains focus on releasing the will to live. Christian mythology (for example, in Genesis) informs its followers that human beings are "fallen" and that nature is corrupt.[2] The goal in both of these systems is to remove yourself from the world and go to wherever deity resides. A natural outgrowth from these systems of thought is a de-emphasis on fostering spiritual relationships with the physical world of forms.

On the other hand, in spiritual paths such as shamanism, Taoism, Zen, and Western mystery traditions such as Gnosticism and Wicca, the world of forms is the culmination of deity. Sacredness is not somewhere else, but right here in whatever is before you (whether you like what is before you or not). These systems of spiritual development work to foster your relationship with everyday sacredness and your connection to the natural world.

The idea of fostering a spiritual alliance with all of nature is nothing new among mystic practitioners, particularly shamans. Among magical people both past and present, an alignment with nature has meant adopting the perspective of whatever appears to be "other." Magical folk across cultures and across time have called this alignment "transformation," "enlightenment" or "shape-shifting." For example, the fifth century Celtic shaman Taliesin said that he had adopted many forms. Among the forms he assumed were eagle, fox, buck, bull, crane, a grain of wheat, a blossom, fire, mist, and stars.[3] The priestesses of the Oracle at Delphi spoke with the voices of the Greek nature deities. The Egyptian *Book of the Dead* instructed the departed to assume the traits of the many gods.[4] And to this day in indigenous cultures globally, shamans often perform dances and wear the skins or bones of a totem animal to sustain a mystic relationship with tribal food sources.[5]

In our culture it might not be appropriate to dress in a buffalo hide, but you still have the ability to link with nature and commit to your own deep experiences of life. This means committing to those things and people that you usually think of as "other." When you open to this experience, a transformation of your consciousness, spirit, and heart takes place. The magical consciousness is one that once referred to everything outside of itself as "it," but now sees the world as a "thou."[6]

If you are committed to each relationship, then you become responsible for it. You begin to demonstrate respect, reverence, and empathy. It is difficult to pollute or to endanger a species when you have respect. It is nearly impossible to harm another person or thing when you have empathy. You live in a focused, powerfully gentle way when you honor and commit to each relationship. Each choice you make in life is an important event when you are committed to your relationships. Each relationship enriches your experience, and in this magical state, the potential for living is abundant.

Abundance is the specialty of the goddess Demeter. In Greek mythology, Demeter is the goddess of seasons, cycles, and fertility. Her myth shows how relationships are central to empowerment. The sacred texts of Demeter involve her daughter, Persephone, and the god of the underworld, Hades. In the tale, Hades fell in love with Persephone, who did not accept the favors of the underworld god. Nevertheless, Hades captured the young goddess and took her to the underworld. When Demeter discovered her daughter missing, she wept, and the earth became barren. Demeter descended into the underworld in her search for her daughter. But Hades would not release her readily, so together they struck a bargain. One half of the year Persephone would spend with her mother. Because of the joy of reestablishing their relationship, the earth would blossom and become abundant. Persephone would spend the other half of the year with Hades, and during these months the earth would lie fallow because the sacred relationship was severed.

The message of the myth is clear. Demeter is an earth goddess, and as such she represents the physical world. When you link with Demeter—the physical world—your life becomes abundant. When you disconnect from your relationships to the physical world, your life becomes fallow.

The Enchantments

The Wheel of the Year

In spiritual practice, knowledge of timing is knowledge of relationships. The flow from one season to the next delineates a path to power. Of course, every moment is sacred, but there are certain times within the year that hold distinctive magical and symbolic significance, times that help point us toward understanding our relationship to the whole of life.

Magical people base these special times on the ancient agrarian and astronomical calendars of our ancestors. These celebrations sprang up around the Danube before the arrival of the Roman empire. During this period, seasonal changes were an integral part of everyday life, holding both earthly and spiritual significance. When our primitive ancestors initially learned to cultivate crops and to know when it was time to sow and time to reap, it meant the difference between life and death, feast and famine. Crops could not come to full fruition if seeds were sown too late in the year. Early farmers chanced the loss of their food supply if they did not harvest crops before the arrival of the winter frosts.

Not only that, but seasonal customs and lore handed down across the ages point out that our ancestors associated the seasons with the passages and phases of human life. For example, people who lived in close communion with nature associated spring with birth, summer with fecundity and the prime years of adulthood; fall with old age and wisdom; and winter with the passage through death. Because our ancestors' lives were so attuned to the calendar year, knowledge of timing was wisdom of the highest order in agrarian societies.

Contemporary magical people celebrate eight seasonal passages that are based on this calendar of Old Europe. The four oldest of these celebrations are rooted in the agricultural cycles and they coincide with the mysteries of life—namely germination, fecundity, birth, and death. Contemporary celebrants consider these venerable feast days the major observances for magical practice. Later in history, when our ancestors learned to keep precise astronomical records, four other feast days were added to the magical calendar. These days coincided with the passage of the sun through the heavens and they mark the solstices and equinoxes.

Contemporary magical folk call the progression of seasonal celebrations the Wheel of the Year. In each ceremony, magical folk draw parallels between what is happening in the season with their own lives. In this way, life itself becomes a sacred mandala, and celebrants can recognize the workings of deity in their own lives. In my own practice, I have come to see the Wheel as a simple framework upon which we weave the intricate web of our lives. It points me in the direction of establishing a firm relationship with the earth, sea, and sky. It shows me how to relate to deity as well as to the people around me. The mystic Wheel of the Year turns continuously and as it spirals, it offers each of us the chance to strengthen our relationship to the life that is before us.

By observing the seasons in a sacred way, you can cultivate awareness of your own life as a thread in the immense tapestry of existence. You come to see that you are made up of nothing but this existence, this moment, and everything in it. Blooming flowers, the sunshine that warms your skin, autumn leaves, the snow, birth, and death are all part of who you are. Through this magical work, you can discover that the turning of the seasons is the cycling of your own life, your energy, and your psyche.

Below are the eight celebrations and their spiritual significance as I have learned them from my teachers. Because the emphasis of these celebrations is on fostering relationships, I have presented them here (with permission from my elders) as celebrations for a collective—a spiritual community. You can easily adapt them for an individual spiritual practice.

Celebration I: Feast Day of the Dead

Why would anyone want to celebrate death? It seems like such a celebration would be a gloomy, morbid, even frightening affair. Nonetheless, it is impossible to celebrate life without acknowledging its final moment. Fear of death is only natural. We fear the unknown and death causes us to speculate about what may happen after our own final breath.

This is not an issue raised solely by contemporary minds. In fact, the oldest celebrated mysteries and rituals in the history of mythic, religious, and spiritual systems across the globe are those associated with death.[7] Archaeologists have linked the first signs of spiritual thinking with the issue of death in the Neanderthal period of human development, about 60,000 years ago. In northern Iran and Iraq, some of the most ancient of human burial sites filled with grave gear, flowers, and the remains of medicinal herbs have been unearthed. It appears that death and its meaning weighed heavily on the minds of even our most primitive ancestors. In later centuries, the mysteries of death so fascinated the folk of Old Europe that they marked the beginning of their year with a feast day of death that they called Samhain (pronounced *sow-en*). Thousands of years later, the subject of death continues to shadow the way many people live day to day. It fuels anxiety and fear.

When we first realize that the human body will not last forever, often we begin to struggle and fight the inevitable. What we do not see is that death is not a problem that can be solved or overcome. The only problem with death is the human struggle against it. Yet, each of us struggles in a thousand different ways every day. Most of our struggles arise from the belief that we will live another day. Unfortunately, it is rare that we are given any notice at all of our own death. The Feast Day of the Dead offers each of us the chance to examine how we are living presently in the face of our death. This celebration is not religious; its tone is existential, human. It awakens you to living fully in the life that you have before you. When you do, you will open up to a renewed life.

Feast Day of the Dead

Date: October 31
Awakening: Death as a magical teacher, the mysteries of life revealed through the mysteries of death
Also Called: Samhain, Hallows, Halloween, Dia de Los Muertos
Magical Scent: Patchouli
Incense: White Desert Sage, Dittany of Crete
  What you'll need:

- A pen
- A large, blank piece of paper
- A drum (or other percussive instrument)

To begin, create sacred space. After this, the person acting as a group leader says:

> *We are in a time that is not a time*
> *In a place that is not a place.*
> *On a day that is not a day.*
> *We are between the worlds and beyond.*

Next, have everyone sit on the floor with a pen and place the large sheet of paper on the floor so that all celebrants can reach it. On this paper, each person should write the names of relatives and friends who have died. When all are finished, one or more group members begin a steady, slow drumbeat. If no one has a drum, have everyone mark time by slapping their thighs or stomping their feet on the ground. Between each beat, individuals take turns calling out the names of their dead friends and relatives. If you are alone, place your list of names where you can easily see it while you drum and read the names aloud. Imagine the faces of each of the people who have died as you say their names. When you have finished the list, add the names of each person present in the circle to the bottom and say them aloud. Elect someone to stand in the west of your sacred space. From that symbolic place of endings and death, this person calls out in a clear voice:

Welcome mighty ancestors! From you we have all come forth.
Be with us now on this sacred night
To teach us of the passage into your realm.

Next, divide the group into partners. One of each pair will be the "seer"; the other will be the querent. The seer's job is to receive messages for the querent from the loved ones who have passed away. The following technique is easy and simple to do. It often produces surprising and insightful results.

To begin, have the querent lay on the floor. The querent should think of issues in his or her life that need addressing. It is best to focus on general life issues rather than specific questions (e.g., "Address the subject of relationships" as opposed to "When will I get married?"). In my experience, focusing on general life areas such as career, romance, spiritual development, family, etc. allows for more creative answers.

The seer sits cross-legged and cradles the querent's head. To do this, the seer should rest his or her hands palms upward on his or her lap and the querent rests his or her head on the upturned palms. The seer closes his or her eyes and breathes deeply. Begin to visualize people gathering around the body of the querent. Even if you cannot see their faces, "know" or sense their presence. Do not struggle to clarify the vision. The vision is less important than the message. Ask the spirits present if they have something to say to the querent. Listen carefully and remember as much as you can of what they tell you. People often feel as though they are making up the whole vision. Do not let this feeling deter you. When the spirits are finished speaking to you, open your eyes and relay what you remember to the querent.

Finally, the seer and querent switch roles and the process is repeated.

When all have finished, have each member of the group write down an answer to this question: *If you had only one day left to be alive and you have no more resources than what you have in your pocket right now and the clothes on your back, what things would you do on this last day?*

Have the members say aloud what they would do on their last day. Finally, ask the celebrants to state what it is that keeps them from fulfilling the actions of this final day right now.

When you have finished, close your sacred space.

Feast Day of the Dead Observances

- Celebrate the memory of your ancestors by holding a "dumb supper." Hold a party for friends who want to remember their loved ones. At the party, provide table settings and serve food to the spirits of people who have passed away. Make a "guest list" of spirits whom you would like to commemorate during the dinner. Take time to reflect upon your spirit guests' lives and see how they have touched your own.

- Honor an elderly person or someone who is terminally ill on this night. Take time to learn from his or her wisdom on All Hallows Eve.
- Do a candle divination. Halloween is a traditional time to seek spiritual guidance and insight regarding the future. Begin by filling a deep bowl with cold water. Light a black candle in the name of those who have passed through the veil of death before you. Ask for their guidance in your magical work. Close your eyes and think of an issue for which you would like insight. Concentrate and tilt the candle toward the bowl of water so that wax drips into the bowl. Keep your eyes closed and hold the candle very still so that you don't drip wax anywhere but inside the bowl. When you feel that sufficient time has passed and that the spirits have answered your question, look at the wax drippings inside the bowl. Look at the patterns that the wax has created. On a piece of paper, write down the images that you first see. Go with your initial impressions, even if they do not appear to be related to your issue. When you have written what you see, begin to make associations with the imagery. Describe the image on paper as though you were describing it to someone who had never heard of the image you saw. For example, if you saw a bird, describe a bird and everything re-lated to a bird that you can think of. You might say, "a bird is an animal that makes a nest, lays eggs, and flies through the sky." Of course there are infinite variations on how to describe a bird, but the words you choose reveal something about you and your issue. From your own words, you can begin to draw mean-ing and insight regarding your issue.
- Carve jack-o'-lanterns out of pumpkins or gourds. This is a wonderful tradition at Hallows that has magical meaning.

When you place a candle or light inside the pumpkin, it is a symbol for the "spirit" of the gourd. Allow the face of the jack-o'-lantern to remind you that all of life has a "face." The face should remind you that nothing in the world is an "it." Everything is sacred.

Feast Day of the Dead Consciousness

On this day, let your own death be your counselor. In other words, if you had full knowledge of your own death as an imminent reality, how would you live this day? What would be different for you regarding your actions, your mood, and your relationships? If you allow the reality of your death to influence your daily life, chances are that you will take more risks to be genuine. You will most likely work toward achieving personal goals because you are aware that time does not stand where it is, nor does it move backward. If death is your counselor, then you will most likely be more open to people and experiences as they come up without worrying that they can harm you or benefit you personally. If death advises you, you don't have time to dwell on your history, your personal resentments, or your preferences. When death counsels you, you must act with precision—no time or effort is wasted while in that frame of mind. On this day, ponder the question: *What is death?*

Celebration II: The Yuletide

People who celebrate the winter solstice also refer to this nature festival by its ancient Anglo-Saxon name, Yule (which is derived from the Norse *Iul*, meaning "wheel"). Most people associate the Yuletide with decorating a tree, roasting chestnuts, gathering mistletoe, and receiving gifts from Santa Claus. What most people do not know is that many of the customs that we observe today were inherited and adapted from ancient pagan practices.

The symbol and spiritual core of the winter solstice focuses on the rebirth of light from darkness. Our ancestors stressed the theme of the return of light in this celebration because, astronomically speaking, the number of daylight hours decrease from the time of the summer solstice to the winter solstice. By the time of Yule, the northern hemisphere countries experience the shortest calendar day and the longest night. Each Yule custom signifies the return of sunlight and the promise of longer, warmer days. At Yule our ancestors represented the return of the sun by burning bonfires, Yule logs, and the lighting of candles. Evergreens and mistletoe became central to Yuletide because they were signs of immortality; they were evidence of life sprouting in the midst of death. The contemporary Santa Claus comes from Saint Nicholas, the bishop of Myra, Lycia, in Asia Minor. His name is linked with "Old Nick," which is another name for the Anglo-Saxon god Wotan. At Yule, Old Nick would give gifts of fruit and nuts, which symbolized the potential of bounty as the sunlight returned.

Celebrants today interpret Yule as a symbolic reminder that even in the darkest times in our lives, there is always some light, some balance. Light comes forth from darkness. The symbols of Yule tell us that nature never leaves any of us in the "dark." We are never alone, abandoned, or lost in our lives. No matter how dark our lives look, they cannot stay that way forever.

Yuletide Rite

Date: December 20–22 (when the sun enters Capricorn)

Awakening: Release, inner movement, silence

Also Called: Yule, winter solstice, Alban Arthan, Meán Geimhridh

Magical Scent: Fresh pine

Incense: Pine bark, cinnamon, myrrh

What you'll need:

- A red or gold candle in a small holder
- A cauldron or a deep pot
- Pine essential oil (or any other scented oil that reminds you of the season)
- Votive candles (one for each group member)

This rite is best done during night hours. All participants gather in a darkened room and each lights a single red or gold-colored candle.

Create your sacred space as a group. Have everyone stand in a circle and anoint one another with pine essential oil. I usually anoint the energy point at the center of the brow, but be creative in your ritual process.

When this is complete, elect someone to stand at the center of the circle with the single lit candle. This person places the candle into the cauldron (or deep pot) and says aloud:

From the darkness of night
Comes the birth of light.

Participants take turns entering the center of the circle and announcing a dark aspect of their lives that they release to the void of night. For example, someone might say, "I release my sorrow to the night," or "I release my anger to the night."

For a more dramatic effect, have each person place his or her hands on the cauldron as he or she announces what he or she would like to release.

Next, pass out votive candles to participants who take turns lighting their votives from the single candle within the cauldron. As they do this, they state an aspect of their life that they would like to grow with the birth of the sun. For example, someone might say, "May optimism be born with the sun," or "May love be born with the sun." When everyone has had their turn, set all of the votive candles in the east of your circle to announce the birth of light with the coming dawn. When you are finished, close your circle.

To add a festive flair to your ritual, have everyone dress in solar colors like red, orange, yellow, and gold. Or have participants assist in the decorating of an evergreen tree with fruit, nuts, and sweets just before you begin the ceremony. At the end of the rite, you might have participants toast the birth of light with hot cider and cinnamon.

Yuletide Observances

- Prepare a Yule log made of an appropriate magical wood:
  Aspen—to invoke understanding and empathy in the coming year.
  Birch—to invoke new ideas, new starts, and revisions in your life during the coming year.
  Holly—to invoke visions or to come to terms with your past during the coming year.
  Oak—to invoke healing, strength, and wisdom during the coming year.

Pine—to invoke knowledge of the eternal during the coming year.

Willow—to invoke love during the coming year.

Magical people sometimes carve images from their dreams or images of their power on the special wood. When you burn the Yule log, keep in mind what it represents.

- Drink hot cider with mulling spices: dried orange peel, cloves, and cinnamon. The hot, spiced cider and its ingredients represent the warmth of the sun.
- Fasten some mistletoe above the front door to your home. Or, if you have enough of the magical herb, make a wreath from it and place it on the front door. Mistletoe is an herb sacred to the Druids—it represents life blossoming in the midst of death.

Yuletide Consciousness

In the world of myth and symbolism, the sun represents immortality. The darkness of night represents the release of hope. Remember, the release of hope is not hopelessness or despair. It is the release of inertia and dreaming that yield either non-action or inappropriate, self-centered action. When you combine the symbols of night and sunlight, you find that Yule symbolizes the immortal state of being that is born from the release of hope and non-action.

Practice releasing hope by having no expectations of anything or anyone for this day. See how your day goes without holding on to hope. Through this, you will experience a sense of freedom and openness. You might also ponder this question: *To what do I cling?*

Celebration III: Festival of Lights

"Know thyself" was the phrase written above the entrance to the temple at Delphi in ancient Greece. Knowing yourself is a key activity for you if you wish to awaken your full magical ability. Yet, how often do we take the time to really scrutinize our lives? It is harder than you think to take an objective stance and unflinchingly acknowledge both your strengths and deficits—what it is you have to offer the world and what it is you take.

When the magical year turns past Yule and the days become visibly longer, there is a special day set aside where magical folk take the time to become acquainted with their true potential. The feast day in the Wheel of the Year is most commonly called *Candlemas*—a Christian name for the feast of lights that early Europeans celebrated each February. The Gaelic name for this feast is *Imbolc* and it is the celebration of the winter thaw. The sun has steadily gained strength since the time of Yule and the earth and all of her creatures show signs of returning to their annual cycles of outward movement, growth, and blossoming.

One of the most celebrated figures of this holiday is Lucina, a Roman goddess of midwifery and birth. Contemporary celebrants represent her as a young woman crowned with a wreath of lit candles. Lucina symbolizes the "maiden" aspect of womanhood; she is the virgin—an individual who stands at the center of all potential. She is *tabla rasa*. The candles atop her head signify inspiration and illumination that emerge when one realizes one's true potential.

Imbolc was a time when the promise of warmer days was in the air for the folk of Old Europe. In the agricultural cycle, this is the time for the ritual plowing of the field. Often the ancients would place food offerings on their plows to be carried to the friendly nature spirits that made their dwelling places in the earth. In colder climes, the ground is hard and sometimes icy from winter and plowing it up represented a farmer's intention to break through winter's frozen barrier. Today's Festival of Lights celebrants interpret the action of plowing as a symbol of our efforts to break through frozen patterns in our lives at the time of this feast day. It is both literally and figuratively a time to break the ice between what it is you are and what it is you might be.

Festival of Lights Rite
Date: February 2
Awakening: Opening to wonder, discovering your true potential, inspiration
Also Called: Candlemas, Oimealg, Lá Fhéile Bríd, Laa'l Breeshey, Imbolc
Magical Scent: Myrrh
Incense: Benzoin, myrrh, and basil
What you'll need:

- Four white taper candles
- A dish of uncooked oats
- A dish of uncooked rice
- A dish of uncooked barley
- A dish of uncooked wheat
- A cauldron or deep pot filled with water

To begin your celebration, create sacred space. Place the cauldron or large pot filled with water at the center of your space. Take the bowl filled with oats to the eastern edge of your circle and set it on the floor. Place one of the taper candles deeply within the oats, so that it stands with the wick upright. Hold your hands over the oats and candle and say:

Kindle the flame,
Quicken the grain,
Knowledge of self
We seek to attain.

Light the candle. Repeat this with the barley in the south, the rice in the west, and the bowl of wheat in the north.

Next, each group member will take a turn in "Lucina's Throne." Lucina's Throne is an exercise whereby group members express the potential they recognize in one another. To begin this, have someone volunteer to take a few grains from each of the four bowls.

The volunteer takes grain from the east bowl and casts it into the larger, central pot or cauldron filled with water. While doing this, the volunteer says:

Oat grain for knowledge!

The volunteer repeats this with the barley from the southern bowl. While casting these grains into the central pot, he or she says:

Barley grain for strength!

The volunteer repeats this with the rice from the western bowl. While casting these grains into the central pot, he or she says:

Rice grain for intuition!

The volunteer repeats this with the wheat from the northern bowl. While casting these grains into the central pot, he or she says:

Wheat grain for wisdom!

After all four grains are gathered, the volunteer stands next to the central pot. The other group members take turns anointing the volunteer with waters from the central pot and blessing him or her with words that express the potential they see for him or her. For example, group members might say, "I see you becoming a healthy person," "I see you accomplishing your goals," or "I see you getting emotionally stronger." When all group members have said their blessings, it is time for other group members to take their turn gathering grains and standing at Lucina's Throne.

When everyone has completed this, close your sacred space.

Festival of Lights Observances

- One favorite Celtic tradition is making a "corn dollie" in honor of the maiden goddess, Brigid. People make dollies to bring inspiration and new possibilities into their homes during the Festival of Lights. Make the dollie with dried corn husks that have been soaking in a pot of cold water for a couple of hours. You can use string to shape the various body parts like the head and hands of the dollie. Set the dollie in a place of prominence in your home — above a door or on a central table. A traditional Celtic prayer to "Saint Brigid" — as the Christian church later called this goddess — was usually recited over the corn dollie:

Brigid's bed, Brigid's home,
From afar Brigid's come!
Bless my home, Bless my kin,
Brigid's blessings now begin!

- Make a magical space near a spring or a lake, which are places sacred to the rites of Imbolc. To do this, tie pieces of brightly colored ribbon on bushes and low hanging tree branches. These symbolize potential for the budding and fruition of spring. For each ribbon you tie, imagine that you open to more of your own potential. Also, you can leave a fruit or flower offering to the lake or spring to assure an inspirational year.

Festival of Lights Consciousness

The Festival of Lights celebrates potential. It opens each of us to the power of wondering beyond the rules and strictures that come with culture, ethnicity, age, gender, and other inhibiting factors. Imbolc teases us out of our world of routines and regulations and teaches us that the world is more than what we think it is. On this day, try something that you normally wouldn't. Take a new route to work, talk with new people, eat new foods. Celebrate the day by breaking old habits and by expanding the potential of your existence. On this day, ask yourself the ultimate question: *Who am I?*

Celebration IV: Day of Birth

During the first day of spring, the number of daylight hours is in balance with nighttime hours. In the northern hemisphere this makes the conditions perfect for germination of plant life in the soil. Naturally, the spring equinox signified the time for planting within the seasonal cycle of our rural ancestors. This is the Day of Birth.

The ancient Europeans would celebrate this day by painting eggs scarlet and planting them in the earth to assure fertility and a bountiful harvest. The goddess Eostre (the precursor to the Christian "Easter") presided over spring festivities in the Anglo-Saxon world. The Irish would wear sprigs of *seamróg* (or shamrock) at this time of year to welcome the warmth of the sun and the green of the fields.

Spiritually speaking, the Day of Birth is a time when magical folk plant the seeds of potential that they blessed during the Festival of Lights. This means that the Day of Birth is a time to take action in order to realize one's full potential. The Day of Birth reminds us that a bountiful harvest requires planning, commitment, and movement. It takes attention and action for potential to finally blossom and bear fruit.

It is also wise to keep in mind that if we insist on a particular harvest, we are only setting ourselves up for disappointment. Our action in life is simply to plant seeds, move in one direction, and tend to our lives carefully. Sometimes we are able to harvest results that we prefer and sometimes we are not. Nonetheless, wise ones know that what grows in the garden of our lives is not as important as how attentive we have been to the planting, nurturing, and harvesting process.

The key to individual action on the Day of Birth is balance. Look to the heavens for your inspiration as the sun balances with the moon and light balances with dark. Metaphorically speaking, the arrival of spring shows us that the individual will is best when balanced with the will of life itself. When the power of nature works in tandem with the power of the individual, miracles can happen.

Day of Birth Rite
Date: March 20–22nd (when the sun enters Aries)
Awakening: Taking action without clinging to a result, opening to balance
Also Called: Meán Earraigh, spring equinox, vernal equinox
Magical Scent: Jasmine
Incense: Frankincense and cedar

What you'll need:

- Seeds of any sort
- A bowl
- Small pots with potting soil in them
- A cup filled with water

Create sacred space. Have participants bring various kinds of seeds to the rite. Have them choose seeds that represent some individual potential and take turns sprinkling their individual seeds into a large bowl. While people do this, they can say aloud the potential they plan to work on during the coming season. For example, individuals might say, "I plan to enhance my education," or "I plan to improve my communication."

When the seeds are all blended together, participants next take a slip of parchment paper and write down an action that they are committed to in order to achieve their potential. Then each group member places his or her slip of paper at the bottom of one of the individual planting pots. Fill the pot with potting soil.

Next, everyone sits in a circle and takes a few seeds and plants them in their individual pots. While they do this everyone chants:

> *Plant the seed!*
> *Fruit or weed!*
> *None can know*
> *How it will grow.*

Finally, pass the cup filled with water and have them pour a small amount over their newly planted seeds. As the plants grow into maturity, so will each member's commitment to action.

Close your sacred space.

Day of Birth Observances

- Paint hard-boiled eggs with symbols that represent your potential, such as a flame or a flower, and then place them in a prominent spot in the house. Every time you eat one of the eggs, renew your commitment to taking action toward a goal.
- The night before the spring equinox, find out the times of dawn and dusk. These are the two magical times on this day. Hold vigils at dawn and at dusk, and ask the rising and setting suns what actions are appropriate to take in your life right now. Listen carefully and write down any answers that come to you.

Day of Birth Consciousness

The spring equinox is the season to take action in order to move in the direction of realizing potential. The most important point to keep in mind is that a seed does not bank on becoming a plant. Either it does or it does not. Neither does a seed get angry when it becomes something for which it did not plan. The lesson here is that when we pursue goals, it is best not to cling to the outcome. Movement toward goals and constructive, creative action is fine work in and of itself. Take time today to make progress on a goal. Have no objective in mind other than your task at hand. On this day, ask yourself: *What is correct action?*

Celebration V: Feast of Love

What is love? It is a difficult question to answer. Most people think of love in terms of romance, or the love one might feel for family members. If you look to nature as the Wheel of the Year turns again, you can find an answer that moves beyond the average definition. The Feast of Love, also called *Beltane*, is a celebration of love as the principle of unity. In the natural world, love is the alliance between what appear to be divergent parts: male and female, hot and cold, yin and yang, life and death, center and periphery. The Feast of Love is a time to explore the ways in which you experience natural love and the ways in which you do not. It is the time to establish relationship with whatever (and whomever) seems to be "the other." Celebrants on this day awaken to the awareness that the "other" exists only in their minds. Beyond the limits and restrictions set up by the mind lies the reality that everything is in union. When you step past the barriers of the critical mind, you find that love emanates from the awareness of your connection to everything. This is the great archetypal realization represented in myth and fairy tale as the heiros gamos,[8] or mystical marriage. In Eastern iconography, a frank symbol for this principle is the golden image of the *lingam* and *yoni* in union. The ancient Europeans symbolized this ancient wisdom through dancing around the phallic maypole and even through physical sexual consummation on Beltane.

The Feast of Love is the beginning of summer just as the Feast Day of the Ancestors is the beginning of winter in the Old European magical calendar. Naturally, the ancient celebrants associated the heat of the approaching summer with the element of fire. Beltane gets its name from the Celtic fire god, Bel (also known as Beli and Balor). On this night, the ancient shamans supervised and coordinated the lighting of bonfires on hilltops throughout the countryside.

Fire is a unique symbol of union and the principle of mystical love. Throughout history poets have referred to their love as a burning passion. Both in symbol and in reality fire does not exist without the principle of union. Without fuel, such as wood, you cannot start a fire. Without air you cannot start a fire. It is when these elements unite with heat that the life-giving forces of fire exist.

Feast of Love Rite
Date: May 1
Awakening: Establishing relationships to all around you
Also Called: May Eve, Roodmas, Beltane
Magical Scent: Rose or lilac
Incense: Orris root
What you'll need:

- A staff with ribbons tied to the top
- White taper candles (one for each group member)
- A deep, wide pot filled with sand or soft soil
- A bowl of rose petals

Before beginning this rite, find a pole or staff that is at least six to seven feet tall. Cut lengths of different colored ribbon that match the length of the pole. Tie one end of each ribbon to the top of the pole and allow the other end to dangle freely. Make sure that you tie enough ribbons so that there is one for each participant. If you are solo, tie three ribbons so that their ends dangle freely. On the day of the rite, get out of bed at dawn and gather rose petals. Again, make sure that you have at least one petal for each group participant. Put the petals in a bowl.

Create sacred space. Have everyone sit in a circle. Pass the bowl of rose petals and have everyone take one. One at a time, group members turn to the person on their left and bless him or her with the rose petal, by pressing the flower petal to his or her forehead, cheek, or heart, releasing the rose's fragrance. While you bless the person on your left, say to him or her:

I bless you with my love.

When everyone is blessed, have someone stand at the center of the circle, holding the pole with the ribbons tied to it. Each group member steps forward, grasps a ribbon, and states a particular relationship he or she wishes to honor. For example, participants might say, "I honor my relationship with my mother," or "I honor my relationship to the sea." When each member holds a ribbon, have him or her form two concentric circles. The innermost circle will move in a clockwise direction while the outermost circle will move counterclockwise. As members pass one another while circling, they begin to weave in and out, thus weaving the ribbon around the maypole.

Then have everyone light his or her individual candle. One at a time, each group member steps to the center of the sacred space and announces what he or she plans to contribute to the collective during the coming year. The contribution can be anything. For example, someone might vow to contribute time to organizing the group's events, while someone else might contribute his or her sensitivity and warmth. While individuals announce their contribution to the unity of the collective, they place their candle in the sand-filled pot.

Once everyone has placed his or her candle in the container, have people take turns jumping over the pot of candles. The tradition of leaping over the "bonfire" is an old custom that signifies success, health, and positive action for the coming year.

Close your sacred space when you have finished.

Feast of Love Observances

- Have group members discuss an action that they can take together to improve their community. If the group is too large to facilitate a decision on one collective action, have members divide into smaller "action circles." You can base these action circles on the four compass directions and their symbolic significance. For example, since the east represents knowledge and communication, people of the east action circle might choose to work with a literacy program or volunteer time to a local school. Or, since the north represents the earth, perhaps the north action circle can collectively work to clean up beaches, local parks, or neighborhoods. This kind of action through unity can open a path to empowerment.
- Go to a place in nature where you can safely create a small bonfire. Leap over the flames of the bonfire to assure blessings in the year from now until next Beltane.
- Celebrate Beltane by affirming your relationship to nature. Go to a park and feed the wildlife there. Go to a beach and watch the sunset.
- Renew your vows of marriage, commitment, or friendship with someone special to you.

- A celebration with sexual union is not out of line on the Feast of Love. However, it is important to keep in mind that the purpose of the sexual act is a means of establishing relationship. Making love builds relationship better than simply having sex.

Feast of Love Consciousness

Above all else, the Feast of Love is a day to explore relationships. You have relationships with all that is around you. Make a commitment to that with which you are in relationship. Honor each relationship you forge and see how your day goes. Ask yourself moment by moment this question: *With what am I in relationship?*

Celebration VI: Renewal of Life

Everyone should celebrate life. In every life there is something worth celebrating. The feast of the Renewal of Life celebrates life by questioning it. It is a time to reflect on the mysteries of your existence. At one time or another perhaps you have asked yourself, "What *is* this life?" It's a good question and well worth exploring. It probes the core issues of life and death. It makes us wonder about the meaning of it all—or if, in fact, there is any meaning behind this existence.

The natural cycles of the sun and earth reflect these same themes at the time of the Renewal of Life. The feast day occurs at the summer solstice, which is the longest day and the shortest night in the magical Wheel of the Year. Just when the sun is at its height of power on the solstice, it also begins its decline. To the ancient Europeans the year had two halves—one half was light and the other half was dark. The light half of the year began at the winter solstice and lasted until summer. The dark half of the year began at the summer solstice and lasted until winter. This equal division of the year illustrated that death was just as important as life. No cycle took precedence over another; one worked in cooperation with the other.

Just as the fate of the sun is its decline, it is important for us to recognize the inevitabilities of our own lives. But what are we to do in the face of such a realization? The answer is to live fully within each moment. Our life in the present becomes renewed when we realize that our existence is not within our control. This realization opens us to maximizing the potential of each second of our lives. The feast of the Renewal of Life is a celebration that opens us to living without grasping at the future. Tomorrow may or may not come—who knows? This celebration illustrates for us that the key to a fulfilling life is living presently.

Renewal of Life Rite

Date: June 20–22nd (when the sun enters Cancer)
Awakening: Recognizing the immortal within
Also Called: summer solstice, Meán Samhraidh, midsummer
Magical Scent: Bergamot
Incense: Cinquefoil, lavender, and frankincense
   What you'll need:

- A grapevine wreath
- Fresh chamomile, sunflowers, and roses
- A length of gold cloth-ribbon
- A felt-tip marker

Before the ritual, you can either make a wreath of grapevines and allow it to dry or purchase a ready-made grapevine wreath at a craft store.

To begin, create sacred space. Next, have each of the group members help decorate the wreath with solar flowers: chamomile, roses, and sunflowers. Cut the gold cloth-ribbon into 18-inch segments and pass one piece to each member.

Each group member will use the marker to write on his or her ribbon words that represent physical things, people, or ideas to which he or she clings. Each of us clings to things, people, and ideas because we think there will always be a tomorrow. Some examples of words that may come up are "money," "anger," "resentments," "hope," etc. When each member is finished writing, take turns tying your ribbons onto the wreath and announcing what you are giving away to the waning sun.

Stand in a circle and pass the wreath from person to person. Kiss the person to whom you hand the wreath through its center. This custom assures healing as you release your hold on things, people, and ideas. Cast the wreath either into a bonfire or set it afloat in a river or in the ocean. As you do this have the group say:

> Everything flows, from birth until death;
> That which was here is gone in a breath.
> The secrets of day meet the secrets of night,
> The spiral uncoils to the waning year's light.

Close your sacred space.

Renewal of Life Observances

- If you want to solve the mysteries of your existence on midsummer's eve, make a small circle of tea lights beneath an elder or oak tree. Scatter rose petals within the circle and then sit within your circle.
- Hang a bunch of fresh fennel over the front door to signify the energies of healing and purification in your home on this night.
- Place fresh chamomile herb in a jar filled with water. Place the jar where the summer solstice sun can heat the water to make sun tea. As you drink the tea, awaken to the moment, which is the secret of immortality.
- Make a circular figure from golden straw and twine to represent the sun. Take the figure to a place where you can safely set it ablaze. Gather the ashes and mix them with potting soil. Plant a sunflower using the potting mix and ash to commemorate the passing of the power of the sun.

Renewal of Life Consciousness

Which are you—the sun, a fixed object whose power wanes, or the sun's light which is everlasting? The question has ramifications for each of us. Shall we cling to the physical body, which must return to the womb of earth, or shall we align with that which is non-physical? When you align with the non-physical, you have awakened to the spiritual power of the summer solstice. Go to a place in nature where you can observe the setting of the sun on this, the longest day of the year. While you are there, make a vow to release your hold on the physical side of life. On this day, ask yourself: *What was I before I was born?*

Celebration VII: The Mysteries of Harvest

Everyone enjoys eating a good meal and the celebration of the Mysteries of Harvest makes eating a sacrament. Life feeds on life. It is a difficult thing to say; it is also difficult to hear, but it is a simple fact. We are all killers. We consume animals or plants so that we may live. It may seem gruesome, cruel, or harsh; nonetheless, this is the way physical existence is and always will be. The question is how we can live with this reality and reconcile ourselves with this human condition. This was one of the first spiritual mysteries the early hunting people addressed[9] and it continues to be a relevant point for contemporary contemplation.

The Mysteries of the Harvest, which occur annually with the reaping of the first fruits or grains, is the feast day that addresses this issue. The Mysteries were celebrated in Old Europe as the festival of Lughnasadh (pronounced *Loó-nah-sah*). Lughnasadh is a celebration of the Welsh god, Lugh, who presided over death and rebirth. No matter the name or cultural reference, the Mysteries of the Harvest was a celebration of the bounty of the earth. An old European custom for this day was for a farmer or a young maiden to ritually harvest the first grains of the field and then incorporate them into a loaf of bread. Later that day, the entire community would sacramentally consume this loaf. A bit of the bread would be offered to the fire. The community might even name a Harvest Lord and a Harvest Queen. Usually they were both carted around the village displaying the first fruits and grains.

In symbolic terms, the grain has given its life freely so that we may live. The power behind the Harvest Mysteries awakens in you when you courageously accept this reality. Everything that lives must consume something else in order to survive. There is no other way to exist. This celebration awakens in us an appreciation of that which we consume. The celebration can catalyze the insight that you are made up of the substances that you eat. Once they are inside of you, they become part of you. When we realize that we owe our lives to the plants and animals that we eat, we open to an enduring sense of gratitude.

The Mysteries of Harvest Rite

Date: August 1

Awakening: Accepting life for what it is as opposed to what it is we want

Also Called: Lammas, Lunasda, Lughna Dubh, Loaf-mas, Lughnasadh

Magical Scent: Heather

Incense: Sandalwood, oak, and copal

What you'll need:

- Seven long stems of wheat, tied with a ribbon
- A large, sharp kitchen knife or cleaver
- A chopping block
- A loaf of whole-grain bread

To begin, gather together all of the items for this rite. Some people find that making the bread themselves is a fun part of the festivities of this day. If you decide to make your own bread, try adding sunflower seeds, whole grains of oat or wheat, or dried herbs like rosemary to your dough. You might also enjoy making crowns of long-stem wheat for everyone who plans to attend your Mysteries celebration. Doing this is a reminder that each of us is made up of the wheat, grain, or other food of the earth.

To begin your ritual, create sacred space. The group members then stand in a circle. Ask each person to bring to his or her mind an event in which he or she made a personal sacrifice to help someone else. Stand in contemplative silence for a few moments. After this, elect someone to stand in the center of the circle, hold the grains of wheat high, and say:

> *Behold the grain of life!*
> *The willing sacrifice of the Harvest.*
> *What sacrifice do you bring on this day?*

Pass the sheaves of wheat around the circle. As the wheat is passed around the circle, each person expresses a way in which he or she has sacrificed for the greater good of someone else. When the sheaves of wheat return to the elected facilitator, he or she lays it on the cutting board. The leader then lifts the kitchen knife high and says:

> *One must die, so the other can live.*
> *Open your hearts to the one who must give!*

In a single movement, the leader chops the wheat stalks in half. Then the group passes the loaf of bread around, each taking a piece of it. Before everyone eats the bread, the leader says:

> *The wheat is food for us today*
> *Because it knows we will be food for it tomorrow!*

Everyone eats the bread in silence.
Close your scared space as usual.

The Mysteries of Harvest Observances

- Wear a necklace of dried corn or other dried grain to commemorate the gathering of the first sheaves.

- Eat a pie of fresh fruits or berries to remember the mythical Greenman, whom the ancestors called the spirit of the harvest. He is also the spirit of giving. Keep in mind what it is that you take as you eat.
- Before eating a meal, instead of thanking deity for it, thank the plant or animal that you are about to consume.

The Mysteries of Harvest Consciousness

The idea that life feeds on life is probably not new to you. However, it is a mystery worth keeping in mind. The central question raised by this festival is: how can we live without harming anything? In the usual way of thinking, we must harm something—a plant, an animal—in order to live. However, it is best to remember the lesson of the festival of the Renewal of Life in order to accept the Mysteries of the Harvest. If everything is a manifestation of deity, then our participation in the cycle of life is not "harming." It is doing what nature necessitates. On this day, ponder the question: *What is sacrifice?*

Celebration VIII: Festival of the Sickle

Most people on a spiritual path are familiar with the word *karma*. In fact, this term from Eastern mysticism is so well-known that it is virtually a part of the vernacular of mainstream culture. Karma is the Sanskrit equivalent of the well-known saying, "what goes around comes around." It is the Eastern rendition of the universal golden rule. The people of the ancient agrarian cultures concretized the symbol of this ideology at their great final harvesting and gathering festivals. It was on the first day of autumn that they literally reaped what they had sown in their fields. It was also a time to recognize the conditions that they reaped in their lives as the result of their actions in the world. The final turning of the Wheel of the Year gave rise to the contemporary Festival of the Sickle.

At the Festival of the Sickle, the zodiacal sign of Libra, the balancing scales, symbolically rules all affairs. It is a time of balancing out the scales of justice and of collecting old debts. It is a time to contemplate what it is that you have contributed to the world and what it is that you have consumed. It is a day of reflection and of turning inward to see what it is you have learned over the full cycle of the growing season.

The Festival of the Sickle, like the spring equinox, is a magical holy day marking a time of balance between light and dark. Just as though the festival is hanging on a scale, daylight shares equal time with night at this transitional period. The customs surrounding the final harvest on this day are many. In rural areas around Europe, the last sheaf of corn was called the "Corn Mother." If the crop was of oats, wheat, or barley, the name changed so that the last sheaf was the mother of that crop. Often the harvesters dressed the Corn Mother in women's clothes, ribbons, hats, or scarves and paraded the final sheaf through the town to commemorate the final day of harvesting. Many times, the one who cut the last sheaf was considered lucky and fall equinox lore said that this person would marry within a year. The one who cut the last sheaf of the crop had the privilege of keeping it in his or her barn since this final grain had magical power to keep mice and other vermin away. Alternatively, the harvester placed the Corn Mother on the front door of his or her home for luck. Sometimes the final grains of the last sheaf would be collected by the farmers in a community, and they would sprinkle these grains in the fields during the following spring to assure a good crop.

At the Festival of the Sickle the light from the sun takes on a golden hue. In the northern hemisphere, a chill begins to descend upon the land. Leaves start to turn bright colors and fall from the trees. That which was outwardly expressed in spring and summer begins to move inward. For example, the power of the trees is no longer in their buds and leaves, but in their trunks and sap. The life-giving earth, which provided a bountiful harvest, withdraws from the process of giving in the fall. This is a tide of turning inward for all.

Festival of the Sickle Rite

Date: September 20–22 (when the sun enters Libra)
Awakening: Reaping what we have sewn, turning inward, achieving balance
Also Called: autumn equinox, Meán Fómhair, Mabon
Magical Scent: Oakmoss, vetiver, or patchouli
Incense: Patchouli and oak

What you'll need:

- Harvest fruits and vegetables—or gourds and grains
- Two candles—one black and one white
- A chalice or cup filled with red wine

- River stones or other flat-surfaced stones
- A black felt-tip marker

Since this is a celebration of turning inward, it is appropriate that this celebration be done in private. The following ritual is a solitary one.

Create a small harvest shrine in your home or garden and cover it with local, seasonal fruits and vegetables. On your shrine, place objects that represent events, people, things, or frames of mind for which you would like to express gratitude. When your altar is complete, place the black and the white candles in holders, set them on either side of the altar and light them, saying:

Fire, flame in gratitude's name.

Next, make a list of single words that represent events, people, things, or frames of mind for which you would like to express gratitude. You might want to express thankfulness for such things as contentment, simplicity, or change. Next make a list of words that represent events, people, things, or frames of mind for which you want to express remorse. You might find that you use words like anger, resentment, or waste. Using an indelible black marker, write each word from your lists on a series of smooth, flat river stones. When you are finished, place the stones that represent gratitude beneath the white candle, and place the stones that represent remorse beneath the black candle. Allow both candles to burn all the way out. While the candles burn, take time to contemplate the actions you must take to balance the scales of justice. For example, you might want to personally thank people that have been helpful to you or apologize to people you have harmed.

When the candles are gone, take the stones, your chalice, and some red wine to a favorite tree in some secluded spot. Create sacred space as you normally do with the tree at the center of your circle. Make a ring around the tree with the stones. When you finish making the ring, pour a libation of red wine from your chalice or special cup inside the ring of stones, saying:

> Thanks to my enemies,
> Thanks to my friends,
> Thanks for beginnings,
> Thanks for what ends.

Close your sacred space and leave the stones in place until next autumn. Each time you visit the tree during the year, be sure to review what makes you appreciative about your life. Take any appropriate actions prompted by your words on each of the stones.

Festival of the Sickle Observances

- Tie several sheaves of brightly colored dried corn together with twine and place them on your front door to remind you that it is a season to be thankful.
- At the craft store, buy a cornucopia and fill it with dried gourds, grains, and fruits. Place this somewhere prominent in your home to remind you that you reap what you have sowed.
- Make a charm with a brightly colored autumn leaf. To do this, select a leaf that has turned a beautiful color. Using a gold-ink pen, write a trait you would like to foster in yourself during the coming year on the back of the leaf. For example, you could

write words like openness, friendliness, or consideration. Place the leaf somewhere safe to dry. When the leaf is finally dried, crumble it or pulverize it into a powder with a mortar and pestle. Save the powder in a bottle and sprinkle a bit of it at your front door with the passing of each full moon.

Festival of the Sickle Consciousness

Fall is a good time for contemplation of your life. It is a time to take stock of what it is you have "reaped" during the past year. It is a time of gratitude and of seeing the way that the scales balance out in your life. Like the power of the trees which turns to inward movement, it is time for you to look within your own being to see who you are at the core. Libate a bit of wine at the foot of a tree or in a field and give thanks for all that has happened in your life during the past year. Give thanks for both the things that you liked and disliked, remembering that life itself does not center around you. It is an ongoing process that involves you. Give thanks for the process and take from it what you can learn. On this day ask yourself: *What is correct gratitude?*

1. Joseph Campbell, *Transformations of Myth Through Time* (New York: Harper & Row, 1990), pp. 108–109.
2. Joseph Campbell, *The Hero with a Thousand Faces* (New Jersey: Princeton University Press, 1973), p. 153.
3. John Matthews, *Taliesin: Shamanism and The Bardic Mysteries in Britain and Ireland* (London: Aquarian Press, 1991), p. 152.
4. Campbell, *The Hero with a Thousand Faces* (New Jersey: Princeton University Press, 1973), p. 371.
5. See, e.g., Marie Antoinette Czaplicka, *Aboriginal Siberia*, (London: Oxford University Press, 1969); Hamilton A. Tyler, *Pueblo Animals and Myths* (Norman: University of Oklahoma Press, 1964); Mircea Eliade, *Shamanism: Archaic Techniques of Ecstasy* (New York: Pantheon Books, 1964).
6. Campbell, Betty Sue Flowers, ed., *The Power of Myth* (New York: Doubleday, 1987), pp. 78–79.
7. Campbell, *Transformations of Myth Through Time* (New York: Harper and Row, 1990), p. 8.
8. Campbell, *The Hero with a Thousand Faces* (New Jersey: Bollingen, 1972), p. 109.
9. Campbell, Betty Sue Flowers, ed., *The Power of Myth* (New York: Doubleday, 1987), pp. 72–73.

CHAPTER X

DIONYSUS

INVOCATION

It is a dark August eve. The new moon is hidden behind low-hanging, shadowy clouds. I stand blindfolded, clothed only by the night sky at the edge of a sacred oak grove, and I reach out to touch the divine. Hermes, Hecate, Sin, Muse, Fate, Chaos, Pandora, Saturn, and Demeter are gathered here for the Ceremony of Naming.

I stand alone, vulnerable, but I am not afraid. I focus my attention on a feeling of warmth that grows in my belly. I hear no sound at all except for the occasional crackle of wood burning in a nearby bonfire, but the silence is soft and soothing. Soon, I find myself going in and out of a deep, peaceful trance state.

Without warning, strong arms grab me around the waist and pull me into the circle. The silence is broken and I am greeted with kisses and laughter. Soon I hear Hermes say, "A name holds great magic, for it is a link to the divine. It is the mark of the gods on people of power. By what name shall you be known from this day forth?"

For an instant I wonder if I should trust the name that I received in a recent vision. "Dionysus," I say in a clear, sure voice. All doubt is removed now. As I say the name, I feel a strong current of the divine pulsating throughout my body. I hear whispers of approval from the elders. "I am guided by the mighty one, Dionysus," I announce. The elders collectively begin to hum in a low tone.

"The Twice Born!" Hermes booms with a hearty laugh. "You would do well to know that you are born more than twice." His words catch my attention; "Each day is a birth. Each day is a death. Seeds grow and pass and then they grow again." Hermes removes my blindfold and I am startled by what I see. Each of the elders, my teachers, friends, and mentors stands naked in a ring around me. Stripped of rank and robe, it is clear to see humanity, plain and simple, in this circle. It occurs to me that no matter our religion, custom, or place in the world, all of us are bound together in a ring of relatedness. Wherever we are right now, we all stand naked, without difference.

Hermes uses his hands to make a magical sign in the air just above me. Then I raise my arms and my voice to the heavens and invoke deity:

> *Come forth teacher! You who guide us to see the circle of our lives, bring forth your lessons. Teach us the mystery that there is no beginning and there is no end.*

DIONYSUS' LAW

Rebecca was a young priestess who had been a student in our sacred circle for some years now. She was schooled in the arts and magics that would typify a young priestess' training. She could name the gods and heal with magical herbs. She knew of the season's passages, the ways of charms and amulets, and the arts of prediction. But Rebecca's magical journey would soon change, and once she began on the new path that lay ahead, her life would never be the same. I felt a twinge of sadness as I watched her selecting rocks just a few yards away from me along the stone scattered cove of Mermaid Beach. We were assembling magical stones that day for use in a full moon ritual that night. It was twilight and I paused for a moment to see a small churning wave foam, gently caress the shoreline, and swirl around Rebecca's bare ankles. She looked up from her task and smiled. I must have been watching her too intently because her smile faded into a look of concern. "What's wrong?" she asked.

I realized that this was the moment to speak. I opened my mouth, but I was surprised to find that it was not I who spoke, but the voice of the divine. "It is time to learn the elder lessons," I heard myself say in a tone of voice that reminded me of Hermes. Then I stooped down to pick up a few bright green stones. Rebecca placed her collection into a small basket that she carried and approached me. "What do you mean?" she asked with a confused look.

This is how it begins. I remember. It is a cycle that never ends. "Am I to become an elder?" she asked. "You are to become an apprentice," I answered without looking up from my task.

"I don't understand," Rebecca said. "I have studied magic and the sacred arts for years now and I have gained in my knowledge. Am I to remain an apprentice?" She looked disappointedly into her little basket. I watched her for a moment in silence and then I looked away toward two thin, flat clouds that were luminous with the last rays of the sun.

"We are all apprentices," I heard deity say through me. "Learning never ends. Teaching never ends." I took a stone from her basket and held it up to the fiery sunset. "This stone teaches and I am an apprentice. The sun and the clouds speak and I obey." Then Rebecca looked up at me with silent expectation.

I spoke again, "All who learn the elder's ways must begin by answering this question: what is this life?"

APPENDICES

SATURN THROUGH THE SIGNS
1910 THROUGH 2000

1910
Aries
1/1 through 5/16
Taurus
5/17 through 12/14
Aries
12/15 through 12/31

1911
Aries
1/1 through 1/19
Taurus
1/20 through 12/31

1912
Taurus
1/1 through 7/9
Gemini
7/10 through 11/30
Taurus
12/1 through 12/31

1913
Taurus
1/1 through 3/25
Gemini
3/26 through 12/31

1914
Gemini
1/1 through 8/24
Cancer
8/24 through 12/6
Gemini
12/7 through 12/25

1915
Gemini
1/1 through 5/14
Cancer
5/15 through 12/31

1916
Cancer
1/1 through 10/16
Leo
10/17 through 12/09
Cancer
12/10 through 12/31

1917
Cancer
1/1 through 6/23
Leo
6/24 through 12/31

1918
Leo
1/1 through 12/31

1919
Leo
1/1 through 8/12
Virgo
8/13 through 12/31

1920
Virgo
1/1 through 12/31

1921
Virgo
1/1 through 10/6
Libra
10/7 through 12/31

1922
Libra
1/1 through 12/31

1923
Libra
1/1 through 12/19
Scorpio
12/20 through 12/31

1924
Scorpio
1/1 through 4/5
Libra
4/6 through 9/12

1925
Scorpio
1/1 through 12/31

1926
Scorpio
1/1 through 12/2
Sagittarius
12/3 through 12/31

1927
Sagittarius
1/1 through 12/31

1928
Sagittarius
1/1 through 12/31

1929
Sagittarius
1/1 through 3/14
Capricorn
3/15 through 4/30
Sagittarius
5/1 through 11/29
Capricorn
11/30 through 12/31

1930
Capricorn
1/1 through 12/31

1931
Capricorn
1/1 through 12/31

1932
Capricorn
1/1 through 2/13
Aquarius
2/14 through 12/31

1933
Aquarius
1/1 through 12/31

1934
Aquarius
1/1 through 12/31

1935
Aquarius
1/1 through 2/13
Pisces
2/14 through 12/31

1936
Pisces
1/1 through 12/31

1937
Pisces
1/1 through 4/25
Aries
4/26 through 12/31

1938
Aries
1/1 through 12/31

1939
Aries
1/1 through 12/31

1940
Aries
1/1 through 3/20
Taurus
3/31 through 12/31

1941
Taurus
1/1 through 12/31

1942
Taurus
1/1 through 5/8
Gemini
5/9 through 12/31

1943
Gemini
1/1 through 12/31

1944
Gemini
1/1 through 6/20
Cancer
6/21 through 12/31

1945
Cancer
1/1 through 12/31

1946
Cancer
1/1 through 8/2
Leo
8/3 through 12/31

1947
Leo
1/1 through 12/31

1948
Leo
1/1 through 9/19
Virgo
9/20 through 12/31

1949
Virgo
1/1 through 12/31

1950
Virgo
1/1 through 11/20
Libra
11/21 through 12/31

1951
Libra
1/1 through 3/7
Virgo
3/8 through 8/13
Libra
8/14 through 12/31

1952
Libra
1/1 through 12/31

1953
Libra
1/1 through 10/22
Scorpio
10/23 through 12/31

1954
Scorpio
1/1 through 12/31

1955
Scorpio
1/1 through 12/31

1956
Scorpio
1/1 through 1/12
Sagittarius
1/13 through 5/14
Scorpio
5/15 through 10/10
Sagittarius
10/11 through 12/31

1957
Sagittarius
1/1 through 12/31

1958
Sagittarius
1/1 through 12/31

1959
Sagittarius
1/1 through 1/5
Capricorn
1/6 through 12/31

1960
Capricorn
1/1 through 12/31

1961
Capricorn
1/1 through 12/31

1962
Capricorn
1/1 through 1/3
Aquarius
1/4 through 12/31

1963
Aquarius
1/1 through 12/31

1964
Aquarius
1/1 through 3/24
Pisces
3/25 through 9/16
Aquarius
9/17 through 12/16
Pisces
12/17 through 12/31

1965
Pisces
1/1 through 12/31

1966
Pisces
1/1 through 12/31

1967
Pisces
1/1 through 3/3
Aries
3/4 through 12/31

1968
Aries
1/1 through 12/31

1969
Aries
1/1 through 4/29
Taurus
4/30 through 12/31

1970
Taurus
1/1 through 12/31

1971
Taurus
1/1 through 6/18
Gemini
6/19 through 12/31

1972
Gemini
1/1 through 1/10
Taurus
1/11 through 2/21
Gemini
2/22 through 12/31

1973
Gemini
1/1 through 8/1
Cancer
8/2 through 12/31

1974
Cancer
1/1 through 1/8
Gemini
1/9 through 4/19
Cancer
4/20 through 12/31

1975
Cancer
1/1 through 9/16
Leo
9/17 through 12/31

1976
Leo
1/1 through 1/14
Cancer
1/15 through 6/5
Leo
6/6 through 12/31

1977
Leo
1/1 through 11/16
Virgo
11/17 through 12/31

1978
Virgo
1/1 through 1/5
Leo
1/6 through 7/26
Virgo
7/27 through 12/31

1979
Virgo
1/1 through 12/31

1980
Virgo
1/1 through 9/20
Libra
9/21 through 12/31

1981
Libra
1/1 through 12/31

1982
Libra
1/1 through 11/29
Scorpio
11/30 through 12/31

1983
Scorpio
1/1 through 5/1
Libra
5/2 through 8/24
Scorpio
8/25 through 12/31

1984
Scorpio
1/1 through 12/31

1985
Scorpio
1/1 through 11/16
Sagittarius
11/17 through 12/31

1986
Sagittarius
1/1 through 12/31

1987
Sagittarius
1/1 through 12/31

1988
Sagittarius
1/1 through 2/13
Capricorn
2/14 through 6/9
Sagittarius
6/10 through 11/11
Capricorn
11/12 through 12/31

1989
Capricorn
1/1 through 12/31

1990
Capricorn
1/1 through 12/31

1991
Capricorn
1/1 through 2/6
Aquarius
2/7 through 12/31

1992
Aquarius
1/1 through 12/31

1993
Aquarius
1/1 through 5/20
Pisces
5/21 through 6/29
Aquarius
6/30 through 12/31

1994
Aquarius
1/1 through 1/28
Pisces
1/29 through 12/31

1995
Pisces
1/1 through 12/31

1996
Pisces
1/1 through 4/6
Aries
4/7 through 12/31

1997
Aries
1/1 through 12/31

1998
Aries
1/1 through 6/8
Taurus
6/9 through 10/24
Aries
10/25 through 12/31

1999
Aries
1/1 through 2/28
Taurus
3/1 through 12/31

2000
Taurus
1/1 through 8/9
Gemini
8/10 through 10/15
Taurus
10/16 through 12/31

RESOURCES

The resources listed here are the most commonly used within the pagan and Wiccan community. Neither I nor the publisher endorse any of the businesses mentioned below.

Herbs
The American Herbalist's Guild
P.O. Box 1683, Soquel, CA 95073
(408) 464-2441
Web site: www.healthy.net/herbalists/
Provides links to herb sites to help you find herb resources.

Seeds of Change
P.O. Box 15700, Santa Fe, NM 87506-5700
Web site: www.seedsofchange.com
Herbs for health and some for magic.

Aphrodesia
28 Carmine St., New York, NY 10014
Send for their catalogue of magical herbs. Most rare and unusual herbs can be found here.

Circle Sanctuary Herbs
P.O. Box 219, Mt. Horeb, WI 53572
Send for a catalogue of magical herbs.

Magical Tools/Supplies
White Light Pentacles
P.O. Box 8163, Salem, MA 01971-8163
Wide collection of jewelry and magical tools.

Pagan Organizations/Resources/Contacts

The EarthDance Collective
Web site: www.earthdancecollective.org
Southern California. Wiccan training, open and private pagan festivals, full moon celebrations, meditation groups, community outreach.

Covenant of the Goddess
P.O. Box 1226, Berkeley, CA 94701
Web site: www.cog.org
Internationally recognized organization with chapters/chartered groups. Provides public with information and referrals to many kinds of pagan groups; has a national pagan festival and a newsletter.

Church of All Worlds
P.O. Box 8247, Toledo OH 43605
(419) 697-1919
Web site: www.caw.org
Legally recognized international church with chapters/chartered groups.

Circle Sanctuary
P.O. Box 219, Mt. Horeb, WI 53572
(608) 924-2216
Web site: www.circlesanctuary.org
International shamanic Wiccan church and pagan resource. Hosts several large pagan gatherings throughout the year. Offers networking and a well-known periodical, *Circle Magazine*.

Foundation for Shamanic Studies
P.O. Box 1939, Mill Valley, CA 94942
(415) 380-8282
Web site: www.shamanism.org
Classes and workshops for serious shamanic studies.

Magical Music

Talking Drum Records
1223 Wilshire Blvd #503, Santa Monica, CA 90403
(310) 396-6941
Web site: www.talkingdrumrecords.com
Carries sacred drumming and trance dance music by Jim McGrath.

Celestial Harmonies
P.O. Box 30122, Tucson, AZ 85751
Sells music appropriate for use in a ritual space.

Raven Recording
P.O. Box 2034, Red Bank, NJ 07701
1-800-76-RAVEN
Magical drumming music for shamanic ritual space and trance dance.

Bibliography

Adler, Margot. *Drawing Down the Moon*. Boston: Beacon Press, 1986.

Ardinger, Barbara. *A Woman's Book of Rituals and Celebrations*. San Rafael: New World Library, 1992.

Beatie, Melody. *Codependent No More*. New York: HarperCollins, 1987.

Beck, Charlotte Joko. *Everyday Zen*. New York: HarperCollins, 1989.

_____. *Nothing Special*. San Francisco: HarperSanFrancisco, 1993.

Bernstein, Jerome, S. "The Decline of Masculine Rites of Passage in Our Culture: The Impact on Masculine Individuation" in Louise Carus Mahdi, Steven Foster, and Meredith Little. *Betwixt and Between*. La Salle: Open Court, 1987.

Bulfinch, Thomas. *Bulfinch's Mythology*. New York: Avenel Books, 1989.

Campanelli, Pauline. *Wheel of the Year*. St. Paul: Llewellyn Publications, 1992.

_____. *Ancient Ways*. St. Paul: Llewellyn Publications, 1992.

Campbell, Joseph. *The Hero with a Thousand Faces*. New Jersey: Princeton University Press, 1973.

_____. Betty Sue Flowers. *The Power of Myth*. New York: Doubleday, 1988.

_____. *The Inner Reaches of Outer Space*. New York: Harper & Row, 1988.

_____. *Transformations of Myth Through Time*. New York: Harper & Row, 1990.

Castañeda, Carlos. *A Separate Reality*. New York: Simon & Schuster, 1971.

Chargaff, Erwin. *Serious Questions*, Boston: Birkhäuser, 1986.

Czaplicka, Marie Antoinette. *Aboriginal Siberia*. London: Oxford University Press, 1969.

Eisler, Riane. *The Chalice and the Blade*. San Francisco: Harper & Row, 1988.

Eliade, Mircea. *Shamanism: Archaic Techniques in Ecstasy*. New Jersey: Princeton University Press, 1974.

Ellenberger, Henri F. *The Discovery of the Unconscious*. New York: BasicBooks, 1970.

Farrar, Janet and Stewart. *The Witches' Goddess*. Custer: Phoenix Publishing, 1987.

_____. *The Witches' God*. Custer: Phoenix Publishing, 1989.

_____. *The Witches' Way*. London: Hale, 1984.

Farrar, Stewart. *What Witches Do*. Custer: Phoenix Publishing, 1983.

Friedman, Steven, ed. *The New Language of Change*. New York: Guilford Press, 1993.

Gardner, Gerald. *Witchcraft Today*. New York: Magikal Childe, 1982.

_____. *Meaning of Witchcraft*. New York: Magikal Childe, 1982.

Gimbutas, Marija. *The Language of the Goddess*. San Francisco: HarperSanFrancisco, 1989.

Ginzburg, Carlo. *Ecstasies: Deciphering the Witches' Sabbat*. New York: Penguin Books, 1991.

Goodrich, Norma Lorre. *Priestesses*. New York: HarperPerennial, 1990.

Hanh, Thich Nhat. *Zen Keys*. New York: Doubleday, 1995.

Harner, Michael. *The Way of the Shaman*. New York: Bantam, 1986.

Highwater, Jamake. *The Primal Mind*. New York: Meridian, 1981.

Hopman, Ellen Everet. *A Druid's Herbal*. Rochester: Destiny Books, 1995.

Huson, Paul. *Mastering Witchcraft*. New York: Perigee Books, 1970.

Itard, Jean-Marc Gaspard. (Translated from the original 1799 study by George Humphrey and Muriel Humphrey.) *The Wild Boy of Aveyron*. New York: Prentice Hall, 1966.

Jacoby, Mario, Verena Kast, and Ingrid Riedel. *Witches, Ogres, and the Devil's Daughter*. Boston: Shambala, 1992.

Jung, Carl G. *Man and His Symbols*. New York: Dell Publishing, 1964.

Kapleau, Roshi Philip. *The Three Pillars of Zen*. New York: Anchor Books, 1989.

March, Marion and Joan McEvers. *The Only Way to Learn Astrology* (Vol. 1). San Diego: ACS Publications, 1981.

Matthews, John. *Taliesin: Shamanism and the Bardic Mysteries in Britain and Ireland*. London: Aquarian Press, 1991.

Mitchell, Stephen., ed. *Dropping Ashes on the Buddha*. New York: Grove Press, 1976.

Monaghan, Patricia. *The New Book of Goddesses and Heroines*. St. Paul: Llewellyn Publications, 1997.

Murray, Margaret. *The God of the Witches*, London: Oxford University Press, 1931.

_____. *The Goddess Path*. St. Paul: Llewellyn Publications, 1999.

Reps, Paul, comp. *Zen Flesh, Zen Bones*. New York: Anchor Books, 1989.

Roderick, Timothy. *The Once Unknown Familiar*. St. Paul: Llewellyn Publications, 1994.

_____. *Dark Moon Mysteries*. St. Paul: Llewellyn Publications, 1996.

Roth, Gabrielle. *Maps to Ecstasy*. San Rafael: New World Publishing, 1989.

Rothen, Leo. *Leo Rothen's Jewish Treasury*. New York: Bantam Books, as cited in Jorge Bucay, *Recuentos Para Demian*, Buenos Aires: Editorial del Nuevo Extremo S.A., 1997.

Scott, David and Tony Doubleday. *The Elements of Zen*. New York: Barnes & Noble Books, 1992.

Shunryu Suzuki. *Zen Mind, Beginner's Mind*. New York: Weatherhill, Inc., 1996.

Small, Jacqueline. *Awakening in Time*. New York: Bantam Books, 1991.

Starhawk in *The Spiral Dance*. San Francisco: HarperCollins, 1989.

_____. *Truth or Dare*. San Francisco: Harper & Row, 1987.

Toynbee, Arnold Joseph. *Choose Life*. New York: Oxford University Press, 1989.

Tyler, Hamilton A. *Pueblo Animals and Myths*. Norman: University of Oklahoma Press, 1964.

Valiente, Doreen. *An ABC of Witchcraft*. New York: St. Martin's Press, 1973.

Weinstein, Marion. *Positive Magic*. Custer: Phoenix Publishing, 1980.

White, Michael and David Epston. *Narrative Means to Therapeutic Ends*. New York: W.W. Norton & Company, 1990.

RELATED BOOKS BY THE CROSSING PRESS

A Woman's I Ching

By Diane Stein

A feminist interpretation of the popular ancient text for diving the character of events. Stein's version reclaims the feminine, or yin, content of the ancient work and removes all oppressive language and imagery.

$16.95 • Paper • ISBN 0-89594-857-5

All Women Are Psychics

By Diane Stein

Women's intuition is no myth; women really are psychic. But your inborn psychic sense was probably suppressed when you were very young. This inspiring book will help you rediscover and reclaim your dormant psychic aptitude.

$16.95 • Paper • ISBN 0-89594-979-2

Fundamentals of Hawaiian Mysticism

By Charlotte Berney

Evolving in isolation on an island paradise, the mystical practice of Huna has shaped the profound yet elegantly simple Hawaiian character. Charlotte Berney presents Huna traditions as they apply to words, prayer, gods, the breath, a loving spirit, family ties, nature, and mana.

$12.95 • Paper • ISBN 1-58091-026-2

Fundamentals of Jewish Mysticism and Kabbalah

By Ron Feldman

This concise introductory book explains what Kabbalah is and how study of its text and practices enhance the life of the soul and the holiness of the body.

$12.95 • Paper • ISBN 1-58091-049-1

Fundamentals of Tibetan Buddhism

By Rebecca McClen Novick

This book explores the history, philosophy, and practice of Tibetan Buddhism. Novick's concise history of Buddhism, and her explanations of the Four Noble Truths, Wheel of Life, Karma, Five Paths, Six Perfections, and the different schools of thought within the Buddhist teachings help us understand Tibetan Buddhism as a way of experiencing the world.

$12.95 • Paper • ISBN 0-89594-953-9

Ghosts, Spirits and Hauntings

Ghosts, specters, phantoms, shades, spooks, or wraiths-no matter what the name, Patricia Telesco will help you identify and cope with their presence. Whatever you encounter, Patricia would like you to relate to it sensitively and intelligently, using this book as a guide.

$10.95 • Paper • ISBN 0-89594-871-0

The Heart of the Circle: A Guide to Drumming

By Holly Blue Hawkins

Holly Blue Hawkins will walk you through the process of finding a drum, taking care of it, calling a circle, setting an intention, and drumming together. She will also show you how to incorporate drumming into your spiritual practice. She offers you an invitation to explore rhythm in a free and spontaneous manner.

$12.95 • Paper • ISBN 1-58091-025-4

Physician of the Soul: *A Modern Kabbalist's Approach to Health and Healing*

By Rabbi Joseph H. Gelberman with Lesley Sussman

In a self-awareness program suitable for all faiths, internationally renowned Rabbi Joseph Gelberman reveals wisdom drawn from Jewish mysticism. Exercises in meditation, visualization, and prayer are discussed to promote harmony in mind, body, and soul.

$14.95 • Paper • ISBN 1-58091-061-0

Pocket Guide to Celtic Spirituality

By Sirona Knight

The Earth-centered philosophy and rituals of ancient Celtic spirituality have special relevance today as we strive to balance our relationship with the planet. This guide offers a comprehensive introduction to the rich religious tradition of the Celts.

$6.95 • Paper • ISBN 0-89594-907-5

Shamanism as a Spiritual Practice for Daily Life

By Tom Cowan

This inspirational book blends elements of shamanism with inherited traditions and contemporary religious commitments. An inspiring spiritual call.—Booklist

$16.95 • Paper • ISBN 0-89594-838-9

Shaman in a 9 to 5 World

By Patricia Telesco

A complete guide to maintaining a powerful connection with nature, even when sacred groves and wild rivers are far away. Patricia Telesco adapts an array of ancient shamanic traditions to city life, including fasting, drumming, praying, creating sacred spaces, interpreting omens, and divination.

$14.95 • Paper • ISBN 0-89594-982-2

To receive a current catalog from The Crossing Press
please call toll-free, 800-777-1048.
Visit our Web site: **www.crossingpress.com**